Getting Comfortable With Special Education Law:

A Framework for Working With Children With Disabilities

Getting Comfortable With Special Education Law:

A Framework for Working With Children With Disabilities

Dixie Snow Huefner
University of Utah

Christopher-Gordon Publishers, Inc.
Norwood, Massachusetts

Credits

Every effort has been made to contact copyright holders for permission to reproduce borrowed material where necessary. We apologize for any oversights and would be happy to rectify them in future printings.

The map of the Federal Court Circuits reprinted by permission from West Group.

Description of functional behavioral assessment used by permission of Robert O'Neill, Ph.D. Associate Professor, The University of Utah, Salt Lake City.

Christopher-Gordon Publishers, Inc.
1502 Providence Highway, Suite #12
Norwood, MA 02062
(800) 934-8322

Printed in the United States of America

10 9 8 7 6 5 4 3 2 1   05 04 03 02 01 00

Library of Congress Catalog Card Number: 99-66128
ISBN: 1-929024-03-7

Dedication

This book is dedicated to Bob, Steve, Eric, Julianne, and Martha—my heroes and heroines on the front line of life.

Acknowledgments

Any book draws on the collective wisdom of many people. My colleagues in the field of special education and special education law have enlightened me over the years. My graduate assistant, Kate Nagle, did a yeoman's job in gathering data during the drafting of early chapters of this book. My students helped by reading and commenting on drafts of the book. So did Stevan Kukic, Utah's former director of At-Risk Services in the State Office of Education. The Christopher-Gordon reviewers also made insightful comments. My editor, Sue Canavan, was encouraging, and it was a pleasure to work with her. My thanks to them all.

Short Contents

Expanded Contents

List of Figures and Tables

Tables

Figures

Introduction

This book is about special education law and children with disabilities who are of public school age. It is written for practitioners: special and regular education teachers, principals and superintendents, special education directors, school psychologists and social workers, school board members and board attorneys, parents, and others on the front line. I hope that college and university students and instructors will find the book useful too, although for course work they may want to supplement this book with actual court cases, journal articles, and the statutes and regulations themselves.

The book is designed to provide a framework for understanding why you are asked to do certain things in the public school setting. It also attempts to indicate where special education law is headed. It is not a primer or a cookbook with quick and easy recipes for particular troubles, although it does suggest strategies to prevent problems. The overall intent is twofold: to provide a conceptual foundation for the explosion over the past 25 years of federal law affecting children with disabilities, and to help you be informed about your particular role and the roles of others in educating children with disabilities. The law keeps changing, and even if you were exposed to special education law and disability issues during your time as a university or college student or as a self-taught advocate, you will need to understand the developments that occurred in the late 1990s.

You may find that you want to read the book from start to finish. On the other hand, Part I provides an overview for those who want simply that and no more. Part II describes Section 504 for those who wonder what it does that the Individuals With Disabilities Education Act (IDEA) does not do. Part III, the longest part of the book, describes the major issues that have arisen under IDEA. The first chapter should be read by everyone. After that, you can turn to whatever chapters are of interest to you.

I hope that, whatever use you make of the book, you will understand more completely the needs of children with disabilities; the complexities of the legal relationships between federal and state governments; the contributions being made by legislation, regulations, and court decisions; and the ultimate responsibility that rests with parents and teachers to make appropriate education a reality for children with disabilities.

Common Acronyms Used in Special Education Law

ADA	Americans With Disabilities Act
ADD/ADHD	Attention Deficit Disorder/Attention Deficit Hyperactivity Disorder (sometimes used synonymously)
BIP (bip)	Behavioral Intervention Plan
C.F.R.	Code of Federal Regulations
DOE	U.S. Department of Education
EAHCA	Education for All Handicapped Children Act (also known as Public Law 94-142), enacted in 1975 as Part B of the Education of the Handicapped Act (since renamed the Individuals With Disabilities Education Act)
EHA	Education of the Handicapped Act, the precursor to IDEA
ESY	Extended school year
FAPE (fape)	Free appropriate public education
FERPA (fur-pa)	Family Educational Rights and Privacy Act
FBA	Functional behavioral assessment
HCPA	Handicapped Children's Protection Act (part of IDEA)
IAES	Interim alternative educational setting
IDEA	The Individuals With Disabilities Education Act
IDELR	Individuals With Disabilities Education Law Report
IEE	Independent educational evaluation
IEP	Individualized education program
LEA	Local educational agency (includes a school district, an intermediate educational unit, a public charter school)
LEP	Limited English Proficiency
LoF	Letter of Finding issued by the Office for Civil Rights (OCR)
LRE	Least restrictive environment
OCR	Office for Civil Rights in the U.S. Department of Education
OSEP (o-sep)	Office of Special Education Programs in the U.S. Department of Education
OSERS (o-surs)	Office of Special Education and Rehabilitative Services in the U.S. Department of Education (OSEP is a subdivision of OSERS)
SEA	State educational agency
Section 504	A brief paragraph in the Rehabilitation Act of 1973 prohibiting discrimination against otherwise qualified persons with disabilities in programs or activities receiving federal money
U.S.C.	United States Code
U.S.C.S.	United States Code Service, an annotated version of the U.S. Code

Part I

An Overview of Federal Special Education Law

Chapter 1

What Is Special Education Law and How To Read It

Background

Before the 1970s there was no such thing as a body of special education law. In fact, prior to 1954 and the U.S. Supreme Court's *Brown v. Board of Education* school desegregation decision, there was not much of a body of general school law, either. Education is not mentioned in the U.S. Constitution, and in colonial times education was largely the responsibility of individual families and communities. In the 19th century, with the advent of mass compulsory education, it became largely the responsibility of the states. State constitutions created state educa-

tion systems, and state legislatures delegated authority to state and local boards of education to run those systems with minimal interference. The few existing court decisions came primarily from state courts; they concerned curriculum content and the process by which schools could discipline and exclude students.

Two important interpretations of the U.S. Constitution by the U.S. Supreme Court in the early 1920s did result in the recognition of parental and private school rights that states had sought to curtail. One case prohibited the states from requiring parents to place their children in public school, recognizing the right of parents to select a private school education for their children.[1] The other case recognized the right of private schools to instruct elementary school students in a foreign language.[2]

In other ways, however, student and teacher rights that we now take for granted were not recognized by the courts. For instance, until recent decades there were no court decisions supporting the right of students to be free from unreasonable searches and seizures by school officials. There were no decisions upholding the free speech rights of students or teachers. Furthermore, there were no decisions prohibiting discrimination based on race, sex, or disability. In most ways, school employees and students were subject to all school district rules, as long as those rules were not arbitrary and irrational.

In the aftermath of the desegregation decision in *Brown*, the individual rights guaranteed under the Bill of Rights and the Fourteenth Amendment to the U.S. Constitution were held to apply to students and teachers in school situations. These rights were embedded in the equal protection clause and the due process clause, both of which will be discussed in detail in the chapters that follow. As a result of the expansion of these rights to new populations, the number of discrimination claims against school districts grew. As teacher and student rights expanded, the rights of federal and state government were correspondingly constrained. Disability rights issues emerged in the wake of expanded federal court involvement in education issues, the larger civil rights movement, and the philosophical "deinstitutionalization" movement within the disability community. The right to a nondiscriminatory and appropriate education for students with disabilities resulted from a decade of visible political lobbying and lawsuits. This book is about these rights.

The issue is not just the rights of students with disabilities but also the responsibility of regular education teachers, special education teachers, school administrators, school psychologists and social workers, other auxiliary personnel, and parents to work together for the benefit of children with special needs. Many educators and parents have not had the opportunity to understand the legal sources of the rights of children with disabilities or the limits of those rights. Often they overreact, thinking that the rights are more extensive than they are or that they favor students with disabilities over other students. This book dispels some of these myths while also empowering those who work with students to advocate for all children—both those with and without disabilities.

Before launching into the most essential material, readers need to understand (a) the sources of the laws they must obey, (b) basic special education terminology, and (c) the organization of this book. The remainder of this chapter deals with these three topics.

Statutes, Regulations, and Court Cases

You may recall from your high school civics classes that the United States government is a federal republic divided into three levels of government: federal, state, and local. The federal government has limited powers that are given to it, explicitly or implicitly, by the United States Constitution. Powers not given to the federal government are retained by the states or the people. The balance of power between federal and state governments is called *federalism*. In school law, as in many other areas of law, tensions exist between state and federal levels of government over who should do what and how much power should reside at each level.

Tension also exists between these levels and the local level. Technically, however, local governments are creations of the states because each state government decides whether and how to divide the state into cities, counties, school districts, and so forth. Because the state legislature or the state constitution delegates various responsibilities to these subunits of state government, ordinary citizens think of these units as operating with independent authority. In actuality, however, the authority can be constrained by the "superboss," the state government. Nevertheless, for day-to-day operating purposes, we speak of three levels of government: federal, state, and local.

Within each level, there are three branches of government, created by federal and state constitutions, with separate responsibilities. The three branches are the legislative, the executive, and the judicial. This system of checks and balances is referred to as the *separation of powers*.

The legislative branch is responsible for writing our laws. The bills passed by the legislature are then signed into law by the chief executive officer—the president, at the federal level, or the governor, at the state level. Once enacted, these bills are called *statutes*. When ordinary citizens think of laws, they are thinking of statutory law.

The executive branch—the chief executive officer (CEO) and the departments and agencies that report to the CEO—is responsible for, among other things, ensuring that the statutes are executed (i.e., implemented and enforced). The executive branch is also known as the administrative branch because it administers the laws of the land. As part of this responsibility, the administrative departments are given the authority by the legislature to write more detailed rules and regulations (hereafter called *regulations*). These regulations interpret and clarify the statutes so that those who are affected by them know what they are expected to do. These regulations have the force of law and must be obeyed. The administrative department that writes a regulation has the responsibility to monitor its implementation, to ensure that both the statute and its regulations are obeyed.

At the federal level, the Department of Education (DOE) is responsible for implementing and monitoring federal education statutes. At the state level, the state board of education is responsible for the executive branch functions that affect the public schools. At the local level, local school district boards of education are responsible. These boards generally exercise their functions by establishing policies and regulations and then allowing the school superintendent to implement them.[†]

The judicial branch of both federal and state government is responsible for interpreting ambiguity in statutes, policies, and regulations; determining whether laws are constitutional; and applying the laws to situations that give rise to grievances. This kind of legal interpretation is referred to as *case law*. Most states do not have a local court system in each school district to hear school disputes. Instead, there are usually mechanisms for appointing administrative hearing officers who function like judges to resolve disputes. Hearing decisions can be thought of as similar to case law—quasi-judicial decisions at the local level. Typically, a hearing decision can be appealed to a court.

Although the three branches of government have different responsibilities, their roles in setting policy overlap, and they influence one another. Administrators (regulators) interpret statutes, and so do judges. In turn, legislative statutes set limits on the discretion that can be exercised by the other two branches. Although special interest groups attempt to influence all three branches, it is fair to state that they usually concentrate their efforts on the legislative and executive branches.

[†]The lines between legislative and executive authority frequently blur at state and local levels if school boards are delegated both legislative policy-making authority and administrative policy-implementing authority. Sometimes local school boards even exercise quasi-judicial authority, such as when they act as hearing boards to resolve employment disputes.

When you set out to understand special education law, you need to understand the relevant provisions of the U.S. Constitution and your state constitution. Then you need to know the basic requirements of the special education statutes enacted by the U.S. Congress and your state legislature. Next, you need to know your own school district policies and to be familiar with the regulations that have been issued to clarify and implement the statutes and policies at all three levels. Finally, you need to know the relevant court decisions that interpret the statutes and regulations, because constitutions, statutes, regulations, and court decisions must all be obeyed, and ignorance of the law is no excuse for violating it. Table 1-1 summarizes the various sources of law with which you should be familiar.

Table 1-1. Sources of Public Education Law in the United States

Branches of Government	Levels of Government		
	Federal	*State*	*Local*
Legislative (statutes)	U.S. Congress	State legislature	School board (quasi-legislative policies)
Executive (regulations)	Department of Education	State office of education	School board and/or superintendent
Judicial (case law)	Federal courts	State courts	Hearing officers and boards (quasi-judicial rulings)

The U.S. Constitution overrides the above sources of law. No level or branch of government may violate the U.S. Constitution. This principle of supremacy does not prevent a state or local government from offering *more* protections to its citizens than are required by the federal government, it simply prevents state and local governments from offering fewer protections.

An Introduction to Our Court Systems

Although most educators and parents know something about the work of their state and federal legislatures and their local school boards, and they generally have some experience with the role of government bureaucrats in establishing regulations and enforcing the law, they frequently know very little about the role of the courts.

The federal court system has three levels: (a) the United States Supreme Court at the top, (b) the United States Court of Appeals (with its 13 circuits) in the middle, and (c) more than 100 federal district (trial) courts at the bottom. A court case starts at the bottom of this pyramid and works its way up.

At the bottom level, the trial stage, evidence is introduced, and either a judge or a jury determines the facts of the case. The relevant law is then applied to those facts. Trial courts frequently rely on juries to resolve disputed facts, although in the case of special education law, as in many other kinds of civil disputes, cases are usually tried by a judge alone. Although each federal district court has a number of judges to handle the workload, each case is presided over by only one judge. Each federal district court serves either an entire state or, in more populated states, a geographic region within the state. Its decisions are binding only within the geographic jurisdiction of that court.

At the intermediate, appeals level, the U.S. Court of Appeals neither hears the evidence again nor conducts a new trial with new evidence. Instead, panels of three appellate judges review the records of trial courts and weigh legal arguments to ensure that the facts were correctly determined at the trial stage and that the correct law was applied to those facts. The U.S. Court of Appeals is divided into 11 regional *circuits* (each consisting of a regional grouping of states), another circuit for the District of Columbia, and one specialized "federal circuit" for patent and admiralty claims (Figure 1-1). Decisions from circuits of the U.S. Court of Appeals are binding only within the geographic jurisdiction of the circuit that issues the ruling. Most decisions become final at this stage, although a losing party in the U.S. Court of Appeals may petition the United States Supreme Court to review the circuit decision.

Figure 1-1. The 13 Federal Judicial Circuits

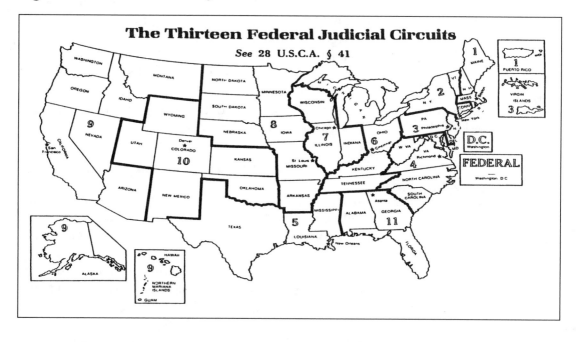

At the top of the pyramid sits the U.S. Supreme Court. It denies most petitions from losing parties in the U.S. Court of Appeals, accepting only those it judges most important. The entire court of nine justices, sitting *en banc* (together), reviews the records of the trial and appellate courts below, hears legal arguments, and issues a ruling. Its decisions establish the legal standard for the whole country and must be followed everywhere.[†]

State court systems are similarly organized into trial courts and appeals courts, although the names selected for these courts vary by state. All states have trial courts to initially try the cases, and most states have an intermediate court of appeals. All have a high court of appeals (usually, but not always, called a supreme court). The decisions of the highest court of a state establish legal standards only for that state. State court jurisdictions do not cross state lines.

One final point about federalism in this country: Although there are areas in which federal law is silent (e.g., much of marriage and divorce law) and therefore state law governs, federal law is supreme over state law

[†]Cases at all three federal levels are featured in this book. Cases below the level of the Supreme Court are discussed when they have been influential in other jurisdictions, but these cases do not establish the law for areas of the country outside the court's jurisdiction. State court cases are rarely discussed in this book, and only if the case provides a particularly helpful interpretation of federal law. Although state courts are authorized to interpret applicable federal law (such as special education law), state courts are more often asked to interpret the law of the state in which the case is brought.

when the two conflict. This principle applies to special education law because the federal government has determined that it has a crucial role to play in ensuring that the rights of students with disabilities are not neglected or violated and because states have accepted federal statutory standards by accepting federal special education money.[†] Similarly, both federal and state special education laws are supreme over local special education law if the local law conflicts with them.

Special Education Acronyms

Special education is full of acronyms, something that confuses individuals new to the field. Familiarity with the acronyms allows easy shorthand references to public agencies, statutes, and principles of special education law. The time to gain familiarity with these acronyms is now—at the beginning of the book. If you forget them, you can refer to the List of Common Acronyms on page xviii. Other terms may be used in your state but are not included in the table because they vary by state. Unless otherwise indicated, the acronyms are pronounced as a series of letters rather than as words. These acronyms will be defined more fully in relevant portions of the chapters to come. The full meaning of some of the less frequently used acronyms is sometimes repeated in chapters where it seems especially helpful to do so.

The Organization of This Book

This book is subdivided into three main parts. Part I has three more introductory chapters, each of which presents a brief overview of a federal law with which you should be familiar: the Individuals With Disabilities Education Act (IDEA), Section 504 of the Rehabilitation Act of 1973, and the Americans With Disabilities Act (ADA). Part I provides a context and necessary background information for the other parts of the book.

Part II is devoted to Section 504 of the Rehabilitation Act of 1973. It contains basic information about the requirements of Section 504 for students of public school age. The chapters in this part of the book explain the nondiscrimination requirements that apply to all students

[†] Notwithstanding the supremacy principle, you will notice as you read this book that there are many places in which you are reminded to consult your own state law. This is because state law sometimes goes beyond the federal law and provides for additional protections for students with disabilities. Moreover, as you will see, the U.S. Congress deliberately left several matters to the discretion of the states. While the federal law provides the framework, major outlines, and numerous details, the states have the ability to fill in remaining details. In an actual lawsuit, you will want to obtain legal advice from an attorney who is not only familiar with federal law and the precise facts of the situation but with relevant state law as well.

with Section 504 disabilities in all schools accepting federal funds, regardless of whether the students receive
special education under IDEA.†

Part III concentrates on IDEA and provides basic
information about its requirements. This is the longest
section of the book because the IDEA requirements are
more detailed, and their impact on the schools has been
more extensive than that of Section 504. Although special educators have assumed primary responsibility for
implementing IDEA, the IDEA chapters heavily implicate regular education teachers because IDEA mandates
their involvement at many points. Principals and regular education teachers ignore Part III at their peril.

†Be aware that regular educators bear the primary responsibility for implementing Section 504 and that the definition of disability under Section 504 is broader than the definition under IDEA. This will be explained in detail in subsequent chapters.

Explanation of the Endnotes and Marginal Notes

Endnotes are included for those who need or want to
know the original source or to share the source with others. Sometimes a statement in an endtnote is included in
parentheses. Such a statement explains the decision in a
court case for the benefit of the reader.

Notes with considerable explanatory material have
been converted to marginal notes and appear close to
the paragraph to which they relate. The remainder of the
notes appear at the end of each chapter. If you want to
understand the source material in the endnotes, you need
to know how to decipher the *citations* to statutes, regulations, and judicial decisions. Citations may seem like
a foreign language until you learn to decode them. How
to do so is explained in the following subsection.

Citations to Primary Source Materials

Court cases are published in volumes called *reporters*.
In this book, when court cases are mentioned in the text,
citations to the reporters are provided. Because this book
is concerned primarily with federal law, most of the citations are to federal cases. The citation indicates the
volume number of the reporter in which the case appears, the abbreviated name of the specific reporter, the
page number, and the specific court (if needed) and year
in parentheses. Without such a citation you would not

know how to locate the decision. For instance, the famous *Brown v. Board of Education* decision, handed down in 1954, is found in volume 347 of the *U.S. Reports* starting on page 483 and is cited as 347 U.S. 483 (1954). Because the abbreviation "U.S." in the citation indicates a Supreme Court decision, no other indication of a specific court is required in parentheses. It takes several years, however, for the official *U.S. Reports* to be published, so sometimes a reference to a Supreme Court decision uses one or both of the unofficial publications—the *Supreme Court Reporter* (S. Ct.) or the *Lawyers Edition* (L. Ed.)—which are available sooner. In either case, the abbreviation indicates that the decision is from the U.S. Supreme Court.

In contrast to Supreme Court citations, a citation for a decision from the U.S. Court of Appeals for a given circuit needs to indicate the specific circuit or court in parentheses. For instance, the Tenth Circuit decision in *Johnson v. Independent School District No. 4* is cited as 921 F.2d 1022 (10th Cir. 1990). The reference to F.2d is a reference to the *Federal Reporter, Second Series.* Current federal appellate cases are found in the *Federal Reporter, Third Series,* abbreviated as F.3d.

Citations to federal district court decisions are comparable to citations to the U.S. Court of Appeals. For instance, the decision in *Sullivan v. Vallejo City Unified School District* is cited as 731 F. Supp. 947 (E.D. Cal. 1990). The reference to F. Supp. is to the *Federal Supplement,* in which federal district court decisions are published, and the specific court indicated in parentheses refers to the federal district court for the eastern district of California. Current federal district court decisions are found in the *Federal Supplement, Second Series,* abbreviated as F. Supp.2d. If a less populous state is not subdivided into eastern, western, northern, southern, and sometimes central districts, the court reference will simply refer to the single district of the given state (D. Utah, for instance).

After their enactment or issuance, federal and state statutes and regulations are organized by subject matter and printed in volumes called *codes.* Citations to federal statutory and regulatory provisions appear in the *United States Code* (U.S.C.) and the *Code of Federal*

Regulations (C.F.R.), respectively. Like case citations, code citations indicate how to locate the source by providing the volume number, the abbreviation for the particular publication, and the page number. The date in parentheses indicates the date on the spine of the code volume. For instance, IDEA is found in volume 20 of the *U.S. Code* starting at section 1400, and continuing through section 1487, so its full cite is 20 U.S.C. §§ 1400–1487. The annotated version is cited as U.S.C.S. (United States Code Service). If the date in parentheses is 1997, it means that the version of the law being cited is the one printed in the 1997 edition of the *U.S. Code.* The IDEA regulations discussed in this book are found in volume 34 of the *Code of Federal Regulations* at Part 300; they are cited as 34 C.F.R. §§ 300.1–.756. The regulations are printed every year, and the date in parentheses indicates which year is being referenced. These sources are generally available in college and university libraries and state court libraries. To the best of my knowledge, all the citations to statutory and regulatory provisions are current as of the date of publication of this book.[†]

When the references in this book are to OSEP, OSERS, or OCR letters and memoranda (see List of Common Acronyms for full names) and state or local administrative hearing decisions under IDEA and Section 504, citations are to the *Individuals With Disabilities Education Law Report* (IDELR, formerly the *Education of the Handicapped Law Report,* or EHLR). IDELR is a comprehensive service that reports decisions and policy statements at the state and federal administrative level. It publishes its material in looseleaf binders that are generally available in law school libraries and state offices of education. An IDELR citation follows the general rule for legal citations: the name of the ruling, the volume number, the abbreviated name of the reporting service, the page number, and the specific administrative body and date in parentheses. For instance, a particular Maryland state educational agency (SEA) hearing decision under IDEA was cited as Frederick County Public Schools, 29 IDELR 1012 (SEA MD 1999).

Table 1-2 summarizes the above information.

Unless otherwise indicated, references to IDEA in this book are to the current version of the statute that is published in the 1998 edition of the *United States Code Service* (U.S.C.S.), an annotated version of the U.S.C.

Table 1-2. Examples of Legal Citations

Federal Court Cases	
Supreme Court	Brown v. Board of Education, 347 U.S. 483 (1954)
U.S. Court of Appeals	Johnson v. Independent School District No. 4, 921 F.2d 1022 (10th Cir. 1990).
Federal District Court	Sullivan v. Vallejo City Unified School District, 731 F. Supp. 947 (E.D. Cal. 1990)
Federal Statutes and Regulations IDEA	20 U.S.C. §§ 1400–1487 (1998)
IDEA Regulations (for Part B)	34 C.F.R. Parts 300 and 301 (1999)
Section 504 of the Rehabilitation Act of 1973	29 U.S.C. § 794(a) (1996)
Section 504 Regulations	34 C.F.R. Part 104 (1997)
OSEP / OSERS / OCR Documents	OCR Senior Staff Memorandum, 19 IDELR 894 (OCR 1992) Letter to Gramm, 17 EHLR 216 (OSERS 1990) Uxbridge (MA) Public School, 20 IDELR 827 (OCR 1993)
IDEA Administrative Hearing Decisions	Cornwall Central School District Board of Education, 17 EHLR 1023 (SEA NY 1991) Conecuh County Bd. of Educ., 30 IDELR 215 (SEA AL 1999)

Conclusion

Now you have enough basic information about special education law to move on to the next three chapters and read about the origins and foundations of IDEA, Section 504, and ADA.

Review

1. What is special education law?

    Simply put, it is the body of rules that govern the publicly funded education of students with disabilities. The rules emanate from statutes, regulations, and case law at federal, state, and local levels. The constitutions of the United States and individual states establish the basic framework for the writing of these rules.

2. What is the difference between a statute and a regulation?

    A statute is a law written by the legislative branch of federal or state government. (At the local level, laws enacted by the legislative branch are usually called *ordinances*.) A regulation is a rule written by the executive branch of government to amplify and clarify statutory ambiguity for those who must comply with the statute. A regulation has the force of law. Regulations are also referred to as administrative rules.

3. Describe the three tiers of the federal court system.

    The federal court has three levels: a trial court (called the U.S. district court); an intermediate appeals court (called the U.S. Court of Appeals), which is divided into 13 circuits, and a high court of appeals called the U.S. Supreme Court. (What else can you remember?)

Notes

[1] Pierce v. Society of Sisters, 268 U.S. 510 (1925).
[2] Meyer v. Nebraska, 262 U.S. 390 (1923).

Selected Supplementary Resources

Thomas, S. B., & Russo, C. J. (1995). *Introduction*. In *Special education law: Issues and implications for the '90s*. Topeka, KS: National Organization for Legal Problems in Education.

Burgdorf, M. P., & Burgdorf, R., Jr. (1975). A history of unequal treatment: The qualifications of handicapped persons as a "suspect class" under the Equal Protection Clause. *Santa Clara Lawyer, 15,* 855–910.

Chapter 2

An Overview of the Individuals With Disabilities Education Act

A History of the Individuals With Disabilities Education Act

Why Did the Federal Government Get Involved in Special Education?

We noted in chapter 1 that public education in the United States has traditionally been the responsibility of state and local governments and that the U.S. Constitution does not mention education. Yet in the 1960s, the federal government began to offer help to the states in educating certain groups of students who were believed to be disadvantaged in one way or another. The federal government got involved for several reasons, but primarily because equal educational opportunity for all students became a national civil rights issue. Advocates for students who were African American female, illegal aliens, disabled, or poor sought enforcement by the federal courts of the right to equal educational opportunity under the Fourteenth Amendment to the U.S. Constitution.

Some groups succeeded in the courts on Fourteenth Amendment grounds better than other groups, but at the same time civil rights advocates lobbied the U.S. Congress for legislation that would address the needs of all these groups. Congress responded in the 1960s and 1970s with a series of civil rights statutes that prohibited discrimination in areas such as voting, housing, employment, and education on the basis of factors such as race, national origin, sex, and disability. Using its Constitutional authority to tax and spend for the general welfare, Congress also enacted a variety of educational funding statutes, offering financial help to the states in return for compliance with federal educational standards. The statutes affected such groups of students as those from families with incomes below the poverty level (Title I programs under the Elementary and Secondary Education Act), students for whom English was not their native language (the Bilingual Education Act), students who were gifted (The Jacob K. Javits Gifted and Talented Students Education Act), and students with disabilities (the Education of the Handicapped Act and its successors). With respect to each of these groups of students, the states were seen as defaulting on their responsibilities, and the legislation was intended to address the special needs of students who did not fit the stereotype of the "typical" student.

Another reason for the federal government's involvement was its own interest in an educated citizenry. The survival and economic well-being of our form of government depends on an educated and self-sufficient citizenry that is capable of earning a living and participating in democratic institutions. In a global economy, it is especially important for the American economy to remain competitive. If certain groups within the society are denied access to an equal educational opportunity, they can become a significant burden on the economy.

The treatment of children with disabilities in the public schools until the 1970s had varied. Prior to the successful challenges under the equal protection clause of the Fourteenth Amendment, the education of children with disabilities had been seen as a privilege rather than a right. For example, in some states, although services in regular schools were provided to children with mild mental retardation, mild speech impairments, and mild emotional problems, children with more severe mental or physical disabilities (including blindness, deafness, mental retardation, and cerebral palsy) were sent to institutions and special schools or otherwise excluded from regular education settings. Children with learning disabilities went unrecognized and were often thought of as lazy or stupid. Many children whose emotional disabilities were severe were simply expelled from school. In other words, what was happening around the country was not uniform, and many school districts had been using essentially a "sink or swim" approach to learning.

The civil rights movement for Blacks was the catalyst for efforts to offer a public school education to all children with disabilities—a public school education that recognized and was suited to their specific needs. Disability advocates argued that if segregation by race was a denial of equal educational opportunity to Black children, then outright exclusion of children with disabilities—all of whom were capable of learning—was also a denial of equal educational opportunity. In addition, it was a further denial of equal opportunity to offer only the same education offered to other children, without any adaptations for the disability.

Two 1972 federal court cases, *Pennsylvania Association for Retarded Children (PARC) v. Pennsylvania*[1] and *Mills v. District of Columbia Board of Education*[2] became "landmark" cases that were influential across the country and in the U.S. Congress. *PARC* focused on children with mental retardation, whereas *Mills* focused on children with many kinds of disabilities, most of which included behavioral problems. Both cases resulted in requiring the public school defendants to provide access to a public school education for children with disabilities. Both cases also resulted in the provision of basic procedural rights—notice and hearing—prior to placing the children in programs separate from regular education students. In particular, the *Mills* decision invoked a line of legal precedents going back to *Brown v. Board of Education*.[3] In *Mills*, the judge reasoned that because segregation into different public schools on the basis of race was unconstitutional, and because using culturally biased measures to place poor children in inferior public school education tracks was unconstitutional, total exclusion by the District of Columbia of thousands of students with disabilities from any education was therefore unconstitutional as well.

The Beginning of Federal Aid for Special Education

Prior to the *PARC* and *Mills* decisions, the U.S. Congress had begun to involve itself in public school education. The watershed year was 1965, when the federal government enacted the Elementary and Secondary Education Act (ESEA).[4] For the first time, the federal government offered direct federal aid to states for the education of students, in this case those whose family incomes were below the poverty level (Title I of the ESEA). Along with Title I came federal initiatives to improve the education of children with disabilities in state schools for the deaf, blind, and retarded. In the 1966 and 1968 amendments to ESEA, indirect aid was provided in the form of grants to state agencies for pilot projects to develop promising methods of serving children with various kinds of disabilities. States could apply for other kinds of discretionary grants as well.

The Education of the Handicapped Act

In 1970, the Education of the Handicapped Act (EHA) was enacted.[5] (At that time children with disabilities were referred to as "handicapped.") EHA consolidated and expanded the earlier federal grant programs and continued to fund pilot projects at state and local levels. At the same time, money was offered to higher education institutions for the development of special education teacher-training programs and to regional resource centers for the delivery of technical assistance to state and local school districts. Congress also authorized grants for special media projects.

In 1974, influenced by the *PARC* and *Mills* cases, Congress expanded EHA to incorporate the concept of a right to a full educational opportunity for handicapped students.[6] The following year, Congress put its money where its mouth was, so to speak. After holding hearings across the country, it amended EHA again by enacting the Education for All Handicapped Children Act, Public Law 94-142, also known as Part B of EHA.

†Public Law 94-142 refers to the 142nd law passed by the 94th Congress. All public laws are numbered in similar fashion.

Public Law 94-142†

Public Law (P.L.) 94-142[7] was Part B of EHA—the part that offered grants to states for direct services to individual students with specified disabilities: learning disabilities, speech and language impairments, mental retardation, serious emotional disturbance, hearing impairments (including deafness), visual impairments (including blindness), orthopedic impairments, and other health impairments. EHA was no longer just an indirect aid program but instead offered grants to participating states for *direct* aid to students with these disabilities. The amount of the grants was based on an annual head count of children served by the program. P.L. 94-142 also elaborated on the educational rights established in the 1974 EHA amendments and expanded the set of procedural safeguards available to students with disabilities and to their parents.

The passage of P.L. 94-142 was a milestone in the education of students with disabilities. The Act engaged the federal government as a partner with the states in educating students with specified disabilities. The federal funding was considered substantial at the time, and the Act held out the promise of steady increases. Funding was authorized to reach 40% of the national average per pupil expenditure. At this level, the funding would have significantly reduced the states' excess cost burden of educating students with disabilities; this burden varied, but it generally exceeded by several thousand dollars the cost of educating students without disabilities.

In reality, during the first 5 or 6 years of the Act, federal funding reached 12% of the national average expenditure per public school student. In the early 1980s it sank to approximately 8%, where it remained until fiscal year (FY) 1997.[8] In FY 1997 and 1998, federal funding rose considerably, but it did not reach its former level of 12%.[†] Although the federal funds are not insignificant, they are everywhere conceded to be inadequate to meet the expectations of the Act.

The basic rights that P.L. 94-142 gave to students with disabilities included (a) the right to a free appropriate public education (FAPE), (b) in a setting that "to the maximum extent appropriate" allowed interaction with regular education students (least restrictive environment, or LRE), (c) governed by a written, individualized education program (IEP), and (d) based on a thorough evaluation of the student's needs. In other words, students with disabilities were to be given access to a publicly supervised and publicly funded education appropriate to their individual needs. All eligible children were to be located, identified, and evaluated. Those previously excluded from public school education were to be served first,

[†]The 1992–93 spending level of $411 per identified student was approximately 8.3% of average per pupil expenditures or just slightly over the 1978 level in constant dollars. Although the FY '97 level rose to $535 per student, that amount was still below the 12% level. See U.S. Department of Education (1998). *Twentieth Annual Report to Congress*, III-43.

along with those with the most severe disabilities. No one was to be rejected ("zero-reject"). Students were to be educated in the setting closest to the instructional mainstream in which an appropriate education could be delivered.

All children with disabilities were considered educable, using a broader definition of educability than just the acquisition of academic skills. The landmark *PARC* case had helped to establish the view that the definition of education included systematic instruction in the skills necessary for living, thereby fostering growth toward goals that meet individual and societal needs. For instance, if a child needed to develop language skills, social skills, or self-help skills like dressing and feeding, and if systematic instruction could result in the acquisition of such skills, then the child was educable. Therefore, the public school system needed to assume responsibility for educating that child.

Along with the basic rights came procedural safeguards to ensure the involvement of parents at key stages of educational decision making. Parents were encouraged and expected to participate as members of the IEP team that designed their child's educational program. Beyond that, the procedural safeguards in P.L. 94-142 built on the *PARC* and *Mills* cases, which had both concluded that removal of children with disabilities from the regular education setting required due process of law under the Constitution—that is, some kind of advance notice and some kind of hearing.

With respect to the notice and hearing rights, P.L. 94-142 provided for notice to parents of what the school proposed to do or not do for their children. It also provided for notice of all their legal rights as parents under P.L. 94-142. This included the right to access their child's records. In addition, if parents disagreed with a school's evaluation of their child, they were entitled, under certain conditions, to an independent education evaluation at public expense. Furthermore, they were entitled to an impartial hearing if they disagreed with the school's actions with respect to the identification, evaluation, placement, or provision of FAPE for their child. If they were dissatisfied with the results of the hearing, they could then seek a review of the hearing decision, first at a state administrative level if the hearing occurred at the local level, and then in federal or state court.

Part B of EHA—the state grant program—is permanently authorized, along with Part A's general provisions and definitions. This means that it does not have to be periodically reenacted by Congress. In contrast, the discretionary grant programs for a variety of research and technical assistance projects must undergo congressional reauthorization every 3 years or so, or they lapse. Partly because these portions of the Act must be reviewed on a triennial basis, the entire Act has remained in the congressional eye. Therefore, amendments to Parts A and B are typically enacted or considered when the rest of the Act is being reauthorized.

The 1986 EHA Amendments

During the 1980s, various other amendments to EHA were enacted by Congress; the most important were enacted in 1986.[9] The 1986 amendments accomplished three major purposes:

1. They extended the rights and protections of P.L. 94-142 to disabled or developmentally delayed preschoolers (ages 3 through 5) over a staged 5-year period (preschool programs), and they provided funding incentives that exceeded the funding available for the education of school-age children.

2. They created an incentive state grant program for experimental programs to serve infants and toddlers (birth through 2) who were experiencing or at risk of developmental delay (early intervention programs).

3. They provided for an award of attorney's fees to parents who prevailed in administrative or judicial proceedings under the Act.[†]

The Individuals With Disabilities Education Act

Four years later, the EHA Amendments of 1990[10] eliminated all use of the term *handicap,* substituting instead the term *disability.* Thus, the Act was renamed the Individuals With Disabilities Education Act (IDEA). Advocacy on behalf of persons with disabilities produced the

[†]The provision that awarded attorney's fees nullified the Supreme Court's ruling in *Smith v. Robinson,* 468 U.S. 992 (1984), which had interpreted P.L. 94-142 to prohibit attorney's fees.

change. Advocates believed that *disability* was a less stigmatizing term than *handicap*. To many, the term *handicap* implied dependence, based partially on the conjecture that the term originated in medieval times when many beggars, with cap in hand, included persons with physical and sensory disabilities. The adjectives *handicapped* and *disabled* were eliminated from the Act as well. "People first" language was preferable because it indicated that all individuals, including those with disabilities, were persons first, with a variety of descriptive characteristics, only some of which might include disability. In other words, no person with a disability should be defined in the eyes of others by the disability alone.

In addition to the terminology changes, IDEA added autism and traumatic brain injury to the other separate categories of disability under the Act, bringing the total to 10. From these 10 statutory categories, the regulations carved out two more: multiple disabilities and deaf-blindness. The regulations also separated the category of hearing impairment from that of deafness, bringing the total of regulatory categories to 13.

IDEA also added a detailed requirement for transition planning by the age of 16 for all IDEA students. Another provision of the law explicitly provided that states were not immune from lawsuits in federal court for a violation of IDEA, thereby preventing states from arguing that the lawsuits in which they were defendants had to be tried in their own state courts.[†] Finally, Congress incorporated requirements concerning assistive technology devices and services into the Act.

Under IDEA, participating states are required to ensure that local school districts comply with the requirements of the statute. If a local agency is unwilling or unable to comply, the state in some circumstances can be held directly responsible for the delivery of FAPE.[11] This is true even if the student is placed out of state.[12][‡]

The IDEA Amendments of 1997

On June 4, 1997, President Clinton signed into law the IDEA Amendments of 1997 (P.L. 105-17, referred to as IDEA '97).[13] The amendments were numerous and substantive. They represented a significant change in focus

---

[†]The provision abolishing state immunity nullified an earlier Supreme Court interpretation of the statute in *Dellmuth v. Muth*, 491 U.S. 223 (1989).

[‡]Residency disputes sometimes can obscure agency responsibility. Usually, the school district where the custodial parent (or person with guardianship) resides is the district responsible for FAPE, even when an out-of-district placement is needed to make FAPE available. In residency disputes, it is important for school officials to check state residency statutes and state and federal court decisions applying to their jurisdictions.

in certain respects and raised outcome expectations for students with disabilities. The changes were consonant with broader federal efforts to encourage clearer state standards and increased national assessment of student achievement. In important ways they paralleled the reform goals embodied in the federal Goals 2000: Educate America Act and the Improving America's Schools Act, both of which preceded IDEA '97. Among the broader goals reflected in IDEA '97 are those to increase school readiness, improve competency in challenging subject matter, improve the safety of the learning environment, increase literacy, improve the professional skills of the nation's teaching force, increase graduation rates, and promote partnerships with parents.

Revisions to Services and Procedural Safeguards   In general, the Amendments focus on efforts to improve the outcomes for students with disabilities, largely by increasing access to general education reforms and the general education curriculum. They also increase the involvement of parents in eligibility and placement decisions, attempt to reduce the opportunities for misidentification and mislabeling, and encourage mediation as a means of dispute resolution. They add major new requirements relating to the development of the IEP and encouraging placement in regular education settings, generating considerable speculation and concern about increased responsibilities for both regular and special educators. The modified requirements for eligibility, evaluation, IEPs, public and private placements, and due process safeguards will be discussed in detail in Part III of this book.

Discipline Amendments   In addition, IDEA '97 expands the mechanisms to facilitate safe schools and focuses attention on behavioral intervention plans and functional behavioral assessments for misbehaving students. The relevant disciplinary amendments were a response to the national concern about violent behavior in school, whether from nondisabled or disabled students. The disciplinary provisions particularly reflected pressures either (a) to allow school officials to discipline students with disabilities more like students without disabilities, or (b) to encourage school officials to do a better job of managing student problem behaviors. The measures were seen as urgently needed because more and more children with behavioral disabilities are being included in regular schools and classrooms. The Amendments codify procedures for suspending and expelling students with disabilities who are dangerous or disruptive, which also has generated a lot of controversy and which will also be discussed in detail in Part III.

Performance Indicators   Additionally, under IDEA '97, the states are now obligated to develop performance goals and indicators for students with disabilities. Indicators include dropout rates, suspension and expulsion rates, and graduation rates.[14] Research had shown that dropout rates are higher and graduation rates correspondingly lower for children with disabilities. Thus, the indicators were required so that the tracking of these students in each state could become more systematic.

State and Districtwide Assessments   Moreover, students with disabilities, with few exceptions, must now be included in state and districtwide assessments of student achievement, with appropriate testing accommodations when necessary.[15] Alternate assessments are to be developed for those who cannot participate in general assessments. In the past, many districts had excluded some students with disabilities from standardized achievement testing so that their scores would not lower the standing of the district schools. Under the new requirements, all districts must include all but their most profoundly disabled students. Concerns have arisen that if some states or districts resist or attempt to manipulate the new mandate, as appears to be the case, it will result in attempts by others to manipulate the mandate as well.

Funding Provisions   A number of other new provisions were added that affect the way that state and local educational agencies (SEAs and LEAs) administer federal IDEA dollars. One applies to public charter schools and specifies that children with disabilities must be served and funds provided in the same manner as they would be in noncharter schools. In other words, Part B must be implemented in public charter schools.[16] Another provision requires states to assure the federal government that if their funding mechanisms are based on the type of setting in which a child is served, the mechanism does not result in placements that violate the principle of LRE.[17] This provision was added out of a concern that many school districts were making placement decisions based on a student's disability label rather than on the IEP.

In response to urging from the LEAs, IDEA '97 allows an LEA to reduce the level of local expenditures below that of the preceding fiscal year if special education personnel voluntarily depart (thereby allowing others to be hired at less expense), if the number of eligible children has declined, if the obligation to provide an exceptionally costly program to a particular child terminates for good reasons, or if expenditures for long-term purchases or construction terminate.[18] The LEA is also allowed to spend federal dollars for special education services that incidentally benefit nondisabled students.[19] For example, the special education staff would be permitted to work with a group of nondisabled children in a regular classroom while simultaneously working with children with disabilities.

Finally, when federal appropriations under IDEA Part B (excluding preschool grants) exceed $4.9 billion, the formula for allocating those dollars will include a calculation based on census data and relative state populations of children living in poverty.[†] Various funding floors and ceilings will be in effect, however, to cushion the impact of the shift in the formula.[20]

All these changes represent a desire to (a) reduce the extent to which students with disabilities continue to be excluded from various aspects of the school program, (b) improve the postschool outcomes for students with disabilities, and (c) forge more extensive links between regular education and special education. A summary of IDEA '97 and its predecessors can be found in Table 2-1 at the end of this chapter.

Many of the IDEA '97 amendments are controversial. Some are ambiguous. Their extensiveness required new regulations, which were not finalized until 21 months later, in March 1999. The regulations are discussed in Part III of this book.

[†]The fiscal year (FY) 1999 appropriation for IDEA Part B (excluding preschool grants) was approximately $4.3 billion, up from $3.8 billion in FY 1998. Source: DOE Website: http://www.ed.gov/offices/OUS/Budget99/pdf

Enforcement, Monitoring, and Technical Assistance

Congress has delegated to DOE the responsibility for monitoring and enforcing the requirements of IDEA. Within DOE, the Office of Special Education and Rehabilitative Services (OSERS) has overall responsibility for IDEA enforcement and implementation. In turn, it delegates to one of its subdivisions, the Office of Special Education Programs (OSEP), the responsibility for writing the regulations implementing the statute. OSEP also has primary responsibility for the actual monitoring and enforcement functions. OSEP staffers monitor the state plans for compliance with IDEA and conduct program audits of SEAs and LEAs. They provide technical assistance in a variety of ways, chief among which are the issuance of formal policy clarifications and informal interpretive guidance in response to inquiries. OSEP also manages the process of applying for and receiving funds under the discretionary grant programs.

Among the more important contributions of OSEP have been the following:

1. The issuance of detailed regulations spelling out the due process protections provided to parents under IDEA

2. The issuance of detailed regulations and an official appendix to the regulations interpreting the intent and requirements of the IEP

3. The issuance of interpretive guidance on such issues as the discipline of children with disabilities and the obligations of public schools with respect to children placed in private schools by their parents

IDEA '97 helps to clarify OSEP's role in interpreting the meaning of IDEA. For instance, the Amendments state that unless OSEP issues a follow-up "policy memorandum," "notice of interpretation," or "notice of proposed rulemaking" within a year of a written request for information, its written response constitutes informal guidance only. In other words, such written responses are restricted to the context of the specific facts presented and are not binding legally.[21] Finally, if the

Secretary of Education wishes to establish a formal rule through policy memoranda or other statements, the Secretary must follow the Administrative Procedures Act,[22] which requires notice and an opportunity for public comment prior to promulgation.

DOE has the authority to withhold IDEA funds in cases where states do not comply with IDEA requirements. Although most disputes are negotiated, occasionally DOE has invoked its authority to withhold funds.[†]

†In *Virginia Department of Education v. Riley,* 86 F.3d 1337 (4th Cir. 1996), the court affirmed the final decision of the Secretary of Education to withhold $50 million in IDEA funds unless Virginia revoked its disciplinary policy that allowed total cessation of services to certain misbehaving students with disabilities.

IDEA Topics in This Book

Part III of this book explores in more detail the various rights and procedural safeguards established under what is actually Part B of IDEA (the state grant program). Part A is also included in the discussion because it contains the definitions of disability categories and services detailed in Part B. Unless other designated, all subsequent references to IDEA are references to Parts A and B. Parts C and D (the early intervention program for infants and toddlers and the discretionary grants program, respectively) are not the focus of this book. Figure 2-1 diagrams the organization of IDEA. IDEA issues are organized around the following 11 topics:

> Eligibility
> Evaluation/Assessment Requirements
> Discipline of Students
> Due Process Protections
> FAPE
> IEPs
> LRE, Mainstreaming, and Inclusion
> Placement of Students in Private Facilities
> Related Services, Nonacademic Services, and
>   Supplementary Services
> Remedies
> Student Records and Privacy Issues

Before reading Part III of the book, you should read the overviews of Section 504 of the Rehabilitation Act of 1973 (chapter 3) and the Americans With Disabilities Act (chapter 4) because they overlap with IDEA, and a basic understanding of their scope and purpose will be helpful.

Figure 2-1. The Organization of IDEA

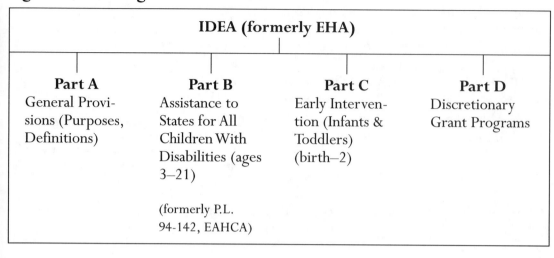

Table 2-1. A Chronology of Major Federal Statutes Relating to the Education of Students With Disabilities

1965 ESEA (Elementary and Secondary Education Act) P.L. 89-10
- Provided direct federal aid for the first time to states for economically disadvantaged regular education students (Title I funds)
- Was the precursor of direct aid for students with handicaps/disabilities

1965 Amendments to Title I of ESEA: P.L. 89-313
- Provided funds for state-operated programs for the "handicapped," such as state schools for the deaf, blind, and retarded

1966 ESEA Amendments of 1966: P.L. 89-750
- Created the federal Bureau of Education for the Handicapped, since renamed the Office of Special Education Programs (OSEP)
- Authorized funds to states to expand their handicapped programs (Title VI)

1968 ESEA Amendments of 1968: P.L. 90-247
- Established the "discretionary" grant programs to serve handicapped students

1970 EHA (Education of the Handicapped Act): P.L. 91-230
- Consolidated Title VI of the ESEA and the discretionary grant programs of EHA
- Expanded basic state grant programs for the handicapped
- Provided indirect aid to handicapped students through discretionary grants for higher education teacher training, regional resource centers, and media programs

1973 Section 504 of the Rehabilitation Act of 1973: P.L. 93-112
- A civil rights provision prohibiting discrimination against "otherwise qualified" handicapped persons in programs or activities receiving federal financial assistance

1974 Education Amendments of 1974: P.L. 93-380
- Expanded the funding base for EHA basic state grants
- Incorporated the rights established in the *PARC* and *Mills* cases

1974 FERPA (Family Educational Rights and Privacy Act) (Buckley Amendment): Title V, § 513(a) of P.L. 93-380
- Gave parents and "eligible" students (over the age of majority) access to the student's educational records
- Prohibited access to unauthorized persons without parental permission

1975 EAHCA (The Education for All Handicapped Children Act): P.L. 94-142
- Extensively amended EHA (EAHCA was EHA Part B)
- Provided for direct federal aid to states for eligible students with one of the specified handicaps
- Elaborated on the right to FAPE in LRE established in P.L. 93-380
- Required an IEP
- Expanded procedural safeguards, such as parental participation, due process hearings, fair and nondiscriminatory assessment, and access to student records (incorporating much of FERPA)

1975 DD Act (Developmentally Disabled Assistance and Bill of Rights Act): P.L. 94-103
- Established a right to treatment and appropriate placement for institutionalized handicapped in states accepting DD funds
- Required creation of protection and advocacy systems in all states, to help the developmentally disabled to pursue legal, administrative, and other remedies

1981 ECIA (Education Consolidation & Improvement Act): P.L. 97-35 (later repealed by P.L. 100-297)
– Continued to fund state-operated programs (formerly P.L. 89-313)
– Consolidated categorical education programs into block grants

1983 EHA Amendments of 1983: P.L. 98-199
– Expanded and extended the discretionary EHA grant programs
– Created a new "transition" program to help handicapped students prepare for employment, independent living, and postsecondary education

1984 Carl D. Perkins Vocational Education Act of 1984: P.L. 98-524
– Provided federal funds to support vocational education programs
– Required equal access to recruitment, enrollment, and placement in vocational education programs for "special needs" students

1986 EHA Amendments of 1986: P.L. 99-457
– Created new incentives for states to educate handicapped infants (birth through 2) via early Intervention Programs
– Extended EHA Part B to 3- to 5-year-olds in participating states
– Extended EHA discretionary grant programs

1986 Handicapped Children's Protection Act: P.L. 99-372
– Amended EHA Part B to provide an award of attorney's fees to parents who prevail in a due process hearing or court case (nullified Supreme Court decision to the contrary)

1990 The Americans With Disabilities Act: P.L. 101-336
– Prohibited discrimination on the basis of disability in public and private employment, public accommodations, state and local government services (including education), transportation, and telecommunications
– Where ADA standards are higher, they replace other provisions in related statutes

1990 Carl D. Perkins Vocational and Applied Technology Act: P.L. 101-392
– Expanded the term "special populations"
– Interwove with EHA (IDEA) to provide full vocational educational opportunity for youth with disabilities

1990 EHA Amendments of 1990: P.L. 101-476
– Renamed EHA the Individuals With Disabilities Education Act
– Extended EHA (IDEA) discretionary grant programs
– Added traumatic brain injury and autism as new categories of disability
– Added IEP requirement for transition planning by at least the age of 16
– Provided that states are not immune under the 11th Amendment to the Constitution from lawsuits in federal court for violations of IDEA (nullified Supreme Court decision to the contrary)
– Redesignated "handicapped students" as "students with disabilities"

1997 IDEA Amendments of 1997: P.L. 105-17
– Added major new IEP requirements
– Added major new discipline procedures
– Modified eligibility and evaluation procedures
– Provided additional avenues for parental participation
– Required states to offer mediation prior to due process hearings
– Required states to develop performance indicators for students with disabilities
– Clarified effect of OSEP policy letters
– Provided more funding flexibility to LEAs
– Established new restrictions on private school placements
– Reorganized Parts C–H into Parts C (early intervention) and D (all discretionary grant programs)

Review

1. Why did the U.S. Congress enact IDEA (EHA)?

    It enacted IDEA (EHA) in response to pressure from advocacy groups to offer equal educational opportunity to children with disabilities by providing financial aid to states to help with the excess costs of special education.

2. What are the basic elements of IDEA that have been consistent across time?

    IDEA provides eligible students with the right to FAPE governed by an IEP and offered, to the maximum extent appropriate, in environments with nondisabled students. FAPE in the LRE with an IEP is based on a multifaceted evaluation of the student's needs. For parents, IDEA provides an extensive set of procedural safeguards to help ensure that their children are given the rights to which they are entitled.

Notes

[1] 343 F. Supp. 279 (E.D. Pa. 1972).

[2] 348 F. Supp. 866 (D.D.C. 1972).

[3] 347 U.S. 483 (1954).

[4] Pub. L. 89-10, 79 Stat. 27 (1965).

[5] Pub. L. 91-230, 84 Stat. 175 (1970).

[6] Pub. L. 93-380, 88 Stat. 580 (1974).

[7] 89 Stat. 773 (1975).

[8] *See* U.S. Department of Education. (1994). *Sixteenth Annual Report to Congress on the Implementation of the Individuals With Disabilities Education Act,* 3–6.

[9] Pub. L. 99-457 (EHA Amendments of 1986), 100 Stat. 1145 (1986); Pub. L. 99-372 (Handicapped Children's Protection Act of 1986), 100 Stat. 796 (1986).

[10] Pub. L. 101-476, 104 Stat. 1103 (1990).

[11] *See* 20 U.S.C.S. § 1413(h) (1998).

[12] Letter to McAllister, 21 IDELR 81 (OSEP 1994) (stating that the SEA has the ultimate responsibility for ensuring that children who are legal residents of the state but who are placed out of state receive FAPE).

[13] Pub. L. 105-17, 111 Stat. 37 (1997) (codified at 20 U.S.C. §§ 1400–1487).

[14] 20 U.S.C.S. § 1412(a)(16).

[15] *Id.* § 1412(a)(17).

[16] *Id.* § 1413(a)(5).

[17] *Id.* § 1412(a)(5)(B).

[18] *Id.* § 1413(a)(2)(B).

[19] *Id.* § 1413(a)(4).

[20] *Id.* § 1411(e).

[21] *Id.* § 1406(d) and (e).

[22] *Id.* § 1406(c).

Selected Supplementary Resources

Ballard, J., Ramirez, B., & Weintraub, F. (Eds.). (1982). *Special education in America: Its legal and governmental foundations.* Reston, VA: Council for Exceptional Children.

Lippman, L., & Goldberg, I. I. (1973). *Right to education: Anatomy of the Pennsylvania case and its implications for exceptional children.* New York: Teachers College Press.

Chapter 3

An Overview of Section 504 of the Rehabilitation Act of 1973

A History of Section 504

Section 504 is a brief but powerful non-discrimination provision included in the Rehabilitation Act of 1973.[1] Section 504 extends to individuals with disabilities the same kind of protection previously extended by the U.S. Congress to individuals discriminated against on the basis of race and sex. Here is the actual language of Section 504:

> No otherwise qualified individual with a disability . . . shall, solely by reason of her or his disability, be excluded from participation in, be denied the benefits of, or be subjected to discrimination under any program or activity receiving Federal financial assistance . . . .[2]

Originally, Section 504 was targeted at employment discrimination, but amendments to the original language extended its reach far beyond employment. Because the implications of Section 504 are so complex and far-reaching, each department within the executive branch of the federal government was required to issue detailed regulations implementing Section 504 for its own recipients of federal funds.

Because virtually every school district in the country accepts federal funds, public education was directly affected by Section 504. Nonetheless, regulations by what was then the Department of Health, Education, and Welfare (HEW) were not issued for several years because of controversies surrounding implementation. In late April 1977, after considerable political pressure, including a media event in which individuals with disabilities chained themselves to the gates of HEW, regulations were finally issued and took effect on June 3, 1977.[3]

†The current Section 504 regulations cover employment practices; program accessibility; preschool, elementary, and secondary education; postsecondary education; and health, welfare, and social services. It is the section on preschool, elementary, and secondary education with which we are concerned in this book.

HEW Section 504 regulations affecting preschool, elementary, and secondary school programs were written in coordination with the first set of special education regulations under Part B of EHA, since renamed IDEA.† The special education regulations were issued in August 1977, and each set refers to the other at various points. After the separate DOE was created in 1980 out of HEW's Office of Education, both sets of regulations were reissued under DOE.[4] For summarizaion purposes, Table 3-1 compares Section 504 regulations with IDEA regulations. You may want to refer to it again after you have read chapters 5–9 (Section 504) and 10–20 (IDEA).

The Scope of Section 504

The scope of Section 504 is broad and extends protection in many areas besides public school education—for instance, higher education, employment, social services, health care, transportation, and physical facilities. In certain programs, such as health and social services, coverage may extend from birth to death.

A Civil Rights Mandate

In contrast to IDEA, Section 504 is not a funding statute, and Congress did not provide funds to help cover the costs of any program adaptations necessary to ensure nondiscrimination. Section 504 simply prohibits discrimination in programs and activities receiving federal money, from whatever source. Nonetheless, as a civil rights statute with enforcement "teeth," it must be taken seriously. In the public school setting, its obligations fall on all school districts because they all receive federal funds. The responsibility not to discriminate applies to all school personnel: administrators, regular education teachers, secretarial and custodial staff, school psychologists, student teachers, and so on.

Although special educators may be involved in protecting the civil rights of Section 504 students, special educators do not have primary responsibility for enforcing the protections of Section 504. The responsibility falls on district- and school-level administrative leaders and on regular education in general.

"Otherwise Qualified" Recipients

Section 504 protects only those individuals with disabilities who are "otherwise qualified" for the program, job, or service in question. In other words, the individual must be qualified in spite of the disability.[†] In employment situations, this means that if an employee with a disability can fulfill the essential functions of the job, either with or without "reasonable accommodations," he or she is "otherwise qualified." An employer who believes that the requested accommodations are unreasonable, however, may invoke the defense of "undue hardship." These standards apply to public school employees.

[†]In *Southeastern Community College v. Davis*, 442 U.S. 397 (1979), the Supreme Court interpreted the "otherwise qualified" language of Section 504 to mean that the person with the disability is able to meet all the program requirements in spite of the disability.

In general, as applied to public education students, an "otherwise qualified" student with a disability simply means such a student of public school age. In cases, however, where competitive criteria are applied in school settings (e.g., eligibility for a competitive athletic team), "otherwise qualified" means that the student has demonstrated that he or she meets the skill criteria in spite of the disability.

Disabled parents of school-age students also must not be discriminated against at school—that is, in their enjoyment of the benefits offered to other parents at school. For instance, the U.S. Court of Appeals for the Second Circuit ruled in 1990 that a school district must provide deaf parents with an interpreter during their parent-teacher meetings.[5] The court reasoned that failure to provide the parents with meaningful communication about academic or disciplinary aspects of their child's educational programming was discriminatory. On the other hand, the court stated that subsidizing parental involvement in voluntary extracurricular activities was not required by Section 504. This judicial decision has been generally accepted across the country as a satisfactory interpretation of the law.

Program Accessibility

Schools must be aware of the architectural requirements under both Section 504 and ADA. In general, all educational *programs* must be accessible to those who need them, but not every *room* in a school building must be accessible to all students.[6] In some situations, this may require moving a given program into an accessible facility or making a portion of a building accessible. If a facility is to be structurally altered in a manner that affects its usability, at that time the altered portion must be made physically accessible. Of course, any newly constructed facilities must be readily accessible to and usable by persons with disabilities. If a separate facility is permissible, then it must be comparable in quality to the facilities used by the nondisabled (see chapter 8).

The Meaning of "Program or Activity"

Early lawsuits attempted to restrict the definition of "program or activity receiving federal financial assistance" to specific programs or activities within an agency. In other words, some recipients of federal money argued that a finding of discrimination in one grant program should not enable termination of federal funding in the recipient's other programs. Although the Supreme Court, in *Grove City College v. Bell*,[7] agreed with this interpretation of Section 504, the U.S. Congress did not. It subsequently amended Section 504[†] by adding language making explicit its view that the definition of a "program or activity" extended to *all* the operations of a recipient of the federal funds.[8] Therefore, if discrimination occurs anywhere within a school district that receives federal funds, all federal funds can be withdrawn, not just those attached to the activity or program in which the discrimination occurs. In other words, Congress apparently did not want to subsidize any institution that was discriminating anywhere within its programs.

[†]The amendment to Section 504 was part of the Civil Rights Restoration Act, 20 U.S.C. § 1687. It not only clarified the definition of "program or activity" under Section 504 but also under Title VI of the Civil Rights Act of 1964 (race discrimination), Title IX of the Education Amendments of 1972 (sex discrimination) and the Age Discrimination Act of 1975.

The Definition of "Disability" Under Section 504

The definition of an "individual with a disability" under Section 504 is one who (a) has a physical or mental impairment that substantially limits one or more major life activities, (b) has a record of such an impairment, or (c) is regarded as having such an impairment.[9] A *physical impairment* includes any physiological disorder or condition, cosmetic disfigurement, or anatomical loss affecting one or more enumerated body systems. A *mental impairment* is defined as "any mental or psychological disorder, such as mental retardation, organic brain syndrome, emotional or mental illness, and specific learning disabilities."[10] If one's "impairment" is not physical or mental but rather a form of cultural or economic disadvantage, then, by definition, it is not a Section 504 disability.

Section 504 regulations describe *major life activities* as functions such as breathing, walking, talking, seeing, hearing, using one's hands, taking care of oneself, working, and learning.[11] Impairments in any one of these life activities (with the exception of working) can require modifications to a child's school program. So, presumably, can impairments to other major life activities because the list is not exhaustive. The Office for Civil Rights (OCR) has declined to define what is meant by a substantial limitation on a major life activity, leaving it up to school districts to determine for themselves.

In the school context, the first prong of the Section 504 definition is usually the relevant one. Schools discriminate against students with disabilities in the following ways: (a) by failing to provide physical access to necessary programs or facilities, (b) by imposing double standards for eligibility for extracurricular activities, and (c) by failing to design regular classroom programs to meet the student's individual needs as adequately as the needs of nondisabled students are met. Even though a student may be learning normally, it will still be discriminatory not to provide access to a private, wider toilet stall for a student with a disability who must use a wheelchair. Similarly, even if a student with a hearing loss is progressing well in class, it will be discriminatory not to provide suitable access to adapted telephone facilities if telephone facilities are made available to nondisabled students. Other examples of discrimination include the failure to provide interpreter services, guide dogs, or service dogs to Section 504 students who need them to help compensate for their substantial limitations in a major life activity. In these situations and others, Section 504 is intended to protect students with disabilities from lack of equal opportunities to benefit from educational programs and facilities.

Occasionally, the second prong of the definition also applies. For instance, if a school refuses to allow an otherwise qualified student to participate in a sports activity on the basis of a history of leukemia that has since gone into remission or on the basis of a history of past (but not current) drug abuse, the student would be protected from such discrimination. If the student meets the competitive criteria in spite of the disability, then the student must be given an opportunity to participate. Unsubstantiated fears about the health or safety of the student should not bar participation.

The third prong can also apply if a school incorrectly treats a child as disabled and discriminates against the child on that basis when no physical or mental impairment is present, such as when a child has limited English proficiency. The third prong can also be relevant when a physical or mental impairment substantially limits a major life activity only because of the attitudes of others. Examples might be a student with a cosmetic disfigurement or asymptomatic AIDS (HIV virus).

Coverage

As the Section 504 regulatory definition of "otherwise qualified" individuals makes clear, IDEA students automatically qualify as having a Section 504 disability.[12†] The Section 504 protection covers all aspects of the IDEA student's curricular and extracurricular life at school. Because the IDEA protections are more specific than those of Section 504, the Section 504 protections usually apply only when an IDEA remedy is not applicable, such as when discrimination occurs in areas of an IDEA student's education outside the IEP.

†See chapter 10 for the definition of children with disabilities under IDEA.

Because the Section 504 definition of disability is broader than the IDEA definition, it extends to another significant group of students who are not IDEA eligible, either because their condition does not fall within an IDEA category or because even if it does, they do not need special education as a result. These students are sometimes referred to as Section 504 *stand-alone* students. Among them are students with attention deficit disorders (ADD/ADHD), epilepsy, AIDS and HIV infection, allergies (e.g., asthma), arthritis, heart disease, diabetes, Tourette syndrome, and even broken limbs under some circumstances. Of course, all these students must show that their impairment substantially limits a major life activity; the impairment or condition alone is insufficient. Certain students with dyslexia or reading disability might be eligible if, although they do not meet the state's test of severe discrepancy for IDEA eligibility as learning disabled, their impairment nonetheless substantially limits their learning in the regular classroom. Also potentially eligible would be a student with a visual impairment who does not require special education but who does need large-print books or additional time to read texts and do assignments in order to succeed in the regular classroom.

Figure 3-1 shows the relationship among the student populations.

Figure 3-1. IDEA Students as a Subset of Section 504 Students, and Section 504 Students as a Subset of All Public School Students

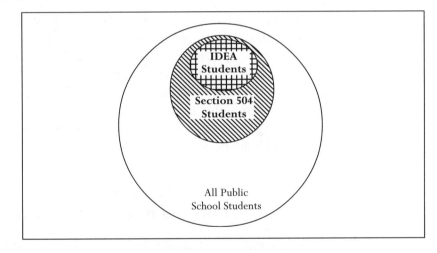

Advocates for students with ADD/ADHD had hoped that ADD/ADHD would be recognized as an IDEA disability in its own right, but Congress declined to extend such recognition and instead funded more research on ADD/ADHD. Also, OSEP, OCR, and DOE's Office of Elementary and Secondary Education (OESE) issued a joint policy memorandum explaining that ADD/ADHD students could be eligible for IDEA services only if they qualified under another label, such as "learning disability," "emotional disturbance," or "other health impairment."[13] Otherwise, if their impairment was a disability because it substantially limited their learning, they could seek programming modifications or other supplementary aids and services that addressed their needs as Section 504 students.

In 1990, the U.S. Congress specified that a current illegal drug user is not considered a person with a disability under Section 504.[14] On the other hand, a former, rehabilitated drug user is protected by the second prong of the definition and cannot be discriminated against on the basis of the former drug use. Also, although students currently *addicted* to alcohol may be protected from discrimination, current *users* of alcohol at school or school functions are not protected from school disciplinary action comparable to that taken against nondisabled students, even if a separate disability would protect them in other ways.[15]

Judicial Rulings on Coverage

Many court cases have ruled that students with HIV infection or AIDS are eligible for protection under Section 504. A number of the cases involved attempts to exclude the students from school or regular classrooms when the child did not present a significant risk of contagion (see chapter 6). In general, the few court cases dealing with other eligibility issues concern the failure to evaluate under Section 504.

Administrative Enforcement and Monitoring

OCR enforces Section 504 in educational institutions that receive federal funds. OCR has regional offices throughout the country and is also responsible for enforcing a number of other civil rights statutes in educational institutions. In addition to providing technical assistance, it performs two major roles: (a) it sometimes conducts compliance investigations on its own initiative, and (b) it investigates complaints of discrimination from individuals or groups. Most of its time is spent investigating complaints and issuing findings to the agency investigated. Usually, OCR negotiates for compliance, although occasionally it issues remedial orders. In extreme circumstances it will initiate administrative enforcement proceedings to terminate federal funds or will refer a case to the Justice Department for litigation. Any school district that has undergone an OCR investigation will tell you that it involves tedious data collection, is very time consuming, and is worth avoiding by resolving discrimination complaints internally whenever possible.

Source Materials

Section 504 statutory provisions and regulations, OCR policy memoranda, OCR compliance letters and complaint Letters of Finding (LoFs), and Section 504 court cases are all published in the *Individuals With Disabilities Education Law Report* (IDELR). This book cites IDELR when providing references to OCR policy memoranda and letters. Otherwise, citations refer to the regular statutory and judicial reporters.

Section 504 Topics in This Book

Part II of this book contains five chapters explaining in more detail the obligations that arise under Section 504. The chapters discuss: (a) evaluation issues, (b) contagious diseases, (c) FAPE and programming issues (instruction and related aids and services), (d) discipline and placement issues, and (e) due process and dispute resolution.

Table 3-1. Comparison of IDEA and Section 504 Public Education Standards

	IDEA: Special Education Law	Section 504: Civil Rights Law
Eligibility	Evaluation for specific disability conditions Need for special education LEP & teaching cannot be primary factors —	Evaluation for functional disability No special education requirement — Broader coverage (IDEA students and others)
Evaluation	Qualified professionals Multiple measures Valid tests Educational measures Relevant areas: functional, developmental Tests that measure what they purport to measure Tests administered in native language Administration and scoring that avoid racial bias Input from parents	Trained evaluators Multiple measures Valid tests Educational measures — Tests that measure what they purport to measure — — —
Procedural Safeguards	Notice of procedural safeguards Prior written notice Informed consent for initial evaluation & initial provision of special education, & for reevaluation Access to educational records Parental input into eligibility/evaluation, IEP, & placement Independent educational evaluation Surrogate parent Stay-put procedure Mediation & due process hearing Review process SEA complaint procedure	Informal notice — No explicit consent requirement, but Office for Civil Rights (OCR) interpretation requiring consent Access to educational records — — — — Due process hearing Review process OCR complaint procedure
FAPE	Special education + related services Benefit standard	Regular or special education + related aids & services Comparability standard

	IDEA: Special Education Law	**Section 504: Civil Rights Law**
Placement	Preference for regular classroom with supplementary aids Continuum of placement options Justification needed for removal from regular classroom —	Same preference as IDEA — — Reevaluation before significant placement change
IEP	Required	Optional (Section 504 plan instead)
Discipline	10 consecutive school-day suspension limit without IDEA protections Other short-term removals allowed if no pattern of placement change Manifestation determination required for disciplinary placement change 45-day removals for drug & weapon offenses or dangerous behavior Longer removal possible if behavior is not a manifestation of disability No cessation of services as a result of a placement change Procedural safeguards for placement changes based on drug & alcohol use	Comparable 10-day rule Same Same — Long-term removal possible if behavior is not a manifestation of disability Cessation allowed if behavior is not a manifestation of the disability No special protection for drug & alcohol use
Federal Administering Agency	OSEP	OCR
Funds	Federal IDEA funds toward excess costs of educating children with disabilities	No federal 504 funds
Overall Responsibility	SEA Special education	LEAs Regular education

Review

1.   What is the definition of an individual with a disability under Section 504?

The individual has a physical or mental impairment that substantially limits one or more major life activities, has a record of such an impairment, or is regarded as having such an impairment.

2.   What are the key differences between Section 504 and IDEA?

Section 504 is a federal civil rights (nondiscrimination) statute; IDEA is a federal funding statute.

Section 504 requires the recipients of federal funds to refrain from discriminating against individuals with disabilities who are otherwise qualified for the service or program in question. This may or may not require the expenditure of money, depending on what kinds of program modifications are needed to provide an equal educational opportunity. In contrast, IDEA requires participating states to ensure that students with eligible disabilities receive special education and other kinds of services necessary for students to benefit from their special education. This does require an expenditure of money.

Section 504 protects more people. It covers more students in the public schools than does IDEA because its definition of disability is broader. Unlike IDEA, it also protects individuals of all ages and extends to many government programs other than education programs.

Implementation and compliance with Section 504 in public schools is the primary responsibility of each school district, not the special education staff and *not* the state office of education. Both regular and special education teachers share the same obligation not to discriminate. In contrast, under IDEA, primary responsibility for implementation and compliance is turned over to the special education section of the state office of education and, in turn, to special education staff within each school district.

3.   What public school students are eligible for protection under Section 504?

IDEA students, other students with a physical or mental impairment that substantially limits a major life activity, and students with a record of such an impairment or who are treated as if they have such an impairment are eligible.

Notes

[1] Pub. L. 93-112, 87 Stat. 394.

[2] 29 U.S.C. § 794(a)(1996). The original language referred to "handicapped person" but was amended to conform with the terminology used in IDEA.

[3] 42 Fed. Reg. 22676 (1977).

[4] Section 504 regulations are now found at 34 C.F.R. Part 104. IDEA Part B regulations are found at 34 C.F.R. Parts 300 and 301.

[5] Rothschild v. Grottenthaler, 907 F.2d 286 (2d Cir. 1990).

[6] 34 C.F.R. §§ 104.21–.23 (1997).

[7] 465 U.S. 555 (1984).

[8] 29 U.S.C. § 794(b)(1996).

[9] 29 U.S.C. § 706(8)(B); 34 C.F.R. § 104.3(j)(1).

[10] 34 C.F.R. § 104.3(j)(2)(i).

[11] *Id.* § 104.3(j)(2)(ii).

[12] *Id.* § 104.3(k)(2).

[13] Joint Policy Memorandum, 18 IDELR 116 (OSEP, OCR, OESE, 1991).

[14] Pub. L. 101-336, 104 Stat. 327, Title V, Sec. 512 (1990), codified at 29 U.S.C. § 706(8)(C). The same exception applies under the Americans With Disabilities Act.

[15] *See* 29 U.S.C. § 706(8)(C)(iv).

Selected Supplementary Resources

Council of Administrators of Special Education. (1999). *Section 504 and the ADA promoting student access: A resource guide for educators* (2nd ed.). Albuquerque, NM: Author.

Zirkel, P. A., & Kincaid, J. (1993). *Section 504, the ADA, and the schools.* Horsham, PA: LRP.

Chapter 4

An Overview of the Americans With Disabilities Act

Provisions of the Statute

The Americans With Disabilities Act (ADA),[1] enacted in 1990, is the latest in a series of civil rights laws protecting various groups of persons from discrimination by American society. You will recall that under Section 504 of the Rehabilitation Act of 1973, recipients of federal funds are prohibited from discriminating against otherwise qualified individuals with disabilities in areas such as employment, public school and higher education, and health and social services. Under ADA, private employers and commercial enterprises serving the public are also among those obligated not to discriminate. In other words, the protections against discrimination are not limited to those served by programs or activities receiving federal funds. In effect, ADA expands the reach of Section 504.

The U.S. Congress used its authority to regulate interstate commerce as the tool for extending ADA to the private sector. Most private businesses engage in interstate commerce, as the term has come to be defined, and therefore Congress may prohibit most private businesses from discriminating against employees or job applicants with disabilities. It may also prohibit private businesses that accommodate the public from discriminating against members of the public who have disabilities.

The ADA definition of an individual with a disability is essentially the same definition used by Section 504—that is, an individual with a mental or physical impairment that substantially limits a major life activity, one with a record of such an impairment, or one who is regarded as having such an impairment.[2] Parts 2 and 3 of this definition are particularly applicable to job discrimination situations. For instance, an individual who has been hospitalized for a heart attack will have a record of a physical impairment but may no longer have the impairment itself. The record does not constitute a basis for discrimination. Neither does the employer's perception that anyone who has had a heart attack should be considered unable to do certain kinds of work, regardless of the current state of the employee's physical fitness. The definition reflects the view that evidence of current ability to perform is what matters, not stereotypes or dated information.

Title I

ADA contains five separate titles, or major sections. Title I prohibits employment discrimination against "qualified" individuals with disabilities, which is defined as those who can perform the "essential functions" of the job "with or without reasonable accommodations." The prohibition extends to hiring, firing, advancement, compensation, and job training. Only when an accommodation creates an "undue hardship" may employers be excused from providing it. Public employees, such as school teachers, are already protected under Section 504 from employment discrimination against qualified persons with disabilities.

Title II

Title II applies to public services and extends the Section 504 nondiscrimination requirements to all subdivisions of state and local government, including those that do not receive federal financial aid. Government agencies are expected to make "reasonable modifications" to their rules, policies, and practices so that otherwise eligible persons with disabilities can participate in government services, programs, or activities. What constitutes a "reasonable" modification is subject to judicial interpretation. Students in public schools are covered under Title II as well as Section 504. In fact, the provisions and regulations are similar in most respects. Title II also applies to public transportation.

The Supreme Court Narrows the Interpretation of Disability Under ADA

In June 1999, the Supreme Court handed down three ADA decisions that narrowed the interpretation of disability under ADA. In the key ruling, *Sutton v. United Air Lines*, 119 S. Ct. 2139 (1999), the Court held that mitigating circumstances had to be weighed in deciding whether twin sisters with severe nearsightedness were individuals whose physical impairments "substantially limited" a major life activity. With corrective lenses, sisters' vision was 20/20, but they were nonetheless rejected by United Air Lines for employment as commercial pilots. The Court invalidated ADA interpretive guidelines that individuals should be evaluated for disability in their uncorrected state. The twin sisters, whose myopia was completely correctable with their prescription lenses, were deemed not to have an ADA disability, and their claim against United Air Lines was dismissed. Together with the two companion cases, *Sutton* stands for the proposition that if, with corrective measures, including devices and medications, an individual's physical or mental impairment does not substantially limit a major life activity, the individual does not have a disability under ADA. (The second and third prongs of the definition of disability are not involved here.)

The effect of these rulings on children of school age is uncertain. The Section 504 definition of disability is essentially the same as the ADA definition, so commentators are wondering if some children covered under Section 504 might now be vulnerable. For instance, children with ADD/ADHD who take ritalin to reduce their symptoms might not be considered to have a substantial limitation on their learning if the ritalin allows them to function reasonably well in the classroom. Of course, as the Supreme Court pointed out, each decision must be an individualized one, and many individuals with ADHD, vision impairments, hearing impairments, physical impairments, and so forth are disabled under ADA even with the use of a corrective device or medication.

It is important to realize that the Supreme Court decisions were all employment cases, and the major life activity under consideration was working rather than activities such as learning, seeing, or hearing. We will have to wait to see how the ADA rulings are applied in the public and private school context for students who are not covered under IDEA. The IDEA definition of disability is different from that of ADA and Section 504, so the ADA decisions do not implicate IDEA coverage.

Title III

Title III affects public accommodations, which are defined as private businesses serving the public. It requires these businesses to make "reasonable modifications" to their policies, practices, and procedures for persons with disabilities. Such persons are to have ready access to public accommodations such as professional offices, shops, retail stores, food establishments, places of public lodging, entertainment facilities, and secular private schools. Architectural modifications to buildings and grounds are required in order to achieve facilities that are "readily accessible" to persons with disabilities. Religious entities and private clubs are exempt from Title III requirements, for the most part. (Note that private schools are *not* exempt unless they are controlled by religious organizations.)

Title IV

Title IV governs telecommunications practices and requires common carriers that provide intrastate or interstate telephone service to provide dual-party telephone relay services. The relay services must be "functionally equivalent" to the telephone services available to hearing persons. Title IV also requires television public service announcements to be closed captioned if they are produced or funded in whole or in part by the federal government.

Title V

Title V contains a series of miscellaneous provisions, including the following: ADA shall not be construed to apply lesser standards than those applied under Section 504; states are not immune under the Eleventh Amendment to the U. S. Constitution from lawsuits in federal court for ADA violations; ADA applies to the U.S. Congress; and a person who is currently an illegal drug user is not considered to be a person with a disability.

ADA Court Cases Interpreting Student Rights

For public school students, the protections of Section 504 are generally coextensive with those of ADA, and compliance with Section 504 regulations generally satisfies ADA requirements. Nonetheless, students with disabilities sometimes "test the waters" to see if ADA provides more extensive coverage than that provided by

Section 504 or IDEA. Students complaining about their treatment in public schools sue under Title II, while private school students sue under Title III. Although courts have not issued many rulings, in most cases ADA claims have been dismissed.

Cases Under Title II

Federal courts have ruled that if an ADA claim seeks relief that is already available under IDEA, it is subject to IDEA's requirement for "exhaustion of administrative remedies." This means that aggrieved persons must use the IDEA hearing process before going to court. Several cases have resulted in dismissal of ADA claims for failure to request a hearing. One in particular, *Glen v. Charlotte-Mecklenburg School Board of Education,* held that a special education student who was suspended for bringing a gun clip with live bullets to school could not circumvent IDEA requirements by bringing an ADA discrimination claim.[3]

On the other hand, if relief is not available under IDEA, then the case may be brought directly under Section 504 or Title II of ADA, and exhaustion of administrative remedies is not required under either one. Such a case was *Bechtel v. East Penn School District of Lehigh County,*[4] in which a student with spina bifida sought access to school facilities, including the football stadium. When the school district renovated its facilities, it failed to meet ADA access standards in spite of having been informed of them. The ADA claim was allowed to proceed.

At least two courts have ruled that ADA does not extend beyond the programming or placement standards of IDEA. In *Conner v. Branstad,*[5] the court ruled that Title II of ADA creates no mandate for deinstitutionalization of the entire class of mentally and physically disabled individuals in Iowa intermediate care facilities. The case, a long-standing class action, is continuing on other grounds.

The other case was *Urban v. Jefferson County School District R-1,*[6] in which the parents of an IDEA student were unable to convince the court that they had a right under ADA to a neighborhood school placement for their child. The federal district court concluded that ADA was not designed to result in alterations of the pre-existing and more specific framework of IDEA, notwithstanding ADA language encouraging the provision of services in the "most integrated setting appropriate to the student's needs." According to the court, giving parents control over where their child attends school would cause the school district to lose control over the utilization and allocation of its resources and would go beyond IDEA placement requirements. The decision in *Urban* was affirmed by the U.S. Court of Appeals for the Tenth Circuit in 1996.[7]

Perhaps the best known Title II case to date is *Petersen v. Hastings Public Schools.*[8] In *Petersen*, a modified Signing Exact English II system (SEE-II) was upheld as a means of implementing the IEPs of three IDEA students with hearing impairments. The parents had sought an exact SEE-II system, not a modified one. The federal district court ruled that, under IDEA, the modified system provided FAPE because the students were clearly making progress at school.

Then the court ruled on whether Title II of ADA required something else. The relevant Title II regulation specifies that the parents' choice of auxiliary aids and services (here stipulated to include a specific signing system) should be honored unless another effective means of communication is available.[9] The court concluded that the modified SEE-II system was an effective alternative to the parents' choice. On appeal, the Eighth Circuit upheld the lower court's decision that the school district's choice of signing method met the ADA requirement of providing an effective means of communication. It appears that an "effective" means of communication may be comparable to IDEA's requirement for an "appropriate" means of communication.

The district court in *Petersen* did allow the parents an opportunity to demonstrate that the LEA's choice of the modified SEE-II was not as effective as their own choice, a burden they were unable to meet. The Eighth Circuit upheld this legal approach. The result opens the door to the possibility that another plaintiff might be able to meet the burden, thereby requiring an LEA to select a communication system that not only is effective but is as effective as the parent's preference.

Another Title II case concerning the mental health system is included here because some may find it analogous to the needs of some deaf students in the public schools. In *Tugg v. Towey*,[10] the issue was whether the use of sign language interpreters in providing mental health counseling to persons who were deaf or hard of hearing violated ADA and Section 504. Advocates for the deaf argued that the use of sign language interpreters in a therapeutic setting did not produce mental health services equal to those provided to the nondisabled because reliance on the interpreters and the inability of the counselors themselves to use sign language created too many miscommunication possibilities. The court issued a preliminary injunction ordering the state Department of Health and Rehabilitation Services to provide counselors who could use American Sign Language (ASL) and who had an understanding of the mental health needs of the Deaf community—that is, those who identify themselves as culturally deaf, for whom ASL is the primary language.

Finally, several cases challenging age-eligibility and other eligibility rules imposed by high school athletic associations have been filed under both Title II and Title III as well as Section 504. One question has been whether athletic associations whose members are dues-paying high schools are public entities or private associations. Another question has been whether the dues they receive make them a recipient of federal financial assistance under Section 504. In *Bingham v. Oregon School Activities Association*, a 1999 federal district court case, the court ruled that the Oregon School Activities Association was a public entity under Title II (but not a public accommodation under Title III) and not a recipient of federal aid under Section 504.[11] The case relied, among other things, on a 1999 Supreme Court ruling that dues paid to the NCAA by postsecondary recipients of federal aid did not make the NCAA a recipient of federal financial aid under Title IX.[12] If the Oregon case is a harbinger of things to come, then the future may see more athletic discrimination claims brought under Title II than under Section 504.[†]

†The court in the *Bingham* case ordered a waiver of the eight-semester rule as a reasonable modification for a student with learning disabilities and ADHD. The student was still age-eligible and was retained in 10th grade for academic and not athletic reasons. The evidence indicated that his athletic participation was important in coping with his disability and would not result in a competitive advantage for him or his team. (You will want to compare the material in chapter 7 on sports participation under Section 504.)

Cases Under Title III

A few cases have arisen that test the extent of the responsibility of secular private schools to provide auxiliary aids and services to students with disabilities in order to assure "full and equal enjoyment of the goods, services, facilities, privileges, advantages, or accommodations"[13] of the private school. Title III excuses the private school from this obligation only when the provision of such goods and services would fundamentally alter the nature of the program or result in an undue burden on the school.[14]

One case that tested the limits of Title III is *Roberts v. Kindercare Learning Centers.*[15] Kindercare, a public accommodation, denied admission to a 4-year-old with multiple disabilities on the basis that it had no legal duty to provide one-on-one care during the times when a personal care attendant (PCA) could not be present. The child's IEP called for a PCA, and the paid services of a PCA for 30 hours a week in the daycare center were authorized under a Medicaid program. The parents, however, wanted the center to provide a one-on-one aide for the remainder of the time at the center and when the PCA was ill or otherwise unable to accompany the child. A federal appeals court upheld the district court, ruling that Kindercare's refusal to admit the student did not violate ADA. The appeals court reasoned that the parents were seeking more than a reasonable accommodation by attempting to force Kindercare to provide far more than its usual group child care. To require one-on-one care would fundamentally alter the nature of its business and create an undue financial burden on the center, the court concluded.

Two other interesting cases produced preliminary injunctions in favor of the plaintiffs, but one was later overturned. The first case also involved a Kindercare center. In *Orr v. Kindercare Learning Centers,*[16] a 9-year-old student with severe developmental disabilities who required assistance in eating, walking, toileting, and interacting with others was placed in Kindercare's after-school 2-year-old class. Kindercare gave notice of its intent to terminate the boy on the basis that it could not meet his individual needs in a group care setting. The parents wanted to provide an aide to accompany him and wanted him placed in a school-age class. The court granted a preliminary injunction to the parents, allowing them to keep their son at the facility pending a trial on the merits. The court found no evidence to indicate that a personal aide, paid for with outside funds, would fundamentally alter the nature of the program, and it held that the likelihood of harm weighed in favor of the parents. Whether the aide was a reasonable modification of Kindercare's activities remained an issue, depending on who trained and supervised the aide, among other things. This issue was to be decided at trial.

The second, and more recent, Title III case, *Bercovitch v. Baldwin School, Inc.*,[17] initially resulted in a preliminary injunction that required a private, college preparatory school to continue to enroll an ADHD teenager in spite of his repeated disruptive behaviors. On appeal, however, the First Circuit vacated the preliminary injunction, concluding that the plaintiffs had not shown a likelihood of winning on the merits. According to the appeals court, the parents (and the district court) had expected the school to go far beyond the reasonable modification requirements of ADA in attempting to manage the student's behavior. The expected changes would have produced a fundamental alteration in the school's standards and created an undue hardship on its academic program.

The appeals court held that an arbitration contract voluntarily entered into by the parents and the school was the valid mechanism for ruling on the ADA claims and determining whether the school could expel the student for his repeated misbehaviors. Of particular importance to educators and parents is the court's conclusion that ADA does not require a private, regular education school to adopt IDEA-type programming or standards to manage a student's misbehaviors. Furthermore, the court concluded that a private school need not exempt a student from conforming to the school conduct code when the school has tried a variety of reasonable ways to accommodate a student's misbehavior.

Safety Issues With an HIV-Positive Student

A 1999 case concerning a child who was HIV-positive and who wanted to participate in private group karate lessons may provide useful information to school districts. In *Montalvo v. Radcliffe*, 167 F.3d 873 (4th Cir. 1999), the father of a 12-year-old boy filed a discrimination suit under Title III of ADA against a private karate school that refused to allow the boy to join its group karate classes. The program was a combat-oriented, traditional Japanese martial arts program. Its training methods resulted in many minor abrasions and bloody noses that allowed blood to transfer from one student to another, and the school argued that the boy's blood spillage could present a direct threat to the health and safety of classmates and instructors. It was willing to instruct the boy privately as a reasonable *modification* of its programming that would not require a fundamental *alteration* of its training program.

The Fourth Circuit upheld the district court decision in favor of the karate school. It noted that the district court had considered the specific circumstances and made an individualized assessment of the risk presented by the boy's participation in group classes. Because AIDS can be transmitted by blood-to-blood and blood-to-eye contact, and precautions could not be taken to minimize the risk of transmission in the context of the group training methods, the school did not need to change its methods to accommodate the boy. Even the use of "universal precautions" such as eye coverings and gloves could not eliminate or minimize the otherwise significant risk.

Administrative and Judicial Enforcement Mechanisms Under Titles II and III

Administrative enforcement under Title II is essentially the same as it is under Section 504. This means that when discrimination in education programs is involved, OCR will investigate and monitor compliance. It can refer unresolved complaints to the Justice Department for litigation.

Under Title III, unless a public accommodation is receiving federal funds under Section 504, there will not be a line agency (like DOE) responsible for administrative enforcement and monitoring. Instead, the attorney general of the United States will investigate alleged violations of ADA and initiate compliance reviews. The attorney general is authorized to commence a lawsuit in federal court if there is a pattern or practice of resistance to ADA or if the discrimination raises an issue of general public importance. Otherwise, the aggrieved individual must bring the lawsuit on his or her own behalf.[18]

When an individual believes that a public accommodation, such as a secular private school, is violating ADA, the individual can sue for an injunction to require an auxiliary aid or service; modifications to policies, practices, or procedures; or removal of architectural barriers if "readily achievable." Also, if an individual reasonably believes that a public accommodation is about to remodel a facility without making the alterations or new construction readily accessible to and usable by persons with disabilities, the individual may sue to stop the construction until it is ADA compliant.

In addition to injunctions, other kinds of relief can be ordered by a court, including monetary damages and civil penalties against the entity violating ADA. The court may also award attorney's fees to the party (other than the United States) who prevails in the lawsuit.

ADA encourages what are known as "alternative means of dispute resolution" to the extent that they are authorized by law. Among the alternatives are such methods as settlement negotiations, conciliation, facilitation, mediation, fact-finding, minitrials, and arbitration, each of which is somewhat different from the other. In the *Bercovitch* case described above, an arbitration contract was upheld as the appropriate mechanism for resolving the disciplinary dispute at the private school.

Implications

The body of relevant ADA case law affecting students with disabilities who are already covered by IDEA or Section 504 is small. Early indications are that, to the extent that IDEA and Section 504 provide more specific rights and standards, they will be used instead of the ADA. In a few areas, however, such as discrimination in secular private schools, ADA establishes rights for an additional group of students with disabilities not otherwise covered. In general, case law affecting students under the ADA is not yet well developed. Table 4-1 compares ADA with Section 504 and IDEA.

Table 4–1. A Comparison of IDEA, Section 504, and ADA in Education Settings

	IDEA	Section 504	ADA
Nature of Statute	Funding Statute	Civil Rights Statute	Civil Rights Statute
Jurisdiction	States and school districts accepting money under the statute	Public and private schools (K–12) and higher education institutions accepting federal money	Public sector and parts of private sector (e.g., secular private schools)
Extent of Coverage	Eligible students	Eligible students, employees, and parents	Eligible service recipients and employees
Definition of Disability	13 specific disabilities, if the disability adversely affects the child's education to the extent that special education is necessary (relaxed definition for younger children)	Functional definition (mental or physical impairment that substantially limits a major life activity, record of such, or regarded as having such an impairment)	Functional definition (essentially the same as Section 504)
Age Range	Birth to 21 years	Birth to death	Birth to death
Program Requirements	Free appropriate public education (FAPE) in the least restrictive environment (LRE) with an individualized education program (IEP) for 3- to 21-year-olds	– Nondiscrimination – Reasonable modifications (programs & services) – Reasonable accommodations (employment) – Accessible facilities	Same as Section 504
Enforcement	– Administrative complaint mechanisms – Private right of action in court	– Administrative complaint mechanisms – Inferred private right of action in court	– Administrative complaint mechanisms – Private right of action in court
Administering Agency	OSEP	– OCR – EEOC – Department of Justice	Same as Section 504

Review

1.   What is the primary difference between Section 504 and ADA?

ADA is broader in scope. It extends to private sector employment and public accommodations. It also extends to state and local government agencies, regardless of whether they receive federal funds. In contrast, Section 504 is limited to recipients of federal funds.

2.   What are the primary similarities of Section 504 and ADA?

Both use essentially the same definition of disability, and both prohibit discrimination against otherwise qualified persons with disabilities. The two laws use comparable standards in determining what constitutes unlawful employment discrimination and unlawful discrimination in state and local government programs.

Notes

[1] 42 U.S.C. § 12101 *et seq.*(1994).

[2] *Id.* § 12210.

[3] 903 F. Supp. 918 (W.D.N.C. 1995). *See also* Hope v. Cortines, 872 F. Supp. 14 (E.D.N.Y.), *aff'd,* 69 F.3d 687 (2d Cir. 1995).

[4] 1994 U.S. Dist. LEXIS 1327 (E.D. Pa. 1994).

[5] 839 F. Supp. 1346 (S.D. Iowa 1993).

[6] 870 F. Supp. 1558 (D. Colo. 1994).

[7] 89 F.3d 720 (10th Cir. 1996).

[8] 831 F. Supp. 742 (D. Neb. 1993), *aff'd,* 31 F.3d 705 (8th Cir. 1994).

[9] See 28 C.F.R. § 35.160 (1995) and accompanying comments.

[10] 864 F. Supp. 1201 (S.D. Fla. 1994).

[11] 37 F. Supp.2d 1189 (D. Or. 1999).

[12] *See* NCAA v. Smith, 119 S. Ct. 924 (1999).

[13] 42 U.S.C. § 12182(a).

[14] *Id.* § 12182(b)(2)(A)(iii).

[15] 86 F.3d 844 (8th Cir. 1996).

[16] 23 IDELR 181 (E.D. Cal. 1995).

[17] 133 F.3d 141 (1st Cir. 1998).

[18] *See* 28 C.F.R. §§ 36.501–.505.

Selected Supplementary Resources

Equal Employment Opportunity Commission & U.S. Department of Justice. (1991). *The Americans With Disabilities Act handbook*. Washington, DC: U.S. Government Printing Office.

Marczely, B. (1993). The Americans With Disabilities Act: Confronting the shortcomings of Section 504 in public education. *Education Law Reporter, 78,* 199–207.

Morrissey, P. (1993). *The educator's guide to the Americans With Disabilities Act*. Alexandria VA: American Vocational Association.

U.S. Department of Justice, Civil Rights Division. *The ADA Title II technical assistance manual*. Washington, DC: Author.

Wenkart, R. D. (1993). The Americans With Disabilities Act and its impact on public education. *Education Law Reporter, 82,* 291–302.

West, J. (Ed.). (1991). *The Americans With Disabilities Act: From policy to practice*. New York: Milbank Memorial Fund.

Part II

Section 504 of the Rehabilitation Act of 1973

Chapter 5

Disability Evaluation Under Section 504

Notice and Consent

Section 504 regulations require school districts to "take appropriate steps to notify disabled persons and their parents or guardians" of the school district's duty not to discriminate under the relevant regulations, including the duty to evaluate a student for eligibility under Section 504.[1] The specific means are left up to each school district. Many school districts post multiple notices within the school building; others also send notices home to all enrolled students. It is helpful to include information in the notice about evaluation and grievance procedures and about whom to contact for further information. The school must give specific notice to the parent of a child whom school personnel want to evaluate under Section 504. Whether to notify the parent verbally or in writing is left to the discretion of each local school district.[2]

Section 504 regulations do not mention parental consent, in contrast to IDEA evaluation requirements. OCR, however, has taken the position that consent should be obtained before evaluating a student for eligibility and services under Section 504.[3] Because some evaluations can be quite informal and are without implications for a change of status (i.e., from a regular to a special education student), the need to seek consent is not as serious a due process issue as it is under IDEA. Perhaps that is why it is not mentioned explicitly in the regulations. (For more information, see chapter 9.)

Regulatory Requirements

Under Section 504 regulations, any person believed to need special education or related services because of a Section 504 disability must be evaluated "before taking any action with respect to the initial placement of the person in a regular or special education program. . . ."[4] The use of the word *or* emphasizes that some students with Section

65

504 disabilities will not need special education; nonetheless, they must still be evaluated prior to "any action" concerning initial placement in a regular education program. This language is ambiguous; if all that is sought is a related aid or service in a regular education setting, one would assume that a Section 504 evaluation could occur simultaneously with or subsequent to placement in a regular education program. Perhaps all that is meant is that evaluation is required prior to identifying and serving a student as a Section 504 student, regardless of the student's placement.

The regulations are cryptic and leave many details of the evaluation to local school districts. Who should perform the evaluation—a team or an individual—is not specified. The regulations mandate only that the school district establish standards and procedures to ensure that (a) tests are valid for the purpose for which they are used and are administered by trained personnel in conformity with the test instructions, (b) measures of educational need and not just IQ are obtained, and (c) tests measure what they purport to measure and not the disability (except where it is intentionally being measured).[5]

In these latter respects, the Section 504 requirements and IDEA regulations are comparable (see chapter 11). Unlike IDEA, however, the Section 504 requirements do not insist on assessment in all areas related to the suspected disability, on functional and developmental information, or on parental input into the evaluation process. Perhaps these omissions reflect that, for a student who is believed to need only related aids or services in regular education classrooms or activities, a less formal and less comprehensive evaluation of the student's individual needs will suffice to ensure nondiscriminatory programming that is as adequate as that provided to the nondisabled. Of course, if a student is suspected of being IDEA eligible, then the IDEA evaluation process will supersede that of Section 504. In any event, although Section 504 regulations do not so state, it does not make sense to evaluate one's eligibility without also evaluating the need for specific kinds of adaptations.

A Section 504 student must be reevaluated prior to any subsequent "significant change in placement."[6] This requirement does not appear in the IDEA evaluation provisions, but because IDEA students are covered under Section 504, this requirement must be met. As with IDEA, placement teams must ensure that placements allow education with nondisabled students to the maximum extent appropriate. Finally, for Section 504 students who receive special education and related services, provision must be made for "periodic" reevaluation, presumably to determine their continuing need for special education.[7] Actual placement decisions are to be made by a knowledgeable group of persons and not by a single individual.[8]

Judicial and OCR Rulings

Litigation with respect to Section 504 evaluations is sparse. One federal court decision faults school officials for failing to reevaluate two students with hearing impairments prior to recommending a significant change in placement from a residential school for the deaf to a public day school setting.[9]

An alternative to litigation is to file a complaint with OCR, and there are numerous LoFs addressing the failure to evaluate potential Section 504 students. Most of these letters concern students with ADD/ADHD,[10] a group that has sought classroom accommodations under Section 504 if they were not eligible for special education as IDEA students. Other OCR letters have addressed the need to evaluate students with Tourette syndrome, juvenile diabetes, juvenile rheumatoid arthritis, broken limbs, allergies, encopresis (medical disorder resulting in decreased ability to control the bowels), and even obesity when it substantially impairs a major life activity or is perceived by others as doing so.[11]

Potential Evaluation Trigger Points

The following situations are among those that ought to trigger the consideration of a Section 504 evaluation:

* When parents inform school personnel that their child has a physical or mental impairment

Responding to Tourette Syndrome

Tommy was a sixth grader with undiagnosed Tourette syndrome. The teacher noticed that Tommy had some unusual facial tics and grimaces. She also was bothered by his sudden outbursts of swearing in the classroom. Her ordinary instincts were to discipline Tommy for uncivil language in the classroom, but she knew a little about the symptoms of Tourette syndrome and realized that Tommy's actions might be totally involuntary. She referred Tommy for a Section 504 evaluation, which required the expertise of the school district's consulting physician. The evaluation team determined that Tommy had developed Tourette syndrome and that it was substantially limiting a major life activity—controlling his behavior so as not to disrupt his own learning and that of others.

As a result of this determination, Tommy became eligible for modifications to his educational program so that he would not be discriminated against in his regular classroom. He did not need special education. Instead, the team determined that he needed to be allowed to leave the classroom when he felt a "spell" coming on. He needed to have his classmates understand and ignore his outbursts. He needed the teacher to make good-faith attempts to calm him when he seemed to be getting anxious about his work.

Without an understanding of Tourette syndrome and Section 504 responsibilities, Tommy's school might have punished him for behavior out of his control and might have contributed to a decline of acceptable behavior and a worsening of his interactions with other students.

- When the school is about to suspend or expel a student who might have some kind of disability but has not been evaluated
- When a child's behavior deteriorates noticeably over time
- When a student returns to school after a serious illness or injury, especially if the student asks for or needs any extra help
- When a student has been evaluated medically as having ADD/ADHD
- When a student has been referred or evaluated for an IDEA disability but is found not to qualify under IDEA
- When a child has a chronic health condition that may require accommodations
- When alcohol abuse is suspected and learning is substantially affected

- When school personnel consider a child to be "at risk" of failing, being held back a grade, or dropping out but don't know the reason

At these times, it is wise to review the available information and consider whether an evaluation is needed to determine if a Section 504 disability is present.

Implications

Many schools continue to misunderstand their obligation to evaluate students who may be eligible for protection under Section 504, thinking incorrectly that evaluation requirements pertain only to students who are suspected of needing special education under IDEA. Educators should be prepared to evaluate anyone who might meet the Section 504 definition of disability.[12] At the same time, they should recognize that they have considerable freedom to design their own evaluation procedures for those who are not suspected of IDEA disabilities. Medical records are frequently helpful and can often be used to assess both the impairment and the extent to which it limits a major life activity. Regarding the major life activity of learning, however, medical records do not relieve educators of making an independent determination of whether learning has been substantially limited by the impairment. This is especially true for ADD/ADHD, which does not impair other major life activities such as walking, talking, breathing, seeing, and hearing.

During standardized evaluation situations such as districtwide achievement testing or high-stakes testing for high school graduation, it is important for school personnel to remember that a student with a Section 504 disability may need testing accommodations in order to demonstrate what he or she knows. For instance, a student could be allowed to type rather than handwrite answers, be provided with extra time, or be given large-print materials. As long as the validity of the test instrument itself is not compromised, accommodations should be provided. This is an increasingly important issue for educators and is discussed more fully in chapter 11.

Finally, school personnel should realize that if a Section 504 "stand-alone" (non-IDEA) student has been determined to need "special education" (specially designed instruction) or any instructional aids and services to ensure nondiscrimination, they should be provided. Although federal IDEA funds are not available for such a student, that does not relieve the school district of providing any special education or related aids that may be needed and absorbing any extra costs associated with them.

Review

1. Who determines eligibility under Section 504?

    Unspecified school personnel, who must evaluate all students suspected of meeting the disability definition, determine eligibility.

2. What are the basic requirements for a Section 504 evaluation?

    The requirements are trained evaluators who administer valid tests in accordance with test instructions; measures of educational need and not just an IQ score; and tests that actually measure what they purport to measure.

Notes

[1] 34 C.F.R. § 104.32(b) (1997).

[2] *See id.* § 104.36.

[3] Letter to Zirkel, 22 IDELR 667 (OCR 1995).

[4] 34 C.F.R. § 104.35.

[5] *Id.* § 104.35(b).

[6] *Id.* § 104.35(a).

[7] *Id.* § 104.35(d).

[8] *Id.* § 104.35(c).

[9] Brimmer v. Traverse City Area Pub. Sch., 872 F. Supp. 447 (W.D. Mich. 1994).

[10] *See, e.g.,* Farmington (MI) Pub. Schools, 17 EHLR 872 (OCR 1991); Columbia County (GA) Sch. Dist., 17 EHLR 586 (OCR 1991); Fairfield-Suisin (CA) Unified Sch. Dist., 14 EHLR 353:205 (OCR 1989); Rialto (CA) Unified Sch. Dist., 14 EHLR 353:201 (OCR 1989); Cocke County (TN) Sch. Dist., 14 EHLR 353:169 (OCR 1988); Knox County (KY) Sch. Dist., 14 EHLR 353:159 (OCR 1988).

[11] *See, e.g.,* Fontana (CA) Unified Sch. Dist., 14 EHLR 353:248 (OCR 1989) (Tourette syndrome); Bement (IL) Community Unit Sch. Dist. 14 EHLR 353:383 (OCR 1989)(juvenile diabetes); Linden (CA) Unified Sch. Dist., EHLR 352:617 (OCR 1988) (juvenile rheumatoid arthritis); Central (CA) Elem. Sch. Dist., EHLR 352:544 (OCR 1987) (broken leg); Great Valley (PA) Sch. Dist., 16 EHLR 101 (OCR 1989) (encopresis); OCR Senior Staff Memorandum, EHLR 307:17 (OCR 1989) (obesity).

[12] *See* 34 C.F.R. §§ 104.35(a) and (b).

Selected Supplementary Resources

Gorn, S. (1998). *What do I do when . . . : The answer book on section 504.* Horsham, PA: LRP.

Idaho State Department of Education., Special Education Section. (1996). *Technical assistance resource guide for teachers educating students with attention deficit hyperactivity disorder.* Boise, ID: Author. (A complete resource guide, with information on identification, assessment, classroom strategies, and interventions. Includes a resource directory and bibliography of other materials. The State of Washington has a similar guide, on which Idaho's was based.)

OSEP, OCR, & OESE. (1991). *Memorandum to chief state school officers: Clarification of policy to address the needs of children with attention deficit disorders within general and/or special education.* Washington, DC: U.S. Department of Education.

Chapter 6

Contagious Diseases and Section 504

Overview

Public health problems have been a concern of the public schools for many decades. Flu epidemics and measles outbreaks continue to create attendance problems for many school districts, and cases of head lice are still frequent in certain areas. Now, however, such problems are handled routinely by schools and public health authorities. Exclusion of the infected student is only for the brief time during which the condition is

contagious, and quarantine of exposed students is nonexistent in most cases, although students who have received a waiver from a state's immunization law may be asked to leave school during an outbreak of a disease such as measles until they can show evidence of immunization.

On the other hand, when a disease or condition is not only contagious but is perceived as particularly dangerous to the health of the student and others, school districts may become alarmed and attempt to exclude or isolate affected students on a long-term basis. In these cases, the students can usually qualify as a student with a disability under Section 504. In recent years a number of court cases have arisen concerning the treatment of students with diseases such as AIDS and hepatitis B. As is traditional in matters of health, courts balance the rights of these students with the health and safety needs of others in the school environment. Students with potentially life-threatening contagious diseases who are nonetheless well enough to attend school, or who are asymptomatic disease carriers, have the right to be in school as long as other students and staff do not incur significant health risks as a result. Otherwise, they are being discriminated against on the basis of a Section 504 disability.

AIDS

In the mid-1980s, in the midst of public alarm over HIV, the virus that causes AIDS, a number of important court cases established that medically unsupported fears of HIV transmission via school contacts would not suffice to exclude children carrying or infected with HIV from regular or special education classrooms. Two federal court cases are instructive. The first, *Ray v. Desoto County School District*,[1] involved three regular education students with hemophilia who had become HIV positive (AIDS carriers), presumably from infected blood transfusions. A federal district court enjoined the school district from excluding the three Ray brothers. The medical evidence indicated that the boys posed no significant risk to other students; they were thereby entitled to education in a regular classroom. AIDS was determined to be a disabling condition under Section 504, and the boys were protected by Section 504 from discrimination that was based on fear rather than a genuine likelihood of transmission of the AIDS virus.

The second case, *Martinez v. Hillsborough County School Board*,[2] concerned a young student, Eliana Martinez, with mental retardation and AIDS, who was not toilet trained, who sucked her fingers, and who had contracted thrush (a mouth disease that can produce blood in the saliva). Claims of violation of both Section 504 and IDEA were involved in the case. In *Martinez*, a federal appeals court determined that, under Section 504, Eliana's AIDS constituted a disability because it was a physical impairment that substantially limited a major life activity. Therefore, she was protected from discrimination based solely on her disability as long as she was "otherwise qualified" to be in school or in a given activity or program within the school. She was also eligible for special education services under IDEA and to placement in the LRE appropriate to her needs.

The U.S. Court of Appeals for the Eleventh Circuit determined that Eliana was otherwise qualified, in spite of her AIDS, to receive special education services in a classroom for children who were trainable mentally retarded. The court ruled that the lower court had erred in concluding that Eliana's school could isolate her in a glass cubicle within her special education classroom. According to the appeals court, the lower court had incorrectly based its decision on a "remote theoretical possibility" of the risk of AIDS transmission via tears, saliva, or urine. The correct standard should have been whether her presence posed a significant risk of harm to her associates. The appeals court remanded the case for additional findings under the announced standard. Upon remand, the lower court found that the medical evidence suggested no significant risk of transmission and therefore ordered Eliana placed in the special education classroom with her other classmates. Eliana has since died.

At least half a dozen similar cases across the country have invalidated the exclusion of a student who tests positive for HIV or who has AIDS or AIDS-Related Complex (ARC) and is otherwise well enough to attend school.[3] Accumulating medical evidence continues to indicate no documented cases of transmission via contact with saliva, tears, or urine. Contact with someone's infected blood is a concern, but only if the blood enters the other person's bloodstream.

Hepatitis B

In contrast, hepatitis B has been found to be a more contagious disease than AIDS, although the risk of fatality is only approximately 1% of those affected. Two federal courts have assessed the potential risks somewhat differently from each other. A federal district court in New York ordered a school to stop isolating students with mental retardation who were hepatitis B carriers, finding that the risk of transmission via saliva was remote and ruling that isolating retarded carriers was discriminatory when the school did not isolate other hepatitis B carriers.[4] On the other hand, the Eighth Circuit concluded that a retarded, blind, adult carrier of the hepatitis B virus who demonstrated aggressive and maladaptive behaviors created a significant risk of transmission and subsequent harm in his vocational training program.[5] The Circuit ruled that the lower court's mandated inoculation plan was too limited and exposed the uninoculated staff to unreasonable risk. A third decision in a state court ordered a special education placement in school rather than a homebound program for a student with Down syndrome and hepatitis B, based on the school's ability to mitigate the risk of transmission.[6]

Implications

In response to concern about students with contagious diseases, many school districts have adopted the recommendations of the Centers for Disease Control and routinely train staff members to take "universal precautions" when in contact with the blood of any child, with or without a known infectious disease. Careful hygiene and use of disposable gloves should be commonplace in the school setting. Also, vaccinations are frequently required for staff members who are likely to come in contact with hepatitis carriers.

As a general rule, school officials are advised to adopt a policy that does not expel anyone just because he or she has contracted a contagious disease or has become a carrier. Instead, using standards established by the U.S. Supreme Court in *Nassau County School Board v. Arline*,[7] districts should conduct an individualized examination of the student's health, including such factors as how the particular disease is transmitted, how long the carrier is infectious, what the potential harm is to third parties, and the probability of transmission and of various degrees of harm. Only when it is determined that the specific student creates a significant health risk (to self or others) that cannot be reduced by individual accommodations should the student be placed in homebound instruction or in another restrictive alternative.

School officials also need to know that they should not automatically label a student with a contagious disease as a special education student. If the student's health condition does not adversely affect educational performance to the extent that special educational services are required, the student will not qualify under IDEA for the special education label of "other health impaired"— or any other disability label, if there is no independent disability.[8] Instead, the student is likely to be a Section 504 stand-alone student.

The same concerns for the rights of students with contagious diseases apply to school employees as well.

Both ADA and Section 504 require that an employee not be discriminated against on the basis of a disability if the employee is otherwise qualified. This means that the employee is able to perform the essential functions of the job with or without reasonable accommodations.

The Ninth Circuit enjoined the administrative reassignment of a classroom teacher with AIDS because there was no evidence that he could not perform the essential functions of his teaching assignment or that he presented any significant risk of transmission of AIDS to his students.[9] This decision was consistent with the Supreme Court's decision in the *Arline* case that a teacher with inactive tuberculosis (TB) was discriminated against on the basis of her TB when she was "relieved" of her teaching duties without evidence that her TB affected her ability to perform or created a significant risk of harm to her students.

Privacy Rights

School personnel should also be aware of the privacy rights of students with diseases. If a parent discloses a student's medical condition to the school and it is part of the student's educational record, the federal Family Educational Rights and Privacy Act (FERPA) requires that schools obtain written parental consent before disclosing the student's disease to persons such as classmates and their parents (see chapter 14). Only in the case of a medical emergency may the confidentiality requirements be breached. Some states may have laws that go beyond FERPA in restricting access by school employees to a student's school medical records, so you should familiarize yourself with state and local policies on this matter.

Privacy Issue for AIDs Student

The Montgomery County, Maryland, school district was sued for privacy violations under state law because a substitute teacher revealed that a student was infected with the AIDS virus. Apparently ill informed about how AIDS is transmitted, the teacher revealed the information to students who were sharing lip balm. The student in question, who was absent from class when the information was revealed, transferred to a different school and sought $100,000 in civil damages. See "Right to Privacy," *EducationWeek, 15,* 4 (May 22, 1996).

Review

1.   What legal standard should be used in determining whether a student or employee with a contagious disease that qualifies as a disability under Section 504 should be separated from contact with other persons in school?

The standard is whether the person is "otherwise qualified" to receive the service or benefit in question. "Otherwise qualified" includes a determination of whether the person's condition creates a substantial risk of transmission to others.

This decision is based on accepted medical judgment.

Notes

[1] 666 F. Supp. 1524 (M.D. Fla. 1987).

[2] 861 F.2d 1502 (11th Cir. 1988); *on remand,* 711 F. Supp. 1066 (M.D. Fla. 1989).

[3] *See, e.g.*, Doe v. Dolton Elem. Sch. Dist. No. 148, 694 F. Supp. 440 (N.D. Ill. 1988); Robertson v. Granite City Community Unit Sch. Dist. No. 9, 684 F. Supp. 1002 (S.D. Ill. 1988); Parents of Child, Code No. 870901W v. Coker, 676 F. Supp. 1072 (E.D. Okla. 1987); Thomas v. Atascadero Unified Sch. Dist., 662 F. Supp. 376 (C.D. Cal. 1986); District 27 Community Sch. Bd. v. Board of Educ. of New York, 502 N.Y.S.2d 325 (N.Y. Sup. Ct. 1986).

[4] New York State Ass'n for Retarded Children v. Carey, 466 F. Supp. 487 (E.D.N.Y. 1979).

[5] Kohl v. Woodhaven Learning Ctr., 865 F.2d 930 (8th Cir. 1989).

[6] Community High Sch. Dist. 155 v. Denz, 463 N.E.2d 998 (Ill. App. Ct. 1984). *See also* Jeffrey S. v. Georgia State Bd. of Educ., 896 F.2d 507 (11th Cir. 1990) (remanding, for a trial on the merits, the question of the potential harm to students of placing a hepatitis B carrier in a school setting compared to the potential harm of placing the student in a homebound program).

[7] 480 U.S. 273 (1987).

[8] *See* Doe v. Belleville Pub. Sch. Dist., 672 F. Supp. 342 (S.D. Ill. 1987).

[9] Chalk v. United States Dist. Ct., Cent. Dist. Cal., 840 F.2d 701 (9th Cir. 1988).

Selected Supplementary Resources

U.S. Department of Health and Human Services Public Health Service, Centers for Disease Control. (1989). Guidelines for prevention of transmission of human immunodeficiency virus and hepatitis B virus to health-care and public-safety workers. *Morbidity and Mortality Weekly Report, 38* (S-6). Atlanta, GA: Author.

Chapter 7

Free Appropriate Public Education Under Section 504

The Regulatory Definition of Free Appropriate Public Education

Free appropriate public education (FAPE), under Section 504, is not defined by statute but by regulation. The definition of "free" education under Section 504 regulations is educational and related services provided without cost to the student with the disability, or to his or her parents, except for fees that are charged to everybody—disabled and nondisabled alike. The definition of "appropriate" education under Section 504 is "the provision of regular or special education and related aids and services that . . . are designed to meet individual educational needs [of persons with disabilities] as adequately as the needs of [nondisabled] persons are met and [that meet the procedural requirements of Section 504]."[1]

Thus, this definition applies to regular education programs as well as special education programs. Neither "special education" nor "related aids and services" are defined by Section 504 or its regulations, however. Often, OCR rulings borrow the IDEA definition of "special education": specially designed instruction to meet the unique needs of the student with the disability.

Section 504 regulations state that an IEP developed in accordance with IDEA is one way to meet the Section 504 definition of appropriate education.[2] Commentators advise against the development of IEPs for non-IDEA students, however, because it

79

creates confusion in the minds of parents and educators as to whether the student is an IDEA student or a Section 504 "stand-alone" student (one without IDEA coverage). Instead, schools are better advised to develop Section 504 plans, which are frequently referred to as Individual Accommodation Plans.

When a complaint raises an independent Section 504 issue, either for a Section 504 stand-alone student or for an IDEA student, then the Section 504 definition of FAPE applies. On the other hand, if the complaint overlaps with an IDEA issue, students covered under IDEA should seek a remedy under IDEA because its protections are more specific, and the IDEA FAPE definition should be applied. In fact, if IDEA provides a remedy for the alleged harm, IDEA students cannot file a lawsuit under Section 504 without first seeking a ruling from an administrative hearing officer under IDEA. Generally speaking, Section 504 should be reserved for issues and claims that cannot be resolved under IDEA.

It is helpful to realize that the Section 504 regulatory definition of FAPE does not include the term "reasonable accommodations," a phrase that is used in the context of employment discrimination cases brought under Section 504 and ADA. Courts sometimes introduce the term in special education cases, however,[†] which adds confusion to the situation. Nonetheless, OCR, which is responsible for enforcement of Section 504, has reminded school officials that FAPE under Section 504 requires that individual needs be met as adequately as those of the nondisabled are met, which is not necessarily the same thing as simply providing reasonable accommodations.[3] Although Section 504 does not require extensive affirmative remedies (like an IEP) as IDEA does, and although a simple nondiscrimination standard or, in effect, a comparability standard may often suffice, the implication of the OCR position seems to be that in some cases, more than "reasonable accommodations" may be required. One possibility is the provision of special education (individually designed instruction) for non-IDEA students, in which case it would not be federally subsidized by IDEA funds. In fact, OCR has made this point explicitly, although it is hard to think of cases when

[†]The court in *Martinez v. Hillsborough County School Board*, 861 F.2d 1502 (11th Cir. 1988) commented on the need for "reasonable accommodations" to reduce the risk of transmission of AIDS. In *Oberti v. Board of Education*, 801 F. Supp. 1392 (D.N.J. 1992), the court found a failure to provide "reasonable accommodations" to enable a young student with Down syndrome to benefit from inclusive education. Compare *Lyons v. Smith*, 829 F. Supp. 414 (D.D.C. 1993), in which the court determined that Section 504 stand-alone students may be entitled to "substantial accommodations," but only to the extent necessary to prevent discrimination. Note that the *Lyons* decision actually does not use the term "reasonable" accommodations.

a Section 504 student would need special education without being able to qualify under IDEA.

It is important to realize that the Section 504 FAPE requirement is triggered only by the first prong of the definition of disability.[4] Under the second and third prongs, the regulations require only that students with *past* or *perceived* disabilities not be discriminated against, not that they receive special services or aids to address the disability. The distinction makes sense because, under Section 504, one is not obligated to provide program adaptations to someone who, in fact, does not have a disability.

Instructional Services

As school districts are well aware, in regional offices across the country, OCR investigates allegations of discrimination and issues findings, sometimes specifying required remedial action. Usually OCR limits its investigation to a determination of whether the agency has complied with the procedural requirements of Section 504.[5] In other words, except in extraordinary circumstances, it does not attempt to second-guess the school district's judgment as to what actual services should be provided and in what settings. In cases of sustained, deliberate noncompliance with its rulings, OCR will refer the situation to the Justice Department to initiate a lawsuit to terminate all federal funding. Although most investigations result in findings in favor of school district policies or practices, following are some examples of the types of services that OCR has found not to be comparable to those provided to the nondisabled.

Establishment of Academic Standards and Test-Taking Procedures

The dilemma for educators is how to modify academic assessments without destroying the validity of standardized tests or impairing the inferences to be drawn from them. This requires a clear understanding of the purposes of the test and whether accommodations can still can allow those purposes to be realized. Failure to consider whether or how to make an accommodation, however, is likely to be a Section 504 violation.

For instance, OCR has repeatedly ruled that learning disabled students are entitled to individual consideration in determining whether instructional evaluation standards and test-taking procedures require modification to meet their needs.[†] Blanket denials of all requests for accommodations without an individual assessment are an invitation to trouble. Furthermore, OCR has ruled that a student may not be evaluated against a standard that is impossible to attain because of clear limitations related to a disability—for instance, a handwriting grade for a student whose cerebral palsy precluded the ability to write.[6] On the other hand, OCR has indicated that procedures such as weighted or coded grading systems that reflect actual differences in difficulty of courses or grading standards are not discriminatory per se.[7]

Regular Classroom Program Adaptations

Many kinds of program adaptations can be made without significantly interfering with a regular educator's curriculum or orderly approach to instruction. Thousands of teachers have always tried to accommodate individual student needs, and others are learning that program adaptations that help a child with a disability often help others in the class as well. Among the kinds of classroom modifications that are currently in use are the following:

- Changing the seating arrangements to accommodate a student with a visual or hearing impairment or a child with ADD/ADHD. Seating a child in the front of the room can make a positive difference, as can allowing an ADD/ADHD student to work for periods of time at a stand-up desk or in a private study carrel. Similarly, arranging seats in a circle instead of rows can be a significant help to a hearing impaired student, as can positioning yourself so that the sun's glare is not behind you.

- Using a multisensory approach to teacher instructions so that instructions are given both orally and in writing.

- Using cooperative learning and peer tutoring strategies so that students with disabilities (and other students) can learn from each other and receive structured individual attention from someone other than the teacher.

- Reducing the length or difficulty level of homework assignments but still requiring mastery of the material before a child moves on.

- Excusing a child with a speech impairment from reading orally in a group until the child is ready and will not feel humiliated.

- Allowing a child with a visual-motor impairment to copy work from his or her desk instead of from the blackboard or classroom walls.

- Allowing a child who has trouble with mathematical abstractions to use his or her fingers in doing math calculations, if it works for the child.

- Allowing a child with a math disability to use a calculator during math tests if the ability to produce the correct answer is what is being tested and not the ability to demonstrate the correct steps in generating the answer or to demonstrate memorization of the multiplication tables, for instance.

- Teaching a child with spatial problems how to find his or her locker, the cafeteria, the gym, and so on, rather than assuming that all children can teach themselves how to find their way around the school building.

- Allowing an extra rest period for a student with an acute or chronic health impairment that limits vitality and alertness.

- Teaching the other children when and how to ignore the involuntary outbursts of children with Tourette syndrome.

- Providing advance organizers before introducing a new lesson.

- Sending home weekly progress reports to parents so they can monitor and reward their child's improvement at school.

- Allowing a student with a writing disability to submit test answers through a tape recorder or a computer if writing is not what is being measured by the test.

If classroom adaptations require the use of different materials, the design of a different method, or the introduction of new behavioral management techniques, the regular educator should be able to call on the special educator or the school psychologist for collaboration in these efforts. The possibilities are multiple, frequently limited only by the creativity of the staff rather than by budgetary shortages. Although adaptations take time to incorporate, they frequently save time in the long run.

When teachers balk at requests for program modifications, it is usually in the belief that all students should be measured according to the same standards and that students with disabilities must learn this sooner or later. While it is true that the essential content should be mastered by all children in the regular classroom and that the expectations should remain high, it is also true that children (and adults) have multiple ways of learning and of showing what they have learned. Refusal to acknowledge this fact subjects some children to school failure who should never have failed.

Program Accessibility

Programs, when viewed in their entirety, must be accessible to persons with disabilities. OCR differentiates a "program" from a physical facility; it is the program within a facility that must be accessible, not necessarily the entire facility. In the late 1970s, OCR issued a policy memorandum clarifying that carrying a student with a mobility impairment was an unacceptable means of providing the student with access to a program.[8] More recently, it has ruled that when a playground on school premises is not accessible to students who use wheelchairs, it is a violation of Section 504.[9]

One case of particularly extensive failure to make programs accessible to mobility, vision, and hearing impaired students was reported in 1993, when OCR found the following (among other things): excessive pressure required to open classroom and entrance doors; no raised letter or number signage to identify classrooms; safety hazards in rest rooms and physics and home economics classrooms; parking spaces improperly marked; and stages inaccessible to persons in wheelchairs.[10]

Related Aids and Services

No definition of "related services" appears in Section 504 regulations. The term appears only as part of the phrase "related aids and services," which, in turn, is part of the Section 504 definition of FAPE. OCR does not utilize the IDEA definition of related services because, under IDEA, related services can only accompany special education and cannot be provided independently. This is clearly not what is meant by related aids and services under Section 504, as indicated by the fact that evaluation is required prior to placement of a student who is believed to need either special education or related services.[11] The use of the word *or* indicates that related services can be severed from special education under Section 504.

OCR rulings variously describe the meaning of "related" aids and services as aids and services necessary (a) to meet individual needs as adequately as the needs of the nondisabled are met, or (b) for the student to benefit from either regular or special education in a way that provides equal opportunity. When OCR rulings invoke the first explanation, they are using the Section 504 FAPE definition. When they invoke the second explanation, they are using the more general Section 504 regulation prohibiting discrimination that denies an "aid, benefit, or service" to an otherwise qualified individual with a disability.[12] Either explanation produces virtually the same result.

Among the related aids and services that have been ordered in given situations are transportation to and from school, the administration of ritalin to ADD/ADHD students at school,[13] special dietary accommodations at school for students with diabetes,[14] use of a service dog for a student with cerebral palsy,[15] provision of FM wireless hearing sets for classroom teachers and students with hearing impairments; provision of large-print books for students with certain kinds of visual impairments, and provision of in-class word processors for students with writing problems. The first two have resulted in numerous OCR rulings, so more information about them follows.

Transportation

Certain widespread problems in providing comparably for the needs of Section 504 students with disabilities were addressed in a 1992 letter to public school administrators from then OCR Director Michael Williams. The provision of nondiscriminatory transportation services was singled out as a special challenge. The letter included the following statement:

> Transportation schedules must not result in [Section 504] students spending appreciably more time on buses than nonhandicapped students, and transportation schedules must be designed to ensure arrival and departure times that do not reduce the length of the school day for students with handicaps for whom a shorter school day has not been prescribed on an individual basis.[16]

The Williams letter also mentioned three specific incidents illustrating discriminatory transportation services: (a) the denial of bus transportation to students with disabilities during bad weather, (b) a lack of bus service to mobility impaired students for 5 months, during which time an accessible bus was not available, and (c) a discriminatory 4¾-hour bus trip to school for students with disabilities.

One can see that Section 504 is the vehicle (no pun intended) for ensuring that the length of bus rides for special education students (and sometimes a concomitant shortening of the school day) is not discriminatory.[17] The LEA should be prepared to demonstrate how it has attempted to minimize transportation problems, how it has provided for the transportation of its special education students as adequately as it has provided for its nondisabled students who require busing, and how any shortening of a school day continues to meet the individualized needs of the students affected.

If, in order to meet the Section 504 FAPE requirements, transportation is required to a program not operated by a school district, then the district must ensure "that adequate transportation to and from the program is provided at no greater cost than would be incurred by the person or his or her parents or guardian if the person were placed in the program operated by the recipient."[18] Section 504 public education regulations provide no definition of the word *transportation.*

Administration of Medication

Administration of medication is considered a related service under Section 504 when it is necessary to enable a student to benefit from the education program. This can occur in a number of circumstances—for instance, when failure to administer prescribed medications results in physical illness at school due to asthma or other allergies, or when it results in distractibility, out-of-seat

---

Administering Ritalin: An Interesting Twist

In *Davis v. Francis Howell School District*, 138 F.3d 754 (8th Cir. 1998), a school nurse refused to administer a prescribed dosage of ritalin to a student with ADHD. The student's treating physician had prescribed 360 mg of the drug, and a second doctor had concurred that the dosage was required to control the boy's ADHD symptoms. The school nurse was concerned because the dosage far exceeded the recommended maximum of 60 mg listed in the *Physicians' Desk Reference* (PDR). The nurse coordinator and consulting psychologist agreed with her, and she notified the parents that she would not administer the medication. The assistant superintendent supported her position but offered to let the parents (or their designee) come to school and administer the medication.

The parents' lawsuit alleged that the nurse's refusal to administer the prescribed dosage of ritalin violated Section 504 and Title II of the ADA. The lower court found no evidence of discrimination, because requests by nondisabled students for administration of drugs exceeding the PDR standards were also denied and because requests by students with disabilities for administration of drugs within PDR standards were honored. The court also ruled that the school had offered a reasonable accommodation to the student by allowing the parents to administer the drug.

On appeal, the U.S. Court of Appeals for the Third Circuit upheld the lower court opinion that the PDR was a nondiscriminatory basis for the nurse's decision. If a reasonable accommodation was required (and the court declined to make such a determination), the parents had been offered one. The Circuit concluded that it would be an administrative and financial burden for the school district to have to determine the safety of usage and likelihood of future liability when a prescription exceeded PDR standards.

misbehaviors, and impulsive behaviors. Under those circumstances, the school district must see that medication is provided at school.[19] The increasing need to administer prescription drugs at school has necessitated the adoption of formal, systematized procedures in school districts across the country.

A Special Case of Discrimination?
Do Not Resuscitate (DNR) Orders

Some children with disabilities who are being educated at school have such severe life-threatening conditions that their parents have requested schools to honor medical DNR orders. This has caused extreme concern among school officials, who have argued that they are not medical personnel and should not be asked to behave as if they were. Whether a district chooses to honor a DNR order or not, it is of utmost importance to communicate effectively with the family and let the family know in advance what protocols will be followed in the event that the child stops breathing at school.

A particularly well known case in Lewiston, Maine, resulted in a caution from OCR that honoring the requested DNR order would be viewed by OCR as discrimination on the basis of disability. In response to the controversy, the school district carefully drafted a policy that made no distinction between students with and without disabilities and that allowed school-based multidisciplinary teams to develop individually designed medical resuscitation plans in appropriate circumstances. OCR determined that this policy did not violate Section 504 or Title II of the ADA. The individual medical resuscitation plan for the particular student was also upheld. See *Lewiston (ME) Public School,* 21 IDELR 83 (OCR 1994). More information about the health care needs of medically fragile students found in chapter 16.

Nonacademic Services

Both Section 504 and IDEA require that students with disabilities be provided with an equal opportunity to participate in nonacademic services and extracurricular activities.[20] Such an opportunity encourages social interaction between students with and without disabilities and ensures that disabled students are not denied access to various services extended regularly to nondisabled students. Among the services specified in both sets of regulations are counseling services, recreational athletics, transportation, health services, recreational activities, special interest groups or clubs sponsored by the school, referrals to appropriate outside agencies, and student employment opportunities. Part of the reason for specifying such services is to remind educators to see the "whole child" and not to set expectations that are too low, for instance, by neglecting to provide vocational counseling and employment referrals for students with disabilities.

Cases challenging the provision of equal opportunity in nonacademic services have been brought mostly under Section 504 rather than IDEA, because IDEA merely echos Section 504 unless nonacademic services are specifically included in an IEP. The legal standard does not require an equal participation in all nonacademic activities but rather an equal *opportunity* to participate.

Sports Participation

The most common nonacademic issue is competitive athletic eligibility. Although separate physical education and athletic activities may be created and may serve a valuable purpose for some students with disabilities, Section 504 regulations specify that no qualified student with a disability can be denied the opportunity to compete for athletic teams or, more broadly, the opportunity to participate in physical education and athletic activities that are not separate or different.[21] The regulations make clear that student athletic ability cannot be prejudged on the basis of a disability.[22]

Court cases generally rule in favor of allowing the participation of qualified student athletes with a disability such as a visual impairment, hearing impairment, or loss of a limb or organ (e.g., a kidney). Of course, it is important that the athletes understand the risks and are able to participate with little or no greater threat to health and safety than is true of their teammates.

In *West Virginia ex rel. Lambert v. West Virginia State Board of Education*,[23] a state court held that an 11th-grade deaf girl receiving interpreter services in academic classes was entitled to receive them as a member of the basketball team so that she could understand the directions of her coach. Failure to do so would have been discriminatory, according to the court.

Several circuits of the U.S. Court of Appeals have considered whether enforcement of an age ceiling (typically the 19th birthday) or an eight-semester rule for high school athletes violates Section 504 when applied uniformly to students with and without disabilities. More courts are being asked to weigh in on this issue, and a few state and federal district courts have adopted a case-by-case approach that analyzes whether granting an exception to the age and eight-semester requirements would frustrate the underlying safety and fairness purposes of the requirement. If it would not, then arguably the age and semester ceilings might be waived for a student with a disability whose presence on the team was not due to redshirting and did not create a physical threat to other players because of size or strength related to the student's advancing age. The trend, however, at least at the appellate level, has been to rule that an evenhanded application of the rule to students with disabilities and students without disabilities is not discriminatory and that schools need not undertake burdensome case-by-case determinations.

Also unresolved in some jurisdictions is whether students with disabilities who are denied athletic participation because of insufficient academic credits are being discriminated against because of their disability.[24] Texas's "no-pass, no-play" statute, however, has been upheld by the Texas courts.[25]

Cost Issues

You will recall that federal funds are not available under Section 504 to help pay for related aids and services. Of course, school districts are free to tap whatever sources are available to them, but if the Section 504 student is not IDEA eligible, and if no other outside sources of funding are available, the cost of the related service must be absorbed by the LEA's regular education budget.

Some commentators worry that OCR's FAPE definition, because it does not employ the concept of reasonable accommodations, allows for no cost limitations on what may be required. This contrasts with Section 504 employment regulations, where an accommodation can be deemed unreasonable if it constitutes an undue

A Split of Judicial Opinion

The judge in *Johnson v. Florida High School Activities Association,* 899 F. Supp. 579 (M.D. Fla. 1995) granted a preliminary injunction to a hearing impaired student after evidence that his participation in wrestling and football would not frustrate the fairness and safety purposes of the age requirement. (On appeal, the lower court decision was vacated as moot because the student had graduated by the time the appeal was to be decided, 102 F. 3d 1172 (11th Cir. 1997)). In *University Interscholastic League v. Buchanan,* 848 S.W.2d 298 (Tex. Ct. App. 1993), a Texas court ordered injunctions to allow overage student athletes with disabilities to continue their participation throughout the current season; the court decided that a case-by-case approach would allow "reasonable accommodation" of disability, yet still curtail redshirting and risks of harm due to age maturity. (Also, recall the ADA case, *Bingham v. Oregon School Activities Association,* 37 F. Supp.2d 1189 (D. Or. 1999), in which the court ordered a waiver of the eight-semester rule for a teenager with a learning disability and ADHD (see chapter 4)).

Decisions to the contrary include *Sandison v. Michigan High School Athletic Association,* 64 F.3d 1026 (6th Cir. 1995); (upholding the age ceiling for track and cross-country); *Pottgen v. Missouri State High School Activities Association,* 40 F.3d 926 (8th Cir. 1994) (upholding the age ceiling for baseball); *Cavallaro v. Ambach,* 575 F. Supp. 171 (W.D.N.Y. 1983) (upholding the age ceiling for interscholastic wrestling). See also *Frye v. Michigan High School Athletic Association,* 121 F.3d 708 (6th Cir. 1997) (upholding the eight-semester rule) and *McPherson v. Michigan High School Athletic Association,* 119 F.3d 453 (6th Cir. 1997) (ruling that waiver of the eight-semester rule would create an undue financial and administrative burden).

hardship on the recipient of federal funds. Arguably, however, the Section 504 requirement that FAPE must provide an education that is comparable to ("as adequate as") what is offered the nondisabled introduces its own cost cap, which is pegged to achievement of nondiscrimination and equal educational opportunity. In other words, if facilities or services are inadequate for the nondisabled, then presumably the facilities or services for the disabled need be no better. Although the cost implications are sometimes minor and sometimes more substantial, under this view they are linked to what is being offered to nondisabled students.

Unfortunately, various OCR regional offices across the country do not always use the same language in their rulings. Sometimes the comparability standard seems paramount; at other times, an assessment of individual need independent of comparability seems to have been used. In the latter type of rulings, it appears that OCR has used the IDEA FAPE standard rather than the Section 504 FAPE definition. In addition, some courts ignore the Section 504 definition and continue to borrow the concepts of reasonable accommodation and undue hardship, introducing cost factors into the equation by that means.

Implications

To meet the nondiscrimination requirements of Section 504, often all that is required is a change of attitude, a change in aspects of the classroom environment, or a fairly simple modification in instructional programming. Other times, more expense is involved, and school districts constrained by limited budgets must search for cost-effective ways to meet individual needs. Use of paraprofessionals and volunteers is one way that has been systematized in many districts. The use of in-school assistive technology devices is another. Devices such as computers, tape recorders and audiotapes, headphones, and VCRs and videotapes are already widely available in classrooms and can be adapted to serve the individual needs of students with disabilities while also being used to serve overall classroom needs. In general, education agencies should explore less expensive ways to deliver services effectively before turning to more costly alternatives.

At the same time, school districts should properly evaluate the need of some Section 504 students with disabilities for *personalized* assistive technology devices and services. Although few assistive technology issues have reached the courts, school districts report growing requests for evaluation and provision of personal computer hardware and software, along with refined equipment for the visually or hearing impaired and adapted equipment for those with mobility impairments and self-care needs. A careful evaluation can reveal whether costly technology is necessary or whether low-tech devices or services can be equally effective. High-tech items like personal computers and reading machines should be saved for those students who really need them.

Review

1. What are the basic differences between the Section 504 FAPE definition and the IDEA FAPE definition?

   The Section 504 definition applies to the provision of regular education as well as special education. Also, Section 504 utilizes a comparability standard (requiring that the needs of the student with a disability be met as adequately as the needs of nondisabled students), whereas IDEA uses an individualized standard (identifying and meeting the student's unique special educational needs).

2. What is the difference between related services under Section 504 and under IDEA?

   Unlike IDEA, related services under Section 504 are not limited to those needed to assist a child to benefit from special education. They can include those aids and services needed to help a child receive a regular education that meets individual needs as adequately as the needs of nondisabled children are met.

Notes

[1] 34 C.F.R. § 104.33(b)(1)(1997).

[2] *Id.* § 104.33(b)(2).

[3] *See* Letter to Zirkel, 20 IDELR 134 (OCR 1993).

[4] OCR Staff Memorandum, 19 IDELR 894 (OCR 1992).

[5] *See* 34 C.F.R. Part 104, app. A (analysis of subpart D).

[6] Harrison County (WV) Sch. Dist., 14 EHLR 353:120 (OCR 1988).

[7] Metropolitan (TN) Pub. Sch. Dist., 18 IDELR 971 (OCR 1991); Letter to Ickes, 14 EHLR 305:50 (OCR 1989). *See also* Pueblo (CO) City Sch. Dist. No. 60, 17 EHLR 535 (OCR 1990) (holding that excluding students from competing for honors at graduation when their IEPs and course work did not satisfy graduation requirements did not violate Section 504).

[8] OCR Policy Interpretation No. 4, EHLR 132:02 (OCR 1978).

[9] Hazelton (PA) Area Sch. Dist., 17 EHLR 907 (OCR 1991).

[10] Uxbridge (MA) Pub. Sch., 20 IDELR 827 (OCR 1993).

[11] 34 C.F.R. § 104.35(a).

[12] *Id.* 104.4(b)(1).

[13] *See, e.g.*, Pearl (MS) Pub. Sch. Dist., 17 EHLR 1004 (OCR 1990); Berlin Brothersvalley (PA) Sch. Dist., 14 EHLR 353:124 (OCR 1988).

[14] *See, e.g.*, Digest of Response to Veir, 20 IDELR 864 (OCR 1993) (stating that schools providing food to regular education students must provide special food to students with special dietary needs, the food to be determined on a case-by-case basis).

[15] Sullivan v. Vallejo City Unified Sch. Dist., 731 F. Supp. 947 (E.D. Cal. 1990).

[16] Williams Letter to Colleagues, OCR, May 27, 1992.

[17] *See, e.g.*, Santa Rosa County (FL) Sch. Dist., 18 IDELR 153 (OCR 1991); Lincoln County (NC) Sch. Dist., 17 EHLR 1052 (OCR 1991); Lafayette (IN) Sch. Corp., 16 EHLR 649 (OCR 1990); Caddo Parish (LA) Sch. Sys., 16 EHLR 326 (OCR 1990); Stafford County (VA) Pub. Schs., 16 EHLR 896 (OCR 1990).

[18] 34 C.F.R. § 104.33(c)(2).

[19] San Ramon Valley (CA) Unified Sch. Dist., 18 IDELR 465 (OCR 1991) (administering allergy medication); Pearl (MS) Pub. Sch. Dist., 17 EHLR 1004 (OCR 1991) (administering ritalin for ADHD); Berlin Brothersvalley (PA) Sch. Dist., 14 EHLR 353:124 (OCR 1988) (same).

[20] *Cf.* 34 C.F.R. § 104.37 (Section 504 regulations) and 34 C.F.R. § 300.306 (IDEA regulations).

[21] 34 C.F.R. § 104.4(b)(3).

[22] *Id.* § 104.37(c)(2).

[23] 447 S.E.2d 901 (W.Va. 1994).

[24] *See* Hoot v. Milan Area Sch., 853 F. Supp. 243 (E.D. Mich. 1994) (allowing the case to go to trial).

[25] Texas Educ. Agency v. Stamos *ex rel.* Class of All Pub. Sch. Children, 817 S.W.2d 378 (Tex. Ct. App. 1991) (upholding against a Section 504 claim the Texas statute requiring all students to meet academic eligibility standards prior to participation in extracurricular activities).

Selected Supplementary Resources

Colorado State Pupil Transportation Association. (1996). *Transporting students with disabilities.* Boulder, CO: Author. (Companion video also available.)

Goedert, J. J. (1995). School, sports, and students with disabilities: The impact of federal laws and protecting the rights of students with disabilities in inter-scholastic sports. *Journal of Law and Education, 24,* 403–421.

Gorn, S. (1998). *What do I do when . . . : The answer book on Section 504.* Horsham, PA: LRP.

Zirkel, P. A. (1996). The substantive standard for FAPE: Does Section 504 require less than the IDEA? *Education Law Reporter, 106,* 369–375.

Chapter 8

Placement and Discipline Issues Under Section 504

Placement Requirements

Education With Nondisabled Students

If a student with a Section 504 disability is believed to need special education or related services, then an evaluation must precede the initial placement, even if the setting for the delivery of those services turns out to be a regular classroom. If the student can be provided with an equal opportunity to learn without assessing the need for special education or related services, then presumably a preplacement evaluation is not required. Placement decisions must be made by a knowledgeable group of persons who consider information from a variety of sources, including aptitude and achievement tests, teacher recommendations, physical condition, social or cultural background, and adaptive behavior. A reevaluation is required prior to "any subsequent significant change in placement."[1]

Section 504 education regulations require that students with disabilities be educated with nondisabled students "to the maximum extent appropriate to the needs of the [disabled] person."[2] Public schools must place a student with a disability in the regular educational environment unless education in that environment cannot be achieved satisfactorily with the use of supplementary aids and services. Furthermore, if the school district places a student in another setting, it must take into account the proximity of the alternate setting to the person's home. In all these ways, the placement requirements under Section 504 parallel those of IDEA, although the IDEA requirements go further and add more detail.

Participation in nonacademic and extracurricular services and activities (e.g., meals, recess, clubs, student employment opportunities, counseling, recreational activities, health services, and transportation) must also be with nondisabled students "to the maximum extent appropriate to the needs of the [disabled] person."[3]

Removal From Regular Classrooms and Schools

OCR has recognized the need for removal of Section 504 students from the regular *classroom* in one particular type of situation. It has taken the position that "where a handicapped child is so disruptive in a regular classroom that the education of other students is significantly impaired, the needs of the [disabled] child cannot be met in that environment. Therefore regular class placement would not be appropriate to his or her needs. . . ."[4] This position has been important in allowing removal of children with disabilities from the regular classroom when their behavior cannot be managed, even with the help of supplementary aids and services.

OCR has also recognized the need for removal from regular *schools* in several kinds of situations. In most of these situations, it is difficult to imagine that the student could be anyone but an IDEA student. First, the regulations provide that if a placement in a residential program is necessary to provide FAPE as defined under Section 504, the program, including nonmedical care and room and board, must be provided at no cost to the person and his or her parents.[5] Second, OCR states that if a recipient of federal money places a student in a program other than the one it operates, it remains responsible for ensuring that the Section 504 requirements are met in the other setting.[6] Finally, several OCR rulings have addressed school-district homebound instruction policies. In each situation, OCR has ruled that individual need, not administrative restrictions on number of hours of homebound instruction per week, must dictate the hours provided to each Section 504 student.[7]

Neighborhood School Placements

A Tenth Circuit decision, in *Urban v. Jefferson County School District R-1*, held that no greater right to neighborhood placement exists under Section 504 and ADA than exists under IDEA.[8] As of early 1999, court decisions in other circuits had not addressed the neighborhood placement issue under Section 504 and ADA.

Comparable Facilities

If the school district operates a separate facility for students with disabilities, this facility must be comparable to the district's other facilities.[9] In other words, the quality of the separate facility must approximate that of the regular education facility, and the services and activities available in the separate facility must be comparable to those offered in integrated facilities.

Establishing classes for disabled students in storage rooms, home economics rooms, partitioned offices, and other areas not conducive to learning will constitute a violation of Section 504.[10] So will classroom sizes that are not adequate to accommodate specific educational, physical, and/or medical needs of students with disabilities. School districts should be certain to allocate resources fairly across staff and not deny special education teachers access to adequate supplies, clerical staff, a classroom telephone, and so forth if they supply regular education teachers with such supplies and services. Special education teachers and students can be asked to share in sacrifices made by an entire building staff but should not be singled out for a disproportionate share of such sacrifices, or it will be discriminatory under Section 504.

Private Schools

The general nondiscrimination requirements of Section 504 also apply to recipients of federal funds who operate private schools. More specifically, a student with a disability may not be excluded from the private program if the person can, "with minor adjustments," be provided with an appropriate education by the private school. Only if there is a substantial cost increase to the school may an additional charge be levied for the education of the student with a disability.[11] If the private school operates special education programs, then it must follow the placement provisions applicable to public schools—for instance, placement in the regular education environment, unless that setting is unsatisfactory even with the use of supplementary aids and services.

What Constitutes a Minor Adjustment by a Private School?

Providing a mandatory, scent-free environment for a girl with asthma was considered more than a minor adjustment in *Hunt v. St. Peter School*, 26 IDELR 6 (W.D. Mo. 1997). In response to the mother's concerns, the private parochial school had adopted a voluntary scent-free policy and had allowed the mother to provide education to the class about her daughter's severe asthma and the threat to her breathing caused by various scents. In response, the teacher and students in the child's fifth-grade class had agreed not to wear perfumes and colognes. When her daughter reached sixth grade, the girl's mother asked for a mandatory scent-free policy, which the school thought it could not enforce, among other reasons because the girl's classes were held in four separate rooms, not always with the same students, and the sixth grade used six other classes during the week for other activities and Catholic mass. The court noted the difficulty of imposing a "sniffing test" on the school, commenting that "sniffing may be appropriate in the wild kingdom but not in an elementary school."

The standard for public schools is higher than for private schools; public schools are expected to do more than make minor adjustments. Depending on a student's environmental allergies, reasonable adjustments might include air filters, a rest room free of certain chemicals, and an outdoor physical education area free of pesticides or fertilizers. Dictating to students and staff what scents they can wear, however, would be problematic in the public as well as the private school context.

Discipline Issues

Overview

Disciplining students refers to the ability to enforce school rules and regulations and to punish or otherwise control student misbehavior in order to ensure order and safety at school. It typically encompasses such sanctions as suspension and expulsion, school detention, restriction of privileges, and even corporal punishment in some states. In using any of these methods, you must be sure that you are not doing so in a fashion that discriminates against Section 504 students. Among other things, you must not treat them more harshly or prejudicially than you would treat students without disabilities. Furthermore, no child, disabled or not, should be disciplined arbitrarily or with unreasonable severity.

The Application of Suspension and Expulsion

The Supreme Court has ruled that all children who are suspended or expelled must be provided with notice of the impending action and a chance to provide their own version of the events producing the disciplinary action.[12] This is required by the concept of due process of law, and it avoids the likelihood of an error in the application of the intended discipline.

In addition, OCR has interpreted the meaning of nondiscriminatory suspension and expulsion under Section 504 in a number of specific situations. In general, 10 consecutive school days is seen as the maximum number of days that a student may be suspended without invoking procedures that go beyond notice and a chance to respond.[†] After 10 days, the suspension constitutes a significant change of placement, triggering the evaluation or reevaluation requirement, which to OCR includes the need to determine whether the misbehavior is a manifestation of the disability.[‡] If it is a manifestation, it would be discriminatory for the placement change to be continued solely as a means of discipline. Instead, the placement would have to be determined to be the setting closest to the regular education classroom in which an appropriate education could be delivered. Although this does not foreclose the possibility of removing a disruptive child from the regular classroom, it means that the setting must deliver appropriate educational services. Therefore, long-term suspension or expulsion without any services would be illegal.

Follow-up Issues   A troubling question is whether an expulsion or a suspension of more than 10 school days at a time can be imposed if the misbehavior does *not* relate to the disability. OCR has taken the position that, when this is the case, long-term suspensions and expulsions for misbehavior may proceed on the same basis as they would for students without disabilities.[13] This means that expulsion or long-term suspension of a student with a disability may include the cessation of all educational services to the student with a disability as long as nondisabled students are treated similarly.[14] In other words, all educational services to the student may stop if that is the practice with respect to nondisabled stu-

[†] OCR has followed the Supreme Court's ruling in *Honig v. Doe*, 484 U.S. 305 (1988), that up to 10 days does not constitute a change of placement (under IDEA) and therefore does not invoke additional due process procedures.

[‡] In *Roane County (TN) School District*, 27 IDELR 853 (OCR 1997), OCR found a violation for a 12-day suspension imposed without conducting a manifestation determination. In *Broward County (FL) School District*, 27 IDELR 850 (OCR 1997), OCR concluded that a 3-day suspension did not constitute a change of placement.

dents, as long as state or federal law does not prohibit cessation of services for all students or a given student. This position is in contrast with the statutory requirement for IDEA students that services to implement the student's IEP and to manage the misbehavior must continue, even if the services are delivered in the student's home.

With or without any causal link, those whose misbehavior involves the use of alcohol or illegal drugs may be disciplined for use or possession in the same way that nondisabled students are disciplined, without the need for the due process protections of Section 504. In short, misbehaviors based on alcohol or current illegal drug use are not protected by Section 504 from ordinary discipline procedures.[15] In contrast, such misbehaviors would not prevent an IDEA student from receiving the benefit of IDEA safeguards.[16]

You may wonder what, in addition to a suspension of more than 10 days, constitutes a "significant change of placement." OCR found that a change from a regular school to an alternative school was a significant change, triggering the need for reevaluation of the student.[17] Changes from self-contained settings to inclusive, integrated settings or vice versa usually constitute a significant change of placement. On the other hand, OCR found that a change from one self-contained classroom to another within the same school was not a significant placement change.[18] OCR also found that no significant placement change occurred when a school required a suicidal student to be accompanied by an escort at all times when the student was not attending a class.[19]

Another issue that has arisen is whether multiple (serial) suspensions together totaling more than 10 school days in a given school year are permitted under Section 504 or whether 10 days is the cumulative annual total permitted before a school must evaluate or reevaluate a student prior to the suspension. The OCR position is that a series of short-term suspensions that together total more than 10 school days do not automatically constitute a significant change of placement. Instead, a case-by-case determination is required as to whether a *pattern* of discriminatory exclusion exists. Factors in determining such a pattern include "the length of each suspension, the proximity of the suspensions to one another, and the total amount of time the child is excluded from school."[20] If there is a pattern, then it constitutes a significant change in placement, requiring an evaluation or reevaluation to determine whether the misconduct was caused by the student's disability, in which case a team must determine what the appropriate placement should be. Of course, if your state law or district policy has established a strict maximum of 10 school days of cumulative suspension per year, then it must be followed.

Alternatives to Suspension and Expulsion

An extensive range of alternative disciplinary methods in addition to suspension and expulsion remains available to school officials. Among the traditional tools used for both students with disabilities and students without disabilities are the separation of misbehaving students into private study carrels, limited after-school detention, restriction of privileges, various forms of time-out, and in-school suspension. These methods were mentioned in the Supreme Court's decision in *Honig v. Doe*[21] as ordinary, acceptable alternatives to suspension and expulsion.

A question that has arisen about in-school suspension is whether long-term in-school suspension would also be considered a significant placement change that triggers the need for procedural safeguards. No OCR interpretation on in-school suspension has been issued, and no federal court decision is relevant. Logic would dictate that in-school suspension for more than 10 school days could constitute a significant change of placement just like out-of-school suspension, if Section 504 FAPE requirements are not being implemented during the in-school suspension periods. At least one state court has so held.[22]

Corporal punishment is also an alternative disciplinary method in a number of states. OCR rulings approach corporal punishment from two perspectives. Corporal punishment administered solely because of the disability is discriminatory; that is, the disabled should not be subject to more severe punishment than the nondisabled. Moreover, if the misbehavior is caused by the disability, then any use of corporal punishment should be subject either to Section 504 FAPE requirements (meeting the student's individual needs as adequately as those of the nondisabled are met) or to the IEP process if the student has an IEP.[23] Of course, if your state or school district has prohibited the use of corporal punishment, you need not be concerned about these rulings.

An Example of Discriminatory Corporal Punishment

In one ruling, OCR determined that delays in administering punishments to a first grader with a behavioral disability produced a denial of FAPE under Section 504 because the child had difficulty linking cause and effect. The youngster was difficult to manage and engaged in fights on the playground. He also swore at his teacher and, on one occasion, threw a rock and hit one of the playground instructors. He was spanked by the principal on more than one occasion and spent a good deal of time waiting outside the principal's office for the principal to discipline him. He had also had his recess periods taken away.

Because of the nature of his disability, which included a short attention span and limited impulse control, psychologists testified at his hearing that spankings, long periods of punishment, and time-outs waiting for the principal were ineffective. What was needed instead was a behavioral management plan that imposed immediate consequences for misbehavior and punishments of short duration that the student could link to the misbehavior. *Central Valley (WA) District No. 410,* EHLR 257:166 (OCR 1979).

Other disciplinary methods that actually inflict physical discomfort, such as the administration of bad-tasting substances (like the old technique of washing the mouth out with soap), have been challenged occasionally. Although generally disfavored educationally, they have been upheld by OCR if the treatment is nondiscriminatory in its application. For instance, in *Salina (KS) Unified School District No. 305,* administering alum to a seriously emotionally disturbed student for vulgar language, did not violate Section 504 when the rest of the class was treated the same way.[24]

The Gun-Free Schools Act of 1994

The Gun-Free Schools Act of 1994[25] prohibits any state from receiving federal funds under the Improving

America's Schools Act unless the state enacts a law requiring the expulsion from the current school setting for at least 1 year of any student who brings a "weapon"[†] (including an unloaded gun) onto the school grounds. In addition, the LEA must have a policy requiring referral of such a student to the state's criminal justice or juvenile delinquency system. Exceptions to the expulsion requirement may be made by the school superintendent on a case-by-case basis.

During the enactment of these provisions, a question arose as to their application to students with disabilities who bring a gun to school. Allowing the superintendent to make exceptions to the expulsion requirement was seen by DOE as a way to honor Section 504. (See chapter 19 for the provisions of IDEA that in effect supersede the Gun-Free Schools Act for IDEA students.)

The Application of Section 504 in Private Schools

In the first reported case of its kind, a student at a private school obtained an injunction prohibiting her expulsion during her senior year for shouting expletives. Susceptible to life-threatening bleeding as a result of a serious autoimmune disorder, the student reacted emotionally, even hysterically, when she cut herself with an exacto knife in art class. As a recipient of federal funds, the school was subject to Section 504; as a public accommodation, it was also subject to Title III of ADA. The court concluded that the school was not entitled to discriminate against the student on the basis of her physical disability; the failure to take her disability into account and reasonably accommodate it in determining whether or how to punish her outburst was sufficiently likely to be discriminatory under Section 504 and ADA to justify the injunction.[26] This case is a likely precursor of more challenges to private school disciplinary actions.

[†]A *weapon* under the Gun-Free Schools Act means a firearm, as that term is defined at 18 U.S.C. § 921(a)(3): "(A) any weapon (including a starter gun) which will or is designed to or may readily be converted to expel a projectile by the action of an explosive; (B) the frame or receiver of any such weapon; (C) any firearm muffler or firearm silencer; or (D) any destructive device. Such term does not include an antique firearm."

Review

1. In what educational setting should Section 504 students be placed?

    They should be placed in regular education settings, unless education cannot be achieved satisfactorily there, even with the use of supplementary aids and services.

2. When must an evaluation or reevaluation of a Section 504 student take place?

    It should occur before the initial placement as a Section 504 student in a regular or special education program, if the student is believed to need special education or related services, and before any subsequent "significant change in placement" for such a student.

3. What must be included in a reevaluation?

    According to OCR, it must include a determination of whether the misbehavior is related to the disability.

4. According to OCR, may students with disabilities be disciplined like nondisabled students?

    In general they may, with certain exceptions:

    (a) If expulsion or suspension for more than 10 consecutive school days is contemplated, the Section 504 student must be evaluated and a determination made as to whether the misbehavior related to the disability. If it did, then the placement must be in the setting closest to the regular education classroom in which the student can be educated appropriately. If it did not, then the student may receive the same disciplinary placement as a nondisabled student would receive for the same kind of misbehavior.

    (b) If a child receives other kinds of discipline, such as in-school suspension, time-out, corporal punishment, or other methods that cause pain or discomfort, they must not interfere with the student receiving an appropriate education that is designed to meet the student's individual needs as adequately as the needs of the nondisabled are met.

Notes

[1] 34 C.F.R. § 104.35 (1997).

[2] *Id.* § 104.34(a).

[3] *Id.* § 104.34(b).

[4] *Id.,* Part 104, app., para. 24.

[5] *Id.* § 104.33 (c)(3).

[6] *Id.* § 104.33(b)(3).

[7] *See, e.g.*, Boston (MA) Pub. Sch., 21 IDELR 170 (OCR 1994); Greensville County (VA) Sch. Bd., 14 EHLR 353:118 (OCR 1988); Lee's Summit (MO) R-VII Sch. Dist., EHLR 257:629 (OCR 1984).

[8] 89 F.3d 720 (10th Cir. 1996).

[9] 34 C.F.R. § 104.34(c).

[10] *See, e.g.*, Wayne Co. (WV) Sch. Dist., 16 EHLR 1261 (OCR 1990).

[11] 34 C.F.R. § 104.39.

[12] Goss v. Lopez, 419 U.S. 565 (1975).

[13] *See* OCR Senior Staff Memorandum, 14 EHLR 307:05 (OCR 1988).

[14] *Id. See also* Policy Guidance—Gun-Free Schools Act of 1994, 21 IDELR 899 (DOE 1994).

[15] 29 U.S.C. 706(8)(C)(iv) (1994). *See also* OCR Staff Memorandum, 17 EHLR 609 (OCR 1991).

[16] Letter to Uhler, 18 IDELR 1238 (OSEP 1992).

[17] Hillsborough County (FL) Sch. Dist., 27 IDELR 730 (OCR 1997).

[18] Seattle (WA) Sch. Dist. No. 1, 28 IDELR 763, 10-98-1005 (OCR 1997).

[19] Harlowston (MT) Pub. Schs., 26 IDELR 115 (OCR 1997).

[20] OCR Senior Staff Memorandum, 14 EHLR 307:05 (OCR 1988).

[21] 484 U.S.305 (1988).

[22] *See* Big Beaver Falls Area Sch. Dist. v. Jackson, 612 A.2d 806 (Pa. Commw. Ct. 1993) (holding that continued in-school suspension interfered with a student's right to FAPE).

[23] Nash County (NC) Sch. Dist., EHLR 352:37 (OCR 1985).

[24] EHLR 352:204 (OCR 1986).

[25] Sec. 14601–14602 of Improving America's Schools Act, Pub. L. 103-382, 108 Stat. 3907 (codified at 20 U.S.C. § 8921).

[26] Thomas v. Davidson Academy, 846 F. Supp. 611 (M.D. Tenn. 1994).

Selected Supplementary Resources

Dagley, D. L., McGuire, M. D., & Evans, C. W. (1994). The relationship test in the discipline of disabled students. *Education Law Reporter, 88,* 13–31.

Zirkel, P. A. (1997). Section 504 and public school students: An empirical overview. *Education Law Reporter, 120,* 369–378.

Chapter 9

Due Process, Dispute Resolution, and Remedies Under Section 504

Due Process Safeguards Under Section 504

School districts receiving federal money must establish a set of procedural safeguards under Section 504 that can be used by parents or guardians who feel that their children are being discriminated against on the basis of disability. The safeguards parallel the basic due process safeguards of IDEA but are less extensive and detailed. They apply to issues of "identification, evaluation, or educational placement" of students whose disability creates a need or perceived need for "special instruction or related services."[1] They also apply to issues surrounding the delivery of regular or special education and related aids and services to Section 504 students.[2] In other words, they apply to the provision of appropriate education, as defined by Section 504.

The safeguards include the following:

1. Some kind of advance notice
2. An opportunity for the parent or guardian to examine relevant records
3. An impartial hearing
4. A review procedure

These safeguards are not fleshed out as they are in the IDEA regulations. The contents and nature (oral versus written) of the notice are not specified, nor is the extent of the access to relevant records. The impartial hearing must allow for participation by the student's parents or guardian and for representation by counsel, but no other details are provided. The nature of the review procedure also is not spelled out.

An Example of Acceptable 504 Hearing Procedures

A parent of a student in the Houston, Texas, school district challenged Houston's Section 504 hearing procedures because the district would not allow the parent to cross-examine witnesses or bring a court reporter to the hearing. Instead, the district's procedures provided for an informal, nonadversarial, impartial hearing, and the hearing officer allowed the parent to ask follow-up and clarification questions. The parent was given an audiotape of the hearing. OCR noted that Section 504 required neither cross-examination of witnesses nor a court reporter and concluded that the hearing was conducted properly. See *Houston (TX) Independent School District,* 25 IDELR 163 (OCR 1996).

Certain safeguards that are included in IDEA are excluded from Section 504. Among the exclusions are the following:

- Provision for an independent educational evaluation (IEE)
- Surrogate parent provision when the child is a ward of the state, the parents are unknown, or the parents cannot be located after reasonable efforts
- Stay-put placement provision when placement is being challenged
- Provisions soliciting parental input into the evaluation process and into eligibility and placement decisions
- Provision soliciting parental input into the development of the student's individualized educational services

Compliance with the more complete IDEA safeguards, however, is viewed as automatically meeting the Section 504 requirements.

Not explicitly mentioned in the Section 504 safeguards, though included among the IDEA safeguards, is a consent requirement for preplacement evaluation and initial placement in special education.[3] Commentators have speculated about the absence of a consent requirement. In 1997, OCR offered policy guidance on the subject, concluding that, although the regulations were silent, they should be construed to require parental consent prior to initial evaluation for purposes of identification, diagnosis, and prescription of specific educational services but not for subsequent evaluations. The stated rationale for the policy was that "parental discretion" with regard to these matters was an "appropriate and necessary policy component."[4]

OCR also has taken the position that when a parent refuses to give consent for initial evaluation or initial placement, a school district may use the Section 504 hearing procedure to override the lack of consent but is not required to do so.[5] Instead, presumably, it could simply maintain the status quo.

Sometimes it is the parent who seeks a Section 504 evaluation—over the objection of the school district. If school officials have no reason to suspect a disability, they need not agree to the parental request. If this happens, the district must provide the parent with notice of the procedural safeguards, including the right to a hearing to challenge the school district's refusal to evaluate.[6]

Avenues for Dispute Resolution

Section 504 Coordinator

Under Section 504 regulations, each school district (or other recipient of federal money) that employs 15 or more persons must establish grievance procedures that provide for prompt and equitable resolution of complaints alleging violations of Section 504. An employee must be designated as the grievance coordinator (Section 504 coordinator). Sometimes the coordinator is used only to resolve employee complaints of discrimination on the basis of disability, but the coordinator also should be the person to whom a *parent* turns if the parent thinks a child has been subject to discrimination in school, assuming the parent cannot resolve the issue with the teacher directly.

School district officials may be tempted to ask a special educator to serve as the Section 504 coordinator because they think the special educator will be more knowledgeable about Section 504. This may or may not be appropriate, and school officials should consider seriously who in the school is in the best position to gain the cooperation and support of the entire staff. The hope is that, with the help of the Section 504 coordinator, all parties can understand the law and disputes can be resolved amicably.

Complaints to OCR

Grievances can also be reported directly to the OCR office in your region (see Table 9-1 at the end of this chapter). After screening the written complaint for merit and the appropriateness of an OCR review, OCR will investigate it, typically by asking for documents from the school and, if necessary, by interviewing school officials. The complaint can be brought by either an individual or a group but usually must be initiated within 180 days of the allegedly discriminatory action. The confidentiality of the complainant will be protected to the extent allowed by law.

Except in extraordinary circumstances, OCR investigates only for procedural compliance and avoids second-guessing the substance of a school district's determinations (e.g., evaluation results, placement decisions, the extent of related services or special instruction).[†] If a due process hearing has been initiated under IDEA, OCR will defer automatically to the IDEA hearing decision.

OCR will seek "Early Complaint Resolution," where both parties seek to resolve the disagreement amicably. It can also do a more formal investigation and issue LoFs when violations are found. OCR has the authority to require a monitored, written agreement by the school to remediate a Section 504 violation.[7] It can also punish a school that retaliates against those who engage in a protected activity under Section 504.[‡] Frequently, as a result of an OCR investigation the school will voluntarily undertake to change its procedures to comply with Section 504 requirements, and the complaint will be closed. If a school refuses to comply with an OCR ruling, OCR can begin administrative enforcement proceedings to terminate federal funds or can refer the matter to the Justice Department for enforcement in court.

[†] In *Manteno (IL) Community Unit School District #5,* 27 IDELR 960 (OCR 1997), OCR made clear that it does not resolve educational disputes over the content of the IEP and related aids and services and that such issues should be resolved at a due process hearing. Comparably, in *Virginia Beach City (VA) Public Schools,* 26 IDELR 27 (OCR 1996), OCR stated that a dispute over a Section 504 plan should be resolved at a due process hearing.

[‡] OCR has the authority to punish retaliators by incorporation of the standards of Title VI of the Civil Rights Act of 1964. See 34 C.F.R. § 100.7(e).

Section 504 Hearings

Parents who feel that their child has been incorrectly denied disability status, placed in an inappropriate setting, denied appropriate instruction and services, or discriminatorily excluded from nonacademic activities may request a Section 504 hearing to challenge the school district's action. State law or policy will dictate whether Section 504 claims that are combined with IDEA claims can be handled in an IDEA due process hearing or must be resolved in a separate Section 504 hearing. Obviously, it is convenient to combine IDEA and Section 504 issues in one hearing, although the SEA does not have responsibility for enforcement of Section 504 as it does for IDEA issues. In some states, separate Section 504 hearing officers are trained, whereas in others, IDEA hearing officers are trained to hear 504 disputes as well. Regardless of the specific procedure in a given state, the plaintiffs have the right to go to court to remedy Section 504 violations.

Litigation

For many years, parents litigating under IDEA have attached Section 504 claims to their IDEA claims. The courts typically resolve the IDEA issue first, which often precludes the need to resolve the Section 504 claim. If the issues are independent of one another and produce separate remedies, however, then the courts will also resolve the Section 504 claim. If a civil action is filed under Section 504 seeking relief available under IDEA, then the claim must first be subject to an administrative hearing process;[8] in other words, due process hearings must be conducted first, as is true for IDEA issues. One court has even required a prior hearing for Section 504 stand-alone students, i.e., those who are not covered under IDEA.[†] Section 504 itself does not specify that a Section 504 hearing must precede litigation, so a court requiring such a hearing is borrowing from IDEA. Parents of Section 504 stand-alone students will want to be aware of whether they are in a jurisdiction that requires them to "exhaust" their administrative remedies before going to court. If the Section 504 claim lacks an IDEA remedy, then administrative remedies need not be exhausted.[†]

[†]In *Babicz v. School Board of Broward County*, 135 F.3d 1420 (11th Cir. 1998), two siblings with chronic asthma and other severe allergies that led to multiple absences from school alleged that the school failed to implement their Section 504 plans. The Eleventh Circuit cited cases involving IDEA students for the proposition that Section 504 students who are not covered under IDEA must use IDEA administrative hearing procedures, arguably an incorrect proposition. The cases used to support the decision all involved IDEA students: *Charlie F. v. Board of Education of Skokie School District 68*, 98 F.3d 989 (7th Cir. 1996); *Hope v. Cortines*, 69 F.3d 687 (2d Cir. 1995); and *Waterman v. Marquette-Alger Intermediate School District*, 739 F. Supp. 361 (W.D. Mich. 1990).

An Example of an Independent Section 504 Issue

In *McKay v. Winthrop Board of Education,* 26 IDELR 1100 (D.Me. 1997), a teenager with a chronic connective tissue disorder (Marfan syndrome) who needed a power wheelchair or scooter to move around her high school alleged that the school violated Section 504 by failing to make the school's activities, programs, and facilities accessible. The federal district court held that a due process hearing was unnecessary because no IDEA issues were raised in the complaint, and the monetary damages sought by the student for her alleged pain, suffering, humiliation, and embarrassment were not available under IDEA. The parties subsequently settled the case, and the township paid the student $50,000 and agreed to renovate its schools. It also paid $30,000 to Maine Advocacy Services for the plaintiff's attorney's fees and costs. (Reported in *Review of Special Education Cases 1997,* p. 99, LRP Publications.) For a similar holding, see *Randolph Union High School District No. 2 v. Byard,* 22 IDELR 617 (D.Vt. 1995).

Remedies for Section 504 Violations

The same kinds of equitable relief available under IDEA are available under Section 504—namely, an order to stop violating a student's rights, an order requiring specific changes in the child's educational program, and other forms of equitable relief such as compensatory education. These remedies can be ordered by a hearing officer or OCR as well as by a court. In addition, in some situations, reimbursement of a parent's out-of-pocket costs can be ordered when the parent paid for aspects of the child's education that should have been, but were not, provided for publicly.[9] Attorney's fees for parents who prevail on a disputed issue are also available.

The Supreme Court has not yet ruled explicitly on whether Section 504 provides a monetary damage remedy against recipients of federal aid. Its decision in *Franklin v. Gwinnett County Public Schools,*[10] however, allowing monetary damages under Title IX for sex discrimination, infers that damages would also be available under Section 504 for intentional discrimination.[†] Most lower courts have held that monetary damages for pain and suffering are available if the violation results from intentional discrimination ("bad faith") or gross misjudgment.[11] Mere failure to provide accurate evaluation, appropriate placement, instruction, and services,

[†] In 1996, the Supreme Court ruled that monetary damages are not available against the *federal* government under Section 504 because statutory language does not explicitly waive federal governmental immunity as it does state governmental immunity. Lane v. Pena, 518 U.S. 187 (1996). Interestingly, in *Lane,* the Court, citing *Franklin v. Gwinnett County Public Schools,* seemed to take as a given that monetary damages were available under Section 504 against parties other than the federal government.

or to provide equal opportunity to participate in nonaca-demic activities under Section 504 is insufficient.

Implications

The best way to avoid legal liability is to take seriously the mandate not to discriminate against a student with a mental or physical impairment that is substantially lim-iting a major life activity, including learning. This means finding a way to provide a comparable opportunity for such a student to learn and participate in school activi-ties.

Although the issues surrounding the judicial and administrative remedies can be technical and complex, what you should remember is that a court can assess mon-etary damages against school districts for deliberate or bad-faith refusal to honor Section 504 requirements. Gross misjudgment of a student's eligibility and needs also opens up the possibility of monetary liability.

Table 9-1.   OCR Regional Offices

Eastern Division: Regions I, II, III	Southern Division: Regions IV, V, XI
Regional Office I	Regional Office IV
Connecticut, Maine, Massachusetts, New Hampshire, Rhode Island, Vermont Office for Civil Rights, Boston Office U.S. Dept. of Education J.W. McCormack Post Office & Courthouse Room 222, 01-0061 Boston, MA 02109-4557 Tel (617) 223-9662 Fax (617) 223-9669 TDD (617) 223-9695 e-mail: OCR Boston@ed.gov	**Alabama, Florida, Georgia, South Carolina, Tennessee** Office for Civil Rights, Atlanta Office U.S. Dept. of Education 61 Forsyth St. S.W., Suite 19T70 Atlanta, GA 30303 Tel (404) 562-6350 Fax (404) 562-6455 TDD (404) 331-7236 e-mail: OCR Atlanta@ed.gov
Regional Office II	Regional Office V
New Jersey, New York, Puerto Rico, Virgin Islands Office for Civil Rights, New York Office U.S. Dept. of Education 75 Park Place, 14th Floor New York, NY 10007-2146 Tel (212) 637-6466 Fax (212) 264-3803 TDD (212) 637-0478 e-mail: OCR NewYork@ed.gov	**Arkansas, Louisiana, Mississippi, Oklahoma, Texas** Office for Civil Rights, Dallas Office U.S. Dept. of Education 1999 Bryan St., Suite 2600 Dallas, TX 75201 Tel (214) 880-2459 Fax (214) 880-3082 TDD (214) 880-2456 e-mail: OCR Dallas@ed.gov
Regional Office III	Regional Office XI
Delaware, Maryland, Kentucky, Pennsylvania, West Virginia Office for Civil Rights, Philadelphia Office U.S. Dept. of Education Wanamaker Bldg., Suite 515 100 Penn Square East Philadelphia, PA 19107 Tel (215) 656-8541 Fax (215) 656-8605 TDD (215) 656-8604 e-mail: OCR Philadelphia@ed.gov	**North Carolina, Virginia, Washington, D.C.** Office for Civil Rights, District of Columbia Office U.S. Dept. of Education 1100 Pennsylvania Ave., NW, Room 316 P.O. Box 14620 Washington, D.C. 20044-4620 Tel (202) 208-2545 Fax (202) 208-7797 TDD (202) 208-7741 e-mail: OCR DC@ed.gov

Midwestern Division: Regions VI, VII, XII	Western Division, Regions VIII, IX, X
Regional Office VI	**Regional Office VIII**
Illinois, Indiana, Minnesota, Wisconsin Office for Civil Rights, Chicago Office U.S. Dept. of Education 111 North Canal St., Suite 1053 Chicago, IL 60606-7204 Tel (312) 886-8434 Fax (312) 353-4888 TDD (312) 353-2540 e-mail: OCR Chicago@ed.gov	**Arizona, Colorado, Montana, New Mexico, Utah, Wyoming** Office for Civil Rights, Denver Office U.S. Dept. of Education Federal Building, Suite 310, 08-7010 1244 Speer Blvd. Denver, CO 80204-3582 Tel (303) 844-5695 Fax (303) 844-4303 TDD (303) 844-3417 e-mail: OCR Denver@ed.gov
Regional Office VII	**Regional Office IX**
Iowa, Kansas, Missouri, Nebraska, North Dakota, South Dakota Office for Civil Rights, Kansas City Office U.S. Dept. of Education 10220 N. Executive Hills Blvd., 8th Floor, 07-6010 Kansas City, MO 64153-1367 Tel (816) 880-4200 Fax (816) 891-0644 TDD (816) 891-0582 e-mail: OCR KansasCity@ed.gov	**California** Office for Civil Rights, San Francisco Office U.S. Dept. of Education Old Federal Building, 09-8010 50 United Nations Plaza, Room 239 San Francisco, CA 94102-4102 Tel (415) 556-4275 Fax (415) 437-7783 TDD (415) 437-7786 e-mail: OCR SanFrancisco@ed.gov
Regional Office XII	**Regional Office X**
Michigan, Ohio Office for Civil Rights, Cleveland Office U.S. Dept. of Education 600 Superior Ave. East Bank One Center, Room 750 Cleveland, OH 44114-2611 Tel (216) 522-4970 Fax (216) 522-2573 TDD (216) 522-4944 e-mail: OCR Cleveland@ed.gov	**Alaska, Hawaii, Idaho, Nevada, Oregon, Washington, American Samoa, Guam, Trust Territory of the Pacific Islands** Office for Civil Rights, Seattle Office U.S. Dept. of Education 915 Second Ave., Room 3310, 10-9010 Seattle, WA 98174-1099 Tel (206) 220-7900 Fax (206) 220-7887 TDD (206) 220-7907 e-mail: OCR Seattle@ed.gov

Review

1. How much flexibility is given to school districts to design their own procedural safeguards under Section 504?

    A great deal is given, as long as the basic elements are present—notice, access to records, a hearing procedure, and a procedure to allow review of the hearing decision.

2. When should a parent ask OCR to investigate a district's actions that might be discriminatory under Section 504?

    This should occur when the issue has not been able to be resolved internally and when the issue concerns compliance with the procedures that are required for identification, evaluation, placement, or the provision of FAPE. The issues can include nonacademic activities, program accessibility, and comparability of separate facilities. If the dispute requires a judgment call (e.g., whether the services are sufficient or the results of the evaluation are accurate), a parent should seek a Section 504 hearing.

Notes

[1] 34 C.F.R. § 104.36 (1997).

[2] *Id.* § 104.33(b).

[3] *Id.* § 104.36.

[4] Letter to Durheim, 27 IDELR 380 (OCR 1997).

[5] Letter to Zirkel, 22 IDELR 667 (OCR 1995).

[6] OCR Memorandum, 19 IDELR 876 (OCR 1993).

[7] 34 C.F.R. § 104.6.

[8] *See* 20 U.S.C.S. § 1415(l).

[9] *See* Board of Educ. of Palmyra Borough v. F.C., 2 F. Supp.2d 637 (D. N.J. 1998).

[10] 503 U.S. 60 (1992).

[11] *See, e.g.*, Sellers v. School Bd. of Manassas, 141 F.3d 524 (4th Cir. 1998); Hoekstra v. Independent Sch. Dist. No. 283, 103 F.3d 624 (8th Cir. 1996); K.U. v. Alvin Indep. Sch. Dist., 991 F.Supp. 599 (S.D. Tex. 1998); Monahan v. Nebraska, 687 F.2d 1164 (8th Cir. 1982).

Selected Supplementary Resources

Section 504 Compliance Advisor, a monthly newsletter published by LRP Publications, Department 430, 747 Dresher Road, P.O. Box 980, Horsham, PA 19044-0980. The newsletter provides advice from experts and up-to-date summaries of court cases and OCR rulings.

Part III

The Individuals With Disabilities Education Act

Chapter 10

IDEA Eligibility

Disability Categories

The Individuals With Disabilities Education Act (IDEA) is designed to ensure a full educational opportunity to students with disabilities, but not all students with disabilities are eligible for services under the Act. In deciding to help school districts serve children with disabilities, the federal government specified both the kinds of disabilities and, initially, the percent of students it would serve as disabled.

The reasons were both financial and philosophical. Financially, the federal government did not want to spread its limited funds too thinly, and, until 1997, it capped the number of children for whom it would provide funding at 12% of the school population ages 3 through 17.[†] Philosophically, it did not want to

Chapter Outline

Disability Categories
Other Eligibility Factors
Definitional Issues
    Autism
    Traumatic Brain Injury
    Other Health Impairment
    Specific Learning Disabilities
    Emotional Disturbance
Judicial Interpretations
    Eligibility of Children With Profound
      Disabilities
    Eligibility on the Basis of Emotional
      Disturbance
Reminders for School Personnel
Review
Selected Supplementary Resources

label children with disabilities as "special education" students if they did not need specially designed instruction. Moreover, it did not wish to expand the disability label to other students at risk of school failure or with any kind of impairment. For instance, IDEA does not serve students whose sole difficulty is learning at a slower rate than the average student. Nor does it serve those who develop temporary behavior problems resulting from a family crisis or who simply miss a lot of school because of family moves.

To be eligible for IDEA services, all students over the age of 9 must be determined to have one of the following disabilities: specific learning disability; speech or language impairment; mental retardation; serious emotional disturbance (referred to generally as *emotional disturbance*); other health impairment; orthopedic impairment; hearing impairment, including deafness; visual impairment, including blindness; au-

†Under IDEA, states and the District of Columbia report serving an average of 10.78% of children ages 6 through 17 and 4.64% of children ages 3 through 5 during the 1996–97 school year. U.S. Department of Education. (1998). *Twentieth Annual Report to Congress on the Implementation of the Individuals With Disabilities Education Act*, p. A-33. The cap was removed in the IDEA Amendments of 1997, apparently because Congress no longer believed that it was needed.

tism; or traumatic brain injury.[1] All these conditions are defined in the regulations. Deafness and hearing impairment are defined separately from each other; blindness and visual impairment are defined together. The regulations go beyond the statute to provide additional definitions for deaf-blindness and multiple disability, because they represent special combinations of disabilities.[2] This brings the total number of disability categories to 13 (see Table 10-1 at the end of this chapter).

For children ages 3 through 9, the eligibility categories need not be used. Instead of determining whether a child has one of the specified disabilities, a state may, at its option, include as disabled a child who is experiencing "developmental delays" in one or more of the following areas: physical, cognitive, communicative, adaptive, or social or emotional development. The state may define these kinds of delays for itself, as long as they are measured by "appropriate diagnostic instruments and procedures. . . ."[3] The relaxed criteria reflect the fact that it is often difficult to pinpoint an exact disability during the developmental years and that it may not be wise to force a premature disability classification.

The state may choose to confine the age ranges to which it will apply the term *developmental delay* and to continue to use both the disability categories and the developmental delay category simultaneously—but for different children. If the state chooses not to adopt the term, neither can the LEA.[4] A local school district, however, need not adopt the term *developmental delay* even if the state does so.

Close to 5.8 million children ages 3 through 21 are currently being served under IDEA.[5] Children with specific learning disabilities account for 51% of those served, while children with speech-language impairments, mental retardation, and emotional disturbance account for another 40%.[6] In other words, more than 90% of the children served come from within these four disability groupings; the other nine disability groupings represent low-incidence disabilities.

Other Eligibility Factors

For children evaluated as having an IDEA disability, a determination must be made that the disability necessitates "special education." The existence of the disability alone is insufficient. The general language of the regulations adds that the disability must "adversely affect educational performance" or, in the case of deaf-blindness and multiple disabilities, produce "severe educational problems" that cannot be accommodated in a special education program developed solely for one of the child's disabilities.

Special education is defined as specially designed instruction, at no cost to the parents, to meet the student's unique needs. The statute specifically includes instruction in physical education.[7] The regulations state that it also includes vocational education, travel training, and speech-language pathology services or other related services if they are considered special education under state law.[8] If the effect of the disability is not to require special education, the student may still be eligible for protection under Section 504 of the Rehabilitation Act of 1973.

A student is eligible for IDEA services beginning at age 3. The student continues to be eligible through the age of 21 if he or she has not received a regular high school diploma prior to that age.[9] Otherwise, services will cease when the student graduates from high school with a regular diploma. Because graduation with a regular diploma is a change of placement, advance notice must be given to the parents. Termination of services under these circumstances, however, or when the student is no longer age eligible, does not require a reevaluation of the student as it does in other circumstances.[10]

The statute says that for those ages 3 through 5 and 18 through 21, FAPE need not be available if such application "would be inconsistent with State law or practice, or the order of any court. . . ."[11] In other words, Congress allows state law to override this particular provision of the federal statute.

IDEA requires that a parent of the child be invited to participate with "qualified professionals" in determining the child's eligibility for IDEA services.[12] The deter-

IDEA's Early Intervention Program for Infants and Toddlers

IDEA establishes a separate program of services for infants and toddlers (birth through age 2) under part C. The eligibility criteria and programming requirements for early intervention services for infants and toddlers are not a focus of this book because the services need not be primarily educational in nature and are frequently coordinated by health or social services agencies.

In brief, eligibility is extended to infants and toddlers who have a developmental delay or a diagnosed condition likely to result in developmental delay. At the state's discretion, eligibility can also be extended to those who are at risk of experiencing a substantial developmental delay if early intervention services are not provided. Services are governed by an Individual Family Service Plan (IFSP). The IFSP is similar to an IEP in many ways but also includes a statement of the family's resources, priorities, and concerns, and requires written parental consent for its implementation. In addition, a service coordinator must be identified. Part C is particularly concerned with interagency coordination and a smooth transition from Part C to Part B services when eligible children turn 3.

The early intervention program requires that services be delivered to the maximum extent appropriate in "natural environments, including the home and community settings in which children without disabilities participate." 20 U.S.C.S. § 1432(4)(G). The governor designates the lead agency for implementing and coordinating Part C services and appoints members of a state interagency coordinating council. Funding is based on the ratio of the number of infants and toddlers in a state to the number of infants and toddlers in all states. Services are at no cost to the family except where federal or state law permits the use of sliding fee scales.

State participation in the early intervention program is optional, but its purpose is to minimize the need for (or costs of) special education after infants and toddlers reach school age. The Part C provisions are found at 20 U.S.C.S. §§ 1432–1445.

mination takes place only after a full evaluation of the child's needs (see chapter 11). The eligibility team must determine that the disability is the key factor in the eligibility decision rather than limited English proficiency or lack of instruction in reading and math. If either of these factors produces a need for instructional help separate from special education, the federal funding source is not IDEA.

Another IDEA provision states that "nothing in this Act requires that children be classified by their disability" as long as a student who meets the definition of a child with a disability is actually regarded as such.[13] In other words, even after a determination of eligibility has been made and a report sent to the federal government listing eligibility by category, a school district need not attach a specific label to a student in order to provide services to that student. Giving the school district this option is intended to allow avoidance of the stigma that is sometimes attached to disability labels.

Definitional Issues

Definitions of various disability categories have been examined carefully over the years. Several terms have generated continuing political debate in recent years, particularly, *specific learning disability* and *emotional disturbance* and, to a lesser extent, *autism, traumatic brain injury,* and *other health impairment.* Each is discussed in more detail below.

Autism

Autism is a disability that was initially viewed as a subset of the category of emotional disturbance and then a subset of other health impairment. Due to advances in medical understanding and parent advocacy, autism was recognized in 1990 as a separate disability under IDEA. At that time Congress acknowledged autism as a discrete developmental disability significantly affecting verbal and nonverbal communication and social interaction. Influential in the change was the fact that, by 1990, theories of biochemical causation had gained scientific dominance over the discredited theory that lack of maternal bonding was the cause. Also, methods of treatment had evolved that were significantly different from those used with children who have an emotional disturbance.

The autism definition in the 1999 IDEA regulations acknowledges for the first time that, although the disability is usually evident by the age of 3, a child who manifests the necessary characteristics after that age could be diagnosed as having autism.

Traumatic Brain Injury

The source of controversy in the definition of traumatic brain injury (TBI) is its limitation to an acquired injury caused by "external" physical force.[14] The definition explicitly excludes injuries that are congenital or degenerative, such as those resulting from strokes or induced by birth trauma. OSEP has explained that its restriction of the definition to externally imposed injuries is consistent with use of the term *traumatic* brain injury in professional practice.[15] This raises the question of whether students with nontraumatic brain injuries will be covered under another category of disability. For instance, some students who have contracted central nervous system infections such as meningitis or encephalitis or who have suffered a stroke, heart attack, or brain tumor may have lasting neurological impairments that do not produce limitations on their strength, vitality, or alertness such that they would qualify as "other health impaired." They also may not fall within any other category, such as mental retardation or learning disability. They may have an erratic profile of cognitive strengths and weaknesses that produces a need for special education yet fall between the cracks and be ineligible for coverage under IDEA. Because the number of children with nontraumatic brain injury is small, the controversy over their inclusion has not garnered widespread visibility. Anecdotal evidence suggests that, in practice, these children are categorized as having TBI or "Other Health Impairment" regardless of whether they technically fit the definition.

Other Health Impairment

The category of *other health impairment* (OHI) has generated some misunderstanding in recent years because DOE took the position in a 1993 memorandum that the symptoms of ADD/ADHD might qualify a child as "other health impaired." The definition itself, however, referred to limited strength, vitality, or alertness, and many children with ADD/ADHD appear to have heightened rather than limited alertness. Their heightened alertness, however, can create distractibility and inattentiveness to educational tasks. To clarify DOE's position, the 1999 regulations interpret limited alertness to include "heightened alertness to environmental stimuli, that results in limited alertness with respect to the educational environment."[16] To cement the point, ADD/ADHD are included as examples of conditions that can constitute an OHI.

The categories of autism, traumatic brain injury, and OHI have seen the largest relative increases in numbers of children served under IDEA in recent years. Their total numbers, however, remain small. The OHI category can be expected to grow faster than the others if more children with ADD/ADHD are included in it in the future.

Specific Learning Disabilities

In general terms, the IDEA regulations define *specific learning disability* as a disorder in one or more of the psychological processes involved in understanding or using spoken or written language, including listening, thinking, speaking, reading, writing, spelling, or performing mathematical calculations.[17]

The regulations contain three criteria for evaluating a student as having a specific learning disability: (a) the student's underachievement must not be the result of the school's failure to provide learning experiences appropriate to the student's age and ability levels; (b) a team must find a "severe discrepancy" between the student's achievement and intellectual ability in one or more of the specified language arts and mathematical areas; and (c) the team must determine that the discrepancy is not primarily the result of mental retardation; emotional disturbance; a visual, hearing, or motor impairment; or environmental, cultural, or economic disadvantage.[18]

The term *learning disability* is an educational, not a medical, one applied to children who have average or above-average intelligence but who show idiosyncratic learning patterns that are not attributable to socioeconomic status or poor teaching. To a greater extent than is true of their peers, they are good in some subjects and poor in others, skillful in some areas but not in others. For instance, they may be good in math and struggling in reading, or vice versa. They may be excellent in reading comprehension but extremely poor at decoding words. Because of their fluctuating educational performance, these children can be a real puzzle. Although most of these children fall within normal intelligence ranges, some are gifted.

The statute does not provide criteria for measuring a "severe discrepancy" but leaves the measurement criteria to the states. In some places, such as Texas and Louisiana, state statutes prevent a diagnosis of dyslexia (a specific reading disability) from qualifying a student as learning disabled if the student does not otherwise meet the state criteria for having a learning disability. The lack of uniformity in measuring "severe discrepancy" across the states has been the subject of considerable debate. Also, the Learning Disability Association has criticized the "severe discrepancy" requirement because it forces many young children to fail academically before they can be served under IDEA. DOE is planning to reevaluate the definition over the next several years to determine whether changes are necessary.

In spite of controversy over the definition, the growth in the number of students determined to have a learning disability is largely responsible for the increases in the number of students served under IDEA. At the same time, the numbers of children determined to have mental retardation have declined steadily.

Emotional Disturbance

The most controversial definition in recent years has been that of emotional disturbance. What was formerly referred to as "serious emotional disturbance" is now referred to in the statute and regulations as "emotional disturbance." The word *serious* has been dropped to avoid any unnecessarily negative meaning attached to it because this adjective is not applied to any other disability category. The definition itself, however, remains the same. It includes children with schizophrenia and explicitly excludes those with social maladjustment unless they are found to also have an emotional disturbance.[19] Many SEAs interpret this exclusion to prohibit IDEA funding for students with conduct disorders, that is, antisocial, rule-breaking, aggressive behaviors and disorders like oppositional defiant disorder. Others choose to serve these students by classifying them as having an emotional disturbance.

In either event, any one of the following five characteristics can result in a determination of emotional disturbance, provided that it is exhibited over a long period of time and to a marked degree that adversely affects a child's education performance:[20]

1. Inability to learn that is unexplained by intellectual, sensory, or health factors

2. Inability to build or maintain satisfactory interpersonal relationships

3. Inappropriate types of behavior or feelings under normal circumstances

4. General pervasive mood of unhappiness or depression

5. Tendency to develop physical symptoms or fears associated with personal or school problems

In 1993, the federal government published a more inclusive, proposed regulatory definition of emotional disturbance in the *Federal Register* and invited public comment.[21] The definition seemed to allow the inclusion of students with conduct disorders and social maladjustments if their educational performance, broadly defined, was adversely affected so that they required special education. The proposed definition required that the disability be consistently exhibited in two settings, at least one of which was school related. In other words, any disorder showing up *only* at school would not be considered a genuine emotional disturbance.

The proposed definition generated a polarized response from service providers. Some feared expansion of the category, whereas others believed that many additional students with behavior problems needed special education services. Because of the inability to garner a working consensus, no change in the regulatory definition emerged.

The 1993 Proposed Definition

The 1993 proposed federal definition of "Emotional or Behavioral Disorder" was "a disability that is (a) characterized by behavioral or emotional response in school programs so different from appropriate age, cultural, or ethnic norms that the responses adversely affect educational performance, including academic, social, vocational, or personal skills; (b) more than a temporary, expected response to stressful events in the environment; (c) consistently exhibited in two different settings, at least one of which is school-related; and (d) unresponsive to direct intervention applied in general education, or the condition of a child is such that general education interventions would be insufficient."

Under the proposed definition, the term "emotional or behavioral disorder" would have included "a disability that co-exists with other disabilities such as a schizophrenic, affective, anxiety, or other sustained disorder of conduct or adjustment, if the disorder affects educational performance as described above."

Judicial Interpretations

Eligibility of Children With Profound Disabilities

Relatively few court cases actually raise basic eligibility issues under IDEA. Probably the best known federal case testing the IDEA eligibility criteria is that of *Timothy W. v. Rochester, New Hampshire School District*.[22] In *Timothy W.*, the U.S. Court of Appeals for the First Circuit held that eligibility under the Act did not require determination of a child's ability to benefit from special education. In other words, a child's "need" for special education was distinguished from the ability to benefit from it.

Timothy was a child with multiple disabilities, including cerebral palsy, quadriplegia, cortical blindness, and complex developmental disabilities. The school district argued that Timothy's disabilities were so profound that he lacked the ability to benefit from educational services and therefore did not need to be served by the educational system. The court disagreed, ruling that even children with the most profound disabilities were covered under the Act's "zero-reject" policy and deserved to be given a *chance* to progress, regardless of whether they could, in fact, do so (see chapter 15 for a discussion of what kind of progress is required for an appropriate education.).

Left unanswered by *Timothy W.* was the question of whether, applying the First Circuit's logic, a school must offer sensory stimulation to a comatose child. OSERS has since taken an informal position that special education services can be required even for a comatose student.[23]

A Comatose Student's IEP

In *Wenger v. Canastota Central School District*, 961 F. Supp. 416 (N.D.N.Y. 1997), a student injured in an auto accident suffered traumatic brain injury that left him in a persistent vegetative state. The court determined that his IEP provided FAPE. It was designed to encourage responses to visual, auditory, and multisensory stimuli and to develop a functional range of motion. He received special education services 2 hours per day, plus 30 minutes per week of speech therapy. He was to receive physical therapy and occupational therapy once a week for 8 weeks and then once a month.

Do you think a school district should be required to provide services to a comatose student? What are the options for the student? What if insurance does not cover these services?

Eligibility on the Basis of Emotional Disturbance

Several controversial decisions have arisen in the context of determinations of eligibility on the basis of emotional disturbance. For instance, *Doe v. Board of Education of Connecticut*[24] ruled that a violent, depressed student who performed well in school and demonstrated no academic underachievement was not emotionally disturbed and, therefore, not eligible for IDEA services. In contrast, OSEP has made clear its own position that educational performance covers more than just academic performance.[25]

In a 1998 case, the Second Circuit upheld a lower court decision that a high school student had an emotional disturbance that had been missed by the school district. The result was to make her parents eligible for reimbursement of private school costs.[26] The student was an adopted Thai orphan named Treena who had experienced various speech/language and reading problems during elementary school. She failed multiple subjects in the seventh and eighth grades and exhibited a series of behavior problems in the ninth grade, including cutting classes, failing to complete assignments, staying out late, disobeying her parents, and attempting suicide. She was hospitalized briefly, subsequently treated in a private psychiatric facility, then placed in day treatment, readmitted to the psychiatric facility, and eventually placed in a longer-term residential treatment center and then a private special education school near her home. In between these placements, she was returned to the public school twice, where her behavior each time disintegrated.

During Treena's residential placement, her public school district evaluated her and concluded that she was not IDEA eligible, primarily because she had been diagnosed as having a conduct disorder and because school personnel thought that her depression was not severe enough to affect her ability to learn or to require special education. Private evaluators at different times throughout this period had diagnosed her variously as having a conduct disorder, oppositional defiant disorder, post-traumatic stress syndrome, and major depression coupled with learning disabilities.

At an administrative hearing, a local hearing officer gave credence to information suggesting that the source of the emotional problems was primarily within the family. The officer therefore upheld the school district's determination that Treena did not have an emotional disturbance. The state-level review officer likewise concluded that Treena did not meet the eligibility criteria. A federal district court judge overturned these determinations. On appeal, the Second Circuit also rejected these determinations, stating that the source of the emotional problems was irrelevant if it affected the student's ability to learn in school. Ignoring various medical labels that are not part of the definition of emotional disturbance, the court concluded that the student had amply demonstrated an inability to learn that was partly caused by emotional problems and that she clearly manifested a pervasive mood of unhappiness or depression and a cluster of behaviors that together were inappropriate under normal circumstances. All of these characteristics had been exhibited to a marked degree and over a long period of time. In other words, she demonstrated not just one but three of the five characteristics for eligibility.

Two additional cases demonstrate contradicting approaches to distinguishing social maladjustment from emotional disturbance, highlighting the definitional dilemma. *A.E. v. Independent School District No. 25*[27] ruled that a student with a conduct disorder that included poor impulse control, suicidal tendencies, excessive anxiety, and poor student interactions was socially maladjusted rather than emotionally disturbed for purposes of determining whether her suspension was valid. The court upheld the suspension, finding her misbehavior to be unrelated to her previously diagnosed learning disabilities. Another effect of the decision was to deny services addressing her emotional needs and limit her special education services to academic areas related to her learning disabilities.

The characteristics of social maladjustment in *A.E.* (impulsivity, suicidal tendencies, anxiety, social deficits) contrast with those in *Springer v. Fairfax County School Board*,[28] which produced a similar outcome. In *Springer*, a high school student was determined to be a juvenile delinquent with social maladjustment and conduct disorder rather than emotional disturbance. His misbehavior included truancy, drug abuse, and auto theft. Despite failing grades, he scored in the average-to-superior range of intellectual ability on standardized tests. None of the psychologists who evaluated him argued that he had an emotional disturbance. Even the student acknowledged that his academic success or failure depended on his motivation. The court ruled that the student's educational difficulties resulted from his misbehaviors, not vice versa. What differentiates a social maladjustment from a conduct disorder and a conduct disorder from emotional disturbance is still subject to debate among professionals,[29] so it is not surprising that emotional disturbance should be described in different ways in court cases.

Reminders for School Personnel

The following points are especially important to remember:

1. Only certain disabilities qualify a child for special education under IDEA.

2. Many students at risk for school failure are not covered by IDEA because they do not have an eligible disability, even though they might benefit from special services.

3. No child is eligible without a full initial evaluation.

4. States are *allowed* to adopt the term *developmental delay* for use with children ages 3 through 9, or a subset of that age range. Local school districts can then decide *whether* to adopt the term for children within that age range.

5. A parent must participate in the determination of eligibility.

6. The eligibility team must ensure that the need for special education is not the result of limited English proficiency or lack of instruction in reading or math.

7. Although OSEP requires school districts to submit the number of IDEA-eligible students by disability category, the category itself is not needed in order to provide services and in no way dictates the student's placement. Instead, placement emerges from development of the student's IEP.

8. Eligibility for special education under IDEA can be based on the need for special *physical* education[†] rather than the need for specially designed *academic* or *behavioral* instruction.[30]

[†]In *Pittsburgh Board of Education v. Commonwealth Department of Education*, 581 A.2d 681 (Pa. Commw. Ct. 1990), a state court found that a student's paralysis limited her educational performance in physical education, and the court invalidated the school district's attempt to declassify her on grounds that her academic performance was not adversely affected.

Table 10-1. Regulatory Definitions of Disability Terms

34 C.F.R. § 300.7(c) *Definitions of disability terms.* The terms . . . are defined as follows:

(1) (i) **Autism** means a developmental disability significantly affecting verbal and nonverbal communication and social interaction, generally evident before age 3, that adversely affects a child's educational performance. Other characteristics often associated with autism are engagement in repetitive activities and stereotyped movements, resistance to environmental change or change in daily routines, and unusual responses to sensory experiences. The term does not apply if a child's educational performance is adversely affected primarily because the child has an emotional disturbance, as defined in . . . this section.

(ii) A child who manifests the characteristics of "autism" after age 3 could be diagnosed as having "autism" if the criteria in [the above] paragraph . . . are satisfied.

(2) **Deaf-blindness** means concomitant hearing and visual impairments, the combination of which causes such severe communication and other developmental and educational needs that they cannot be accommodated in special education programs solely for children with deafness or children with blindness.

(3) **Deafness** means a hearing impairment that is so severe that the child is impaired in processing linguistic information through hearing, with or without amplification, [and] that adversely affects a child's educational performance.

(4) **Emotional disturbance** is defined as follows:

(i) The term means a condition exhibiting one or more of the following characteristics over a long period of time and to a marked degree that adversely affects a child's educational performance:

(A) An inability to learn that cannot be explained by intellectual, sensory, or health factors,

(B) An inability to build or maintain satisfactory interpersonal relationships with peers and teachers,

(C) Inappropriate types of behavior or feelings under normal circumstances,

(D) A general pervasive mood of unhappiness or depression,

(E) A tendency to develop physical symptoms or fears associated with personal or school problems.

(ii) The term includes schizophrenia. The term does not apply to children who are socially maladjusted, unless it is determined that they have an emotional disturbance.

(5) **Hearing impairment** means an impairment in hearing, whether permanent or fluctuating, that adversely affects a child's educational performance but that is not included under the definition of deafness in this section.

(6) **Mental retardation** means significantly subaverage general intellectual functioning, existing concurrently with deficits in adaptive behavior and manifested during the developmental period, that adversely affects a child's educational performance.

(7) ***Multiple disabilities*** means concomitant impairments (such as mental retardation–blindness, mental retardation–orthopedic impairments, etc.), the combination of which causes such severe educational needs that they cannot be accommodated in special education programs solely for one of the impairments. The term does not include deaf-blindness.

(8) ***Orthopedic impairment*** means a severe orthopedic impairment that adversely affects a child's educational performance. The term includes impairments caused by congenital anomaly (e.g., clubfoot, absence of some member, etc.), impairments caused by disease (e.g., poliomyelitis, bone tuberculosis, etc.), and impairments from other causes (e.g., cerebral palsy, amputations, and fractures or burns that cause contractures).

(9) ***Other health impairment*** means having limited strength, vitality or alertness, including a heightened alertness to environmental stimuli, that results in limited alertness with respect to the educational environment, that

(i) Is due to chronic or acute health problems such as asthma, attention deficit disorder or attention deficit hyperactivity disorder, diabetes, epilepsy, a heart condition, hemophilia, lead poisoning, leukemia, nephritis, rheumatic fever, and sickle cell anemia; and

(ii) Adversely affects a child's educational performance.

(10) ***Specific learning disability*** is defined as follows:

(i) *General.* The term means a disorder in one or more of the basic psychological processes involved in understanding or in using language, spoken or written, that may manifest itself in an imperfect ability to listen, think, speak, read, write, spell, or to do mathematical calculations, including conditions such as perceptual disabilities, brain injury, minimal brain dysfunction, dyslexia, and developmental aphasia.

(ii) *Disorders not included.* The term does not include learning problems that are primarily the result of visual, hearing, or motor disabilities, of mental retardation, of emotional disturbance, or of environmental, cultural, or economic disadvantage.

(11) ***Speech or language impairment*** means a communication disorder, such as stuttering, impaired articulation, a language impairment, or a voice impairment, that adversely affects a child's educational performance.

(12) ***Traumatic brain injury*** means an acquired injury to the brain caused by an external physical force, resulting in total or partial functional disability or psychosocial impairments, or both, that adversely affects a child's educational performance. The term applies to open or closed head injuries resulting in impairments in one or more areas, such as cognition; language; memory; attention; reasoning; abstract thinking; judgement; problem-solving; sensory, perceptual, and motor abilities; psychosocial behavior; physical functions; information processing; and speech. The term does not apply to brain injuries that are congenital or degenerative, or to brain injuries induced by birth trauma.

(13) ***Visual impairment including blindness*** means an impairment in vision that, even with correction, adversely affects a child's educational performance. The term includes both partial sight and blindness.

Review

1. How is eligibility under IDEA determined?

    The student must (a) be evaluated as fitting within one of the specified categories of disability, (b) need special education, (c) be age eligible, and (d) not have limited English proficiency or lack of instruction in reading or math as the determining factor.

2. Which categories of disability account for more than 90% of the children served under IDEA?

    Learning disabilities, speech or language impairments, mental retardation, and emotional disturbance account for this percentage.

3. Which two disability definitions continue to generate the most controversy?

    Learning disabilities and emotional disturbance remain controversial.

4. What is the difference between the eligibility requirements of IDEA and Section 504?

    Eligibility is narrower under IDEA. The child must not only fit one of the disability categories (or the category of developmental delay) but must need special education as a result. Under Section 504, the definition of disability is not limited to the IDEA categories of disability, nor must special education be required as a result.

Notes

[1] 20 U.S.C.S. § 1401(3)(A)(1998).

[2] 34 C.F.R. § 300.7(a)(1)(1999).

[3] *Id.* § 300.7(b)(1).

[4] *See* 20 U.S.C.S. § 1401(3)(b); 34 C.F.R. § 300.313.

[5] U.S. Department of Education. (1998). *Twentieth Annual Report to Congress on the Implementation of the Individuals With Disabilities Education Act,* p. iii.

[6] *Id.* at A-1.

[7] 20 U.S.C.S. § 1401 (25).

[8] 34 C.F.R. § 300.26.

[9] 20 U.S.C.S. § 1401(3).

[10] 34 C.F.R. § 300.122(a)(3); 34 C.F.R. § 300.534(c).

[11] 20 U.S.C.S. § 1412(a)(1)(B)

[12] 20 U.S.C.S. § 1414(b)(4).

[13] *Id.* § 1412(a)(3)(B).

[14] 34 C.F.R. § 300.7(c)(12).

[15] Letter to Harrington, 20 IDELR 623 (OSEP 1993).

[16] 34 C.F.R. § 300.7(c)(9).

[17] *Id.* § 300.7(c)(10).

[18] *Id.* § 300.541.

[19] *Id.* § 300.7(c)(4)(ii).

[20] *Id.* § 300.7(c)(4)(i).

[21] 58 Fed. Reg. 7938 (1993).

[22] 875 F.2d 954 (1st Cir 1989).

[23] Letter to Gramm, 17 EHLR 216 (OSERS 1990).

[24] 753 F. Supp. 65 (D. Conn. 1990).

[25] Letter to Lybarger, 16 IDELR 82 (OSEP 1989).

[26] Muller v. Committee on Special Educ. of the East Islip Union Free Sch. Dist., 145 F.3d 95 (2d Cir. 1998).

[27] 936 F.2d 472 (10th Cir. 1991).

[28] 134 F.3d 659 (4th Cir. 1998).

[29] H. F. Clarizio. (1992). Social maladjustment and emotional disturbance: Problems and positions. *Psychology in the Schools, 29,* 131–140.

[30] 20 U.S.C.S § 1401(25)(B). *See also* 34 C.F.R. §§ 300.26(a)(1)(ii),(b)(2).

Selected Supplementary Resources

Forness, S. R., & Kavale, K. A. (1997). Defining emotional or behavioral disorders in school and related services. In J. W. Lloyd, E. J. Kameenui, & D. Chard (Eds.), *Issues in educating students with disabilities.* Mahwah, NJ: Erlbaum.

Kaufman, J. M. (1997). *Characteristics of emotional and behavioral disorders of children and youth.* New York: Merrill.

Kavale, K. A., & Forness, S. R. (1995). *The nature of learning disabilities.* Hillsdale, NJ: Erlbaum.

Lerner, J. (1989). *Learning disabilities: Theories, diagnosis, and teaching strategies* (5th ed.). Boston: Houghton Mifflin.

Chapter 11

Evaluation and Assessment Requirements Under IDEA

Child Find

IDEA requires a state receiving money under IDEA to establish policies and procedures to ensure that all children with disabilities who reside in the state are "identified, located, and evaluated."[1] This provision is referred to as the "child find" provision. It applies to all children, regardless of the severity of their disability, including children with disabilities who are attending private schools. The 1999 regulations specify that the child find efforts must extend to highly mobile children with disabilities, such as migrant and homeless children.[2] The regulations also make the point that children suspected of being IDEA eligible should be evaluated even though they are advancing from grade to grade. In other words, social promotions to keep a child

Chapter Outline

Child Find

Initial Evaluation

   Legal Requirements

   School District Refusal to Evaluate

   Judicial Interpretations

Reevaluation

Role of the Regular and Special Educator and Other Professionals

Other Assessment Issues under IDEA

   Continuing Opportunities for Assessment of Progress

   State and Districtwide Assessments of Achievement

Suggestions for School Personnel

Review

Selected Supplementary Resources

with age-appropriate peers do not prevent (a) the need for evaluation and (b) ultimate eligibility.

Among other things, the SEA must monitor the child find procedures of LEAs; obtain the number of children identified, located, and evaluated; and determine the effectiveness of the child find procedures.[3] The child find evaluation requirement is subject, however, to the parental consent provisions discussed below. The purpose of the requirement is to ensure that no child with a disability lacks an opportunity to receive services under IDEA.

Initial Evaluation

Legal Requirements

Evaluation of a child suspected of having a disability is an important part of IDEA because not only is it the mechanism for establishing eligibility for services under the Act but also for determining the nature of needed special services and subsequent placement.[4] No initial placement into a special education program may occur without a full, individualized evaluation of the student's educational needs.[5]

Prior to conducting an evaluation for special education eligibility under IDEA, school officials either must obtain the informed written consent of the parent or use the IDEA mediation or due process hearing procedures (unless they conflict with your state law governing parental consent).[6] In other words, school officials may not act on their own to initially evaluate a student for IDEA eligibility. In deciding whether or not to consent, parents are entitled to descriptions of each evaluation procedure to be used.[7] School district failure to provide explanations can be a serious enough legal error to produce liability.[†]

IDEA is silent about the specific length of time between the date of parental consent for a child's initial evaluation and the time the evaluation must be completed and an IEP developed. The 1999 regulations expect performance within a "reasonable period of time" and require that an IEP be developed within 30 days of an eligibility determination.[8] Some states have adopted their own timelines, but in their absence courts will construe the meaning of a "reasonable" time period.[‡]

The evaluation must use a variety of technically sound tools and strategies that assess the child in all areas of the suspected disability, including cognitive and behavioral, as well as physical and developmental.[††] No single procedure is sufficient. The data generated must include relevant functional and developmental information, including information provided by the parent. If appropriate, the initial evaluation data also should include current classroom-based assessments and observations.[9]

[†]In *Holland v. District of Columbia*, 71 F.3d 417 (D.C. Cir. 1995) the D.C. Circuit returned the case to the lower court for a factual determination of whether the school district responded to a reasonable inquiry from the parents about the specific procedures to be included in a "clinical evaluation" of their troubled teenager; if the district did not provide the requested information, then the parents were within their rights in rejecting the evaluation and were entitled to be reimbursed for private school tuition for their daughter.

[‡]In *Jose P. v. Ambach*, 669 F.2d 865 (2d Cir. 1982) the appeals court upheld the district court's adoption of a 60-day timeline to reduce the waiting lists and delays that had plagued the New York City schools.

[††]The court in *Bonadonna v. Cooperman*, 619 F. Supp. 401 (D.N.J. 1985), invalidated an IEP because it was developed from a single assessment—evaluation by a teacher.

The regulations add that tests and evaluation materials must include those tailored to assess specific areas of educational need and not merely those designed to provide a measure of general intelligence or IQ.[10] The evaluation should be comprehensive enough to identify all the child's special education and related service needs, even if they are not commonly linked with the child's disability category.[11]

Misclassification Issues   In addition to helping to determine IDEA eligibility and the nature of needed services, the evaluation procedures are intended to protect students from being misassessed or misclassified based on race, culture, language difference, or disability itself. Misclassification is an issue of serious proportions, one of real concern to OCR and OSEP. Overrepresentation of certain minority groups in specific disability categories can be evidence of discrimination and can result in restricted access to future educational and employment opportunities if students are given limited access to the general curriculum. In particular, African American students appear to be significantly overrepresented in special education programs serving students with mental retardation and emotional disturbance.[12]

The evaluation procedures attempt to address the problem of misclassification in several ways. The statute specifies two basic means of reducing the risk of misclassification:[13]

1. Standardized tests must be administered by trained and knowledgeable personnel in accordance with instructions provided by the producer.
2. Standardized tests must be validated for the specific purpose for which they are used.

The regulations add that tests must be selected and administered so as to measure what they purport to measure rather than the child's impaired sensory, manual, or speaking skills, if the intent of the test is not to measure those skills.[14] This awkwardly stated regulation means, for instance, that a student with a visual impairment should not be penalized on a reading comprehension test by being asked to read print that is too small for the student to see, nor should a student with handwriting disabilities (e.g., from cerebral palsy) be penalized by having to write the answers if handwriting is not being evaluated. Analogously, a learning disabled student with a visual or an auditory processing deficit should be allowed extra time to complete a test if speed of performance is not part of what is being measured. If school officials do not observe this standard, the performance measures will not adequately reflect the skills of a student with a disability.

In addition to these requirements, IDEA requires that tests be selected and administered so as not to be racially or culturally discriminatory. As part of this process, evaluators must provide and administer tests and other evaluation materials "in the child's native language or other mode of communication, unless it is clearly not feasible to do so. . . ."[15] In evaluating students with limited English proficiency, materials and procedures must measure the extent of any possible disability rather than measuring English language skills.[16] If the administration of a standardized test deviates from standard procedures, details of the deviation should be shared with the eligibility team so that it can evaluate the effects on the reliability and validity of the test scores.[17]

Evaluating Special Education Students Who Are Limited English Proficient (LEP)   The federal mandate to address the language barrier applies to students with disabilities who are also LEP. The challenge is twofold. First, evaluators must identify them correctly and then adapt special education programs to their needs. Too many LEP children have been misidentified as children with mental retardation, learning disabilities, or speech or language impairments. It is particularly discriminatory to administer an intelligence test in English if English is not the child's native language. For Spanish-speaking children, for instance, a Spanish version of a standardized IQ test should be used. If a Spanish version is not available, then school officials should consider using nonverbal tests for measures of cognitive and problem-solving ability or using interpreters to facilitate the testing process. Measures of the child's adaptive behavior at home and when interacting with others who speak the child's language become crucial in helping to determine whether a child who is LEP also has mental retardation.

Second, evaluators need to assess the child's proficiency in his or her native language—the language normally used by the child in the home. If the child is old enough, measures of proficiency should assess not just oral fluency but the child's ability to read, write, and comprehend in his or her native language. If the performance in the native language is satisfactory for the child's age, it tends to indicate that the student does not have a language-based disability. Generally speaking, if the child has significant problems processing written and oral language in his or her native language despite developmentally appropriate opportunities in that language, then the child may be eligible for special education under IDEA.

Services for LEP Students

LEP students were the beneficiaries of an important 1974 Supreme Court ruling in *Lau v. Nichols*, 414 U.S. 563. The Court ruled that the San Francisco School District was violating Title VI of the Civil Rights Act of 1964 by not providing meaningful instruction to many of its Chinese students in a language they could understand. The Court stated that "there is no equality of treatment merely by providing students with the same facilities, textbooks, teachers, and curriculum; for students who do not understand English are effectively foreclosed from any meaningful education." *Lau* and federal regulatory guidelines give discretion to school districts as to the methods they use to rectify the language problem, but rectify it they must.

When an LEP child qualifies for services under IDEA, teachers must consider language and communication adaptations so that the instruction is understandable and meaningful. Otherwise, the special education may result in a violation of Title VI as well as a denial of FAPE.

Parental Input   Parental input in the evaluation process is required, among other reasons because parents frequently can provide data about the child's developmental history, prior school history, and medical history. Also, when parents are involved in the data collection, they are more likely to be comfortable with the evaluation process. You will recall from chapter 10 that after the evaluation data has been gathered, the determination of eligibility is made by a team of qualified professionals and the parent. The eligibility team could be but does not have to be the IEP team, and the determination of which qualified professionals should be used to interpret the evaluation data in individual situations is left to the school districts. Together the qualified professionals and the parent are to make sure that the determination is not based on a child's limited English proficiency or lack of instruction in reading or math.[18] A copy of the evaluation report and the documentation of eligibility must be given to the parent.[19] Who writes the report is left to the discretion of the educational agency.

If honored and implemented in good faith, the above evaluation measures go a long way toward providing the kind of whole-child assessment envisioned by IDEA. To the extent that any of the requirements is not met, the possibility of error is magnified.

Additional Learning Disability Requirements

For a student suspected of having a learning disability, the IDEA regulations require additional procedures, including classroom observations by a team member other than the child's regular teacher, as well as a written team report (with minority reports if consensus is not reached). In addition, the team of qualified professionals must include a regular educator and at least one person qualified to conduct diagnostic examinations of children (such as a school psychologist, speech-language pathologist, or remedial reading teacher). 34 C.F.R. §§ 300.540–.543. These requirements exist for several reasons: the lack of a clear, operational definition of learning disability; congressional fear that students would be overclassified as learning disabled; and parental fear that determinations would be made without the participation of sufficiently knowledgeable individuals.

School District Refusal to Evaluate

Although either school district personnel or a parent may initiate a referral for special education evaluation, sometimes a school district may not see a need to honor a particular parental request. Yet the district may be hesitant to refuse to evaluate the student for eligibility, lest the refusal itself be seen as a violation of IDEA. In the early 1990s, OSEP clarified that a school does not have to evaluate every student at parental request. Instead it may explain, in writing, the reason for believing that the student does not have a disability and does not need an evaluation, thereby meeting the requirement to notify parents when it refuses to perform a requested evaluation.[20] Of course, if the parent disagrees with the school's refusal, the parent may request a due process hearing to contest the school's decision.

Judicial Interpretations

The best known, but now older, cases alleging misclassification of special education students are *Larry P. v. Riles*[21] and *PASE v. Hannon*.[22] *Larry P.* was a class action suit originally filed in the northern district of California in the late 1960s. The class was initially limited to African American students in the San Francisco Unified School District who were classified as educable mentally retarded (EMR) on the basis of standardized intelligence tests. The class was eventually extended to all such students in the state of California. The case, alleging racial discrimination in IQ testing, took almost 15 years to resolve.

In 1984, the U.S. Court of Appeals for the Ninth Circuit upheld the decision of the trial court that school district overreliance on IQ tests to place African American students in EMR classes violated both IDEA and Section 504. Such overreliance failed to honor the multiple evaluation requirements of both laws. More particularly, the defendants failed to establish that the IQ tests were valid for the purpose for which they were used, namely to accurately establish the general intelligence of African American students believed to be retarded.

A moratorium on the use of these tests for placement of African American students in EMR classes or their substantial equivalent remains in effect in the Ninth Circuit, although a subsequent, expanded moratorium on their use for *any* special education placements of African American students has been lifted.[23]

Although the factual circumstances in the *Larry P.* and *PASE* cases were similar, the 1980 ruling in *PASE* contrasts with the ruling in *Larry P.* In *PASE*, the plaintiff African American students were overrepresented in Chicago classrooms for the educable mentally handicapped (EMH—the equivalent of EMR), and they too alleged racial bias in the use of standardized intelligence tests as a part of the EMH placement process. The evidence presented in *PASE*, however, unlike that in *Larry P.*, tended to show compliance with the multifaceted, multidisciplinary assessment process established under IDEA. After examining items on the commonly used intelligence tests, the court concluded that the test scores were unlikely to produce an inaccurate classification when used in conjunction with the other statutorily mandated evaluation procedures.

What both decisions share in common is a belief in the necessity of using multiple measures instead of relying solely on an IQ measure in classifying a student as having mental retardation. These views are reflected in the evaluation procedures written into IDEA. The need for multiple measures is especially important to avoid mislabeling LEP students as disabled when the problem is actually their lack of fluency in the language of the classroom.

More recent evaluation cases have concerned other issues. For instance, legal disputes have arisen over the right of parents to obtain an independent educational evaluation if they disagree with the school's evaluation (see chapter 13). Other disputes have concerned procedural compliance. For instance, *Tice v. Botetourt County School Board*[24] concerned the failure to evaluate a student in a timely fashion. This procedural failure alone (more than 200 days from referral to an initial determination of ineligibility, which was subsequently changed to eligibility) was held sufficient to produce failure to provide FAPE.

Reevaluation

Because the possibility always remains of evaluation errors or a significant change in a child's status over time, IDEA requires a reevaluation for eligibility at least every 3 years, or more often if requested.[25] Nonetheless, in response to complaints about unnecessary reevaluations when a child's disability status (i.e., eligibility) has not changed, Congress simplified the reevaluation process in situations where the parents and school agree that the child's status has not changed. IEP team members and other qualified professionals must still review existing evaluation data. If the school team determines that no additional data are needed to determine a child's continuing eligibility, the school district is not required to conduct a new assessment to redetermine eligibility, unless the parent requests it. If, however, the school team determines that administration of an individualized assessment instrument is needed, the school district must obtain parental consent prior to using the instrument, unless it can show that the parent "failed to respond" to the reasonable measures[†] it used to seek consent.[26]

Reevaluation also requires assessment of the child's progress and any need for modifications in the delivery of special education and related services. In a sense, this requirement duplicates the requirement for continuing measures of the appropriateness of IEPs.

Reevaluation is required if a student is to be terminated from eligibility, except when a student reaches the age limit or receives a regular high school diploma.[27] Such a reevaluation can consist of a review of existing data if that is sufficient.

Role of the Regular and Special Educator and Other Professionals

IDEA does not designate who should perform various evaluation tasks, as long as those administering standardized tests are trained and knowledgeable and as long as the IEP team consists of someone qualified to interpret the instructional implications of the evaluation results. If the student is being referred for initial evaluation after experiencing difficulties in the regular education classroom, however, the regular educator is expected to provide input and to share observations about the child's performance levels in the general curriculum.[28]

The special educator is likely to be a participant any time that the measures of the child's strengths and weaknesses involve the administration of educational diagnostic tests. The school psychologist is likely to be involved if measures of general intelligence and social and emotional functioning are indicated. Depending on the child's particular needs, speech-language therapists, physical therapists, pediatricians, and others may be in-

[†]Reasonable measures to seek parental consent to reevaluate mean measures that are consistent with those used to obtain parental attendance at IEP meetings, for instance, a record of telephone calls, correspondence, and home visits. See 34 C.F.R §§ 300.505(c)(2) and § 300.345 (d).

volved in the evaluation. The point is to take enough care on the evaluation not only to determine eligibility but also to identify the child's specific needs so that appropriate teaching goals, strategies, and services may be designed. It is likely to be time well spent in the long run.

Other Assessment Issues Under IDEA

Continuing Opportunities for Assessment of Progress

Evaluation or reevaluation of IDEA students is meant to determine student eligibility and special educational needs at specific points in time. Other means of assessing and reporting special educational needs on a more continuing basis are built into the IEP process. These mechanisms are not concerned with eligibility but with the student's progress toward his or her special educational goals. For instance, IEPs must be reviewed at least annually. Furthermore, during the year, regular progress reports must be given to parents as often as reports are sent to the parents of nondisabled children. The intent of these requirements is not solely to keep parents informed but to allow the IEP team to make changes in the IEP if the student is not making sufficient progress toward the achievement of annual IEP goals. In other words, continuing assessment of progress or lack thereof is built into the IEP requirements. These forms of continuing assessment are discussed more fully in chapter 12.

State and Districtwide Assessments of Achievement

Under IDEA, special education students must participate in state and districtwide assessments of achievement, in part to reflect the fact that schools are accountable for the achievement levels of special education as well as regular education students. If testing accommodations are necessary for participation, they must be provided. Depending on the purpose of the test, accommodations could include such things as extended time, extra breaks, a separate room or private study carrel, a reader or signer, a large-print version of the text, and assistive technology devices.

If there are special education students whose disabilities preclude participation in the general achievement testing, even with testing accommodations, then the SEA or LEA must develop guidelines for the participation of such children in alternate forms of achievement testing.[29] Finally, the SEA must make available to the public the number of IDEA students participating in regular assessments and the number participating in alternate assessments. It must also make performance data available provided that release of the data would be statistically sound and would protect the confidentiality of the children involved.[30]

An issue that arises in determining appropriate accommodations to general achievement tests is whether a proposed accommodation will destroy the validity of the score on the standardized test instrument. Test producers and SEAs should help with this determination. If a test is not measuring speed of performance, then allowing a student to have extended time may be an appropriate accommodation. If visual acuity is not being measured, generating a large-print version of the test may be acceptable. On the other hand, if silent reading comprehension is being tested, reading the selections aloud to the student will destroy the validity of the test results. Care must be taken to make sure that test accommodations preserve the validity of the test score.

Competency-Based and High-Stakes Testing   Many schools conduct a special kind of districtwide achievement testing with the intent to determine whether students meet certain standards for high school graduation. Sometimes called competency-based testing, minimum competency testing, outcome-based performance testing, and more recently high-stakes testing, the evaluations raise questions as to when, if at all, they discriminate unfairly against students with disabilities. On the one hand, they may discriminate if students with disabilities are not allowed to take the tests and measure themselves against the same standards as the nondisabled. On the other hand, if no accommodations to the test-taking procedures are allowed, the tests may measure the disability rather than what the tests purport to measure.

Generally speaking, courts have upheld competency-based test requirements for students with disabili-

†Two of the most important competency-based testing cases were *Debra P. v. Turlington,* 564 F. Supp. 177 (M.D. Fla. 1983), *aff'd,* 730 F.2d 1405 (11th Cir. 1984), which required that the tests have instructional validity for all students, and *Brookhart v. Illinois State Board of Education,* 697 F.2d 179 (7th Cir. 1983), which required test modifications or accommodations for students with disabilities in appropriate circumstances.

ties, provided that three basic conditions are met: **(a)** sufficient notice must be provided to the students, **(b)** the students must be given an adequate opportunity in school to learn the skills being tested, and **(c)** appropriate testing accommodations must be provided to allow the tests to measure what they purport to measure and not the disability, if the disability is not meant to be measured.†

Suggestions for School Personnel

Those involved in evaluating students suspected of an IDEA disability should take the following precautions throughout the evaluation process:

1. Base the evaluation on multiple measures of educational need, and assess both the student's abilities and disabilities.

2. Be familiar with the validity and reliability measures of standardized test instruments and use those instruments only for the purposes for which they were validated.

3. Consider the need for testing accommodations to ensure that tests measure what they are supposed to measure and not the disability. At the same time, be sure that any individual accommodations do not destroy the validity of the test score.

4. Be sensitive to the possibilities of racial, cultural, and ethnic discrimination in all assessment measures, and select and administer them so they do not unfairly discriminate on the basis of race, ethnicity, or national origin. Of particular concern should be the failure to distinguish between a disability and limited English proficiency or racial and cultural difference. Misclassifications based on flawed evaluations can have serious legal consequences under both special education law and civil rights laws.

5. Remember that assessment of student needs occurs at multiple points and not just during initial evaluation and formal reevaluation stages. It is difficult to program effectively for a special education student if good measures of the student's current lev-

els of performance and the student's strengths and weaknesses are not available. Making time for accurate and continuing assessment enables good programming to follow. In other words, evaluation should drive the programming.

Review

1. How are the IDEA evaluation requirements similar to those of Section 504?

    Both require (a) that tests be valid for the purpose used and be administered by trained personnel in accordance with instructions provided by the test producer; (b) that tests measure what they purport to measure and not the child's impaired sensory, manual, or speaking skills (unless those are factors the test purports to measure); and (c) assessment of specific areas of educational need and not merely a single general intelligence quotient.

2. How do the IDEA evaluation requirements differ from those of Section 504?

    They (a) require functional and developmental information, including information provided by the parent; (b) require assessment in all areas of suspected disability; (c) provide more detail about the nature of the technically sound assessment tools that should be used; (d) address ways to avoid racial and cultural discrimination; (e) encourage classroom-based assessments and teacher observations; and (f) specify additional requirements for evaluation of a learning disability.

    In short, they are far more extensive.

Notes

[1] 20 U.S.C.S. § 1412(a)(3)(1998).

[2] 34 C.F.R. § 300.125(a)(2)(1999).

[3] *Id* § 300.125(b).

[4] 20 U.S.C.S. § 1414(a)(1)(B).

[5] *Id.* § 1414(a)(1)(A).

[6] *Id.* § 1414(a)(1)(C).

[7] *Id.* § 1415(c)(4).

[8] 34 C.F.R. § 300.343(b).

[9] 20 U.S.C.S. § 1414(b)(2) and (3).

[10] 34 C.F.R. § 300.532(d).

[11] *Id.* § 300.532(g) and (h).

[12] U.S. Department of Education. (1997). *Nineteenth Annual Report to Congress on the Implementation of the Individuals With Disabilities Education Act*, pp. I-42–43.

[13] 20 U.S.C.S. § 1414(b)(3)(B).

[14] 34 C.F.R. § 300.532(e).

[15] 20 U.S.C.S. § 1414(b)(3)(A)(ii).

[16] 34 C.F.R. § 300.532(a)(2).

[17] *See id.* § 300.532(b)(2).

[18] 20 U.S.C.S. § 1414(b)(4)and (5).

[19] *Id.* § 1414(b)(4)(B).

[20] Letter to Anonymous, 21 IDELR 998 (OSEP 1994); *see also* Letter to Williams, 20 IDELR 1210 (OSEP 1993); 34 C.F.R. § 300.503.

[21] 793 F.2d 969 (9th Cir. 1984).

[22] 506 F. Supp. 831 (N.D. Ill. 1980).

[23] Crawford v. Honig, 37 F.3d 485 (9th Cir. 1994).

[24] 908 F.2d 1200 (4th Cir. 1990).

[25] 20 U.S.C.S. § 1414(a)(2).

[26] *Id.* § 1414(c)(3); 34 C.F.R. § 300.505(c).

[27] 34 C.F.R. § 300.534(c).

[28] *See* 20 U.S.C.S. § 1414(c)(1); 34 C.F.R. § 300.533(a)(1)(iii).

[29] 20 U.S.C.S. § 1412 (a)(17).

[30] *Id.*

Selected Supplementary Resources

Artiles, A. J., & Zamora-Duran, G. (1997). *Reducing disproportionate representation of culturally diverse students in special and gifted education.* Reston, VA: Council for Exceptional Children.

Gersten, R., & Woodward, J. (1994). The language-minority student and special education: Issues, trends, and paradoxes. *Exceptional Children, 60,* 310–322.

Markowitz, J., Garcia, S. B., & Eichelberger, J. (1997). *Addressing the disproportionate representation of students from racial and ethnic minority groups in special education: A resource document.* Alexandria, VA: National Association of State Directors of Special Education.

Phillips, S. E. (1993). Testing condition accommodations for disabled students. *Education Law Reporter, 80,* 9–32.

Thurlow, M. L., Elliott, J. L., & Ysseldyke, J. E. (1998). *Testing students with disabilities.* Thousand Oaks, CA: Corwin Press.

Chapter 12

Individualized Education Programs Under IDEA

Purpose

An individualized education program (IEP) for each eligible student with a disability is at the heart of IDEA. It is the primary tool for individualizing services for each eligible student, and it commits resources on behalf of the student. It is the key mechanism for gaining participation by parents in the development of the student's specially designed instruction and provides an important opportunity for resolving disagreements between home and school. In addition, it provides a means both to monitor the delivery of special education and to evaluate its effectiveness.

Team Development of the IEP

Development of the IEP is a team effort, requiring both a meeting and the production of a written document; neither without the other is sufficient. An IEP meeting must be held at least annually and an IEP must be in place for each eligible student by the beginning of each school year.[1] Team development of the student's special education, related services, supplementary services, program modifications, and teacher supports is meant to help ensure effective implementation of the IEP by all those with key roles to play.

In the past, the core of the IEP team was typically a special educator, the parent(s), a representative of the LEA, and the student, when appropriate (but at least by the age of 14). Under IDEA '97, the membership has been expanded. First, more than one special educator is explicitly permitted, and a special education provider may take the place of the special educator, if appropriate.[2] The 1999 regulations interpret this to mean that if a related service provider is delivering specially designed instruction to the student and if the instruction falls within the definition of "special education" under state standards, then the related service provider can be considered the special education teacher.[3] The likeliest situation is where a speech-language pathologist is the primary provider of special services, and the student does not receive special instruction from a special education teacher as such.

The teacher membership also has been expanded to include at least one regular educator, "if the child is, or may be, participating in the regular education environment."[4] The teacher should be someone responsible for implementing the portion of the child's IEP that relates to the regular classroom. If the child receives instruction in multiple regular education classrooms, the LEA may select which teacher or teachers to serve on the IEP team.

Adding a regular educator to the team reflects the fact that the overwhelming majority of children with disabilities spend considerable time in the regular classroom, and the regular educator can be an important player in helping the child to meet IEP goals and receive special services in the regular education environment. Although admirable in intent, the requirement has generated considerable concern about increased burdens on regular classroom teachers. IDEA '97 attempts to reassure regular educators by stating that the regular educator shall participate in IEP development "to the extent appropriate." An important way in which regular educators can contribute is to determine appropriate positive behavioral interventions and strategies, supplementary aids and services, program modifications, and needed supports for school personnel.[5] Their understanding of the general curriculum can also be invaluable. The regular educator also participates in the review and revision of the IEP, but again only "to the extent appropriate."[6]

DOE provided further guidance about the role of regular educators in its Appendix A to the 1999 regulations. Appendix A focuses exclusively on how to interpret the IEP requirements. It suggests that the school district and parents should try to agree on the extent of the regular educator's participation on a case-by-case basis.[7] It states that the attendance of a regular educator may be needed for only part of an IEP meeting or not at all, depending on the purpose of the meeting. For instance, if the meeting or a part thereof is to determine related services rather than the child's instructional needs in the classroom, then the regular educator might not have to be present.

Under IDEA '97, the LEA representative's role has been magnified. The representative must be knowledgeable not only about the availability of district resources but also about the general curriculum. In addition, the representative must be qualified to either provide or supervise the provision of special education. This language is more flexible than previous regulatory language in that the LEA representative no longer has to be a supervisor of the provision of special education. In other words, a key administrator need not participate in the IEP meeting as long as a provider of special education knows the general curriculum and the availability of district resources.[†]

†If the LEA representative is not a key administrator, Appendix A (question 22) of the 1999 regulations indicates that he or she must nonetheless have the authority to commit district resources and be able to ensure that whatever services are listed in the IEP will be provided.

The IEP team must also include an individual who can interpret the instructional implications of evaluation results.[8] Prior to 1997, the law required the presence of such an individual only during the initial IEP meeting. Now the individual's attendance is required at each IEP meeting. This individual could be someone already on the team, such as the regular or special education teacher, or it could be someone else, such as the school psychologist.

At the discretion of the parent or the school district, the team may also include others who have "knowledge or special expertise" regarding the child.[9] Whoever (parent or LEA) invites the person to join the IEP team makes the determination that he or she has the requisite knowledge or special expertise.[10] In the case of the LEA, related service providers come immediately to mind. In the case of a parent, an independent evaluator comes to mind, or someone else who has studied the disability or knows the child well.

In IEP meetings with complex educational and support service requirements, it is not unusual for staff from mental health, social service, or vocational rehabilitation agencies to attend. When transition planning or services are involved, representatives of other agencies participating in the planning must be invited.[11] By this stage, if not sooner, the student must also be invited to share in developing IEP goals, objectives, and services, which must consider his or her strengths, weaknesses, preferences, and interests.[12]

At no time should a staff member attend an IEP meeting in the role of a teacher advocate or union representative.[13] The meeting should focus on the student's needs; it is meant as a cooperative venture, not an adversarial proceeding. Also, the school should remain aware of the possibility of overwhelming a parent if too many staff members attend the meeting.

Parent Participation in IEP Development

To demonstrate the seriousness with which DOE views parental participation, the regulations specify that one or both parents must be invited to attend each IEP meeting, and the meeting must be held at a mutually convenient time and place. Moreover, the parents must be notified in advance as to who will be attending. If neither parent can attend, then school officials must use other methods to include them, such as telephone conference calls.† Only when multiple documented attempts to involve the parents have failed may the school proceed to develop an IEP on its own.[14]

Parents must be given a copy of their child's IEP at no cost.[15] Additionally, school officials must make sure that parents understand what is happening at the IEP meeting.‡ This may mean arranging for an interpreter for parents who are deaf or for whom English is not the native language.[16]

Appendix A of the 1999 regulations, which interprets the IEP requirements in considerable detail, addresses a number of questions about the role of parents. It makes the following important points:

1. Parents are to be considered coequal participants in the development of the IEP.[17] Agreement is not a matter of majority rule but rather a process of consensus building.

2. The IEP is not to be completed until the meeting itself, although IEP staff members should come pre-

†The term *parent* is defined in the regulations to also include a guardian, a person acting in the place of a parent, a surrogate parent appointed in accordance with § 300.515, and, in some situations, a foster parent. *See* 34 C.F.R. § 300.20.

‡Compare this requirement with the decision in *Rothschild v. Grottenthaler,* 907 F.2d 286 (2d Cir. 1990), in which the court held that failure to provide an interpreter for deaf parents at parent-teacher meetings concerning academic or disciplinary aspects of the child's education violated Section 504.

pared with their own ideas, written or oral, of what would be appropriate to include.[18]

3. Parental concerns and information must be considered in developing and reviewing their child's IEP.[19]

It's Risky Not to Engage Parents as Partners

In *W. G. v. Target Range School District No. 23*, 960 F.2d 1479 (9th Cir. 1992), the LEA made a number of mistakes. First, it overlooked the learning disability of the plaintiff's fifth-grade son, attributing the boy's school problems to poor attention, forgetfulness, and behavior problems. It then rejected an independent educational evaluation that identified the learning disability. In response, the parents placed their son in a private school, where the school psychologist also evaluated him as learning disabled.

Ultimately, the LEA agreed to develop an IEP in conjunction with the private school, but when private school representatives could not make the meeting, the LEA proceeded to develop the IEP without the participation of the boy's regular classroom teacher or any other representative of the private school. The parents apparently walked out of the meeting when agreement became stalled over methodologies, transportation, location of special education services, and student-teacher ratios. The court decision indicates that the LEA took a firm position in support of the Scott-Foresman reading program and refused to budge. After the meeting stalled, the LEA did not attempt to convene another meeting for 5 months.

The U.S. Court of Appeals for the Ninth Circuit was extremely critical of the public school for failing to consider the recommendations of a knowledgeable teacher, other private school representatives, and his parents. It commented on the 5-month delay and the failure to respond to the parents' specific concerns. Because the IEP had not been developed correctly and was incomplete, the court awarded reimbursement to the parents for private tutoring they arranged for their son during the 1997–98 school year.

This is the kind of problem that should not and need not develop if a school understands the IEP requirements.

Contents of the IEP

IDEA '97 specifies what is to be included in an IEP.[20] The initial component is a description of the child's *present levels of educational performance,* a description that should emerge from the multifaceted, nondiscriminatory evaluation of the whole child and the identified needs for specially designed instruction (see chapter 11). The child's disability classification alone is insufficient and, in fact, IDEA does not require its inclusion in the IEP, although some states may choose to include it.

It is difficult to overstate the importance of a full evaluation of the child prior to the development of the IEP. An accurate evaluation of the child's strengths, weaknesses, and current levels of performance is the basis for all that will follow. If the parents bring an independent educational evaluation (IEE) to the school, the school should fully consider that evaluation in developing its own assessment of the student's needs and goals. A school district is unwise to reject independent evaluation results unless they conflict with its own evaluation and eligibility criteria, and the district has superior documentation. An accurate evaluation of the nature of the child's disability and accompanying needs goes a long way toward allowing the development of an appropriate IEP.

†For preschoolers, the IEP can describe how the disability affects the child's participation in "appropriate activities" rather than the general curriculum.

Under IDEA '97, the statement of the child's present levels of educational performance must include how the child's disability affects the child's "involvement and progress in the general curriculum."[21]† Because lawmakers became convinced that the expectations for students with disabilities were too low, IDEA is far more outcome oriented than it was before the 1997 Amendments. Involvement in the general curriculum is now essential. Although the term "general curriculum" is not defined in the statute, the 1999 regulations define it as "the same curriculum as for nondisabled children."[22] In short, it is what all children study, not some specialized curriculum for special education students.

From the assessment of a child's present levels of educational performance and evaluation results, the IEP team must generate *measurable annual goals,* including either benchmarks (major milestones) or intermediate short-term objectives.[23] The goals must indicate what academic (and, if appropriate, nonacademic) areas must be addressed during the coming school year in order to meet the student's individual needs relating to involvement and progress in the general curriculum. They must also address other educational needs arising from the disability.[24]

Prior to IDEA '97, only the objectives but not the goals had to be stated in measurable terms. Now that the annual goals must be measurable, the IEP must include a *statement of how the child's progress toward the goals will be measured and how the child's parents will be informed of their child's progress as often as the parents of nondisabled students are informed.* Appendix A of the 1999 regulations indicates that benchmarks measure the amount of progress a child is expected to make within specified segments of the year, while objectives generally divide skills described in an annual goal into discrete components.[25] The option to select whether to use benchmarks or objectives gives new flexibility to IEP team members. In either case, if progress is not sufficient to enable the child to achieve the goals by the end of the year, presumably the IEP should be revised. Goals that stay the same from year to year are clearly suspect. Table 12-1 shows one approach to benchmarks and objectives.

Table 12-1. One Approach to the Difference Between Benchmarks and Objectives

Annual Reading Comprehension Goal

By the end of the final reporting period, Peter will verbally answer 90% of the reading comprehension questions correctly in the final units covered in a fourth-grade basal reading book.

Benchmarks (Milestones)

- 75% correct in the units covered by the end of the first reporting period
- 80% correct in the units covered by the end of the second reporting period
- 85% correct in the units covered by the end of the third reporting period
- 90% correct in the units covered by the end of the final reporting period

Short-Term Objectives (Discrete Components of the Skill)

- 90% of the factual questions (who, what, when, and where) correct by the end of the first reporting period
- 90% of the factual questions and questions that differentiate fact from opinion correct by the end of the second reporting period
- 90% of the questions dealing with factual, opinion, and inference questions correct by the end of the third reporting period
- 90% of all reading comprehension questions correct by the end of the final reporting period

The above percentages were selected based on the assumption that Peter is in the sixth grade.

Another section of the IEP requires a statement of the specific *special education and related services,* the *supplementary aids and services,* and the *program modifications* or *supports for school personnel* that are needed to help the student achieve the specified goals, to be involved and progress in the general curriculum, and to participate in extracurricular and nonacademic activities with nondisabled and disabled children.[26] If the child will not be participating with nondisabled children in the regular class and in extracurricular and nonacademic activities, *the IEP must explain the extent of nonparticipation.*[27] Prior to IDEA '97, the requirement was the reverse: the IEP had to state "the extent that the child will be able to participate in regular educational programs."[28] The change enhances the legal support for a philosophy of including children with disabilities in regular classrooms. It means that when a dispute arises with respect to an IEP or placement, the school district's burden of producing evidence has shifted from one of showing when the child *can* participate to one of showing when the student *cannot* participate in regular education activities. The shift is legally significant and creates a presumption against pullout programs.[†] The presumption can be rebutted, however, when there is good reason for the pullout, such as the need for quiet space for one-on-one speech therapy or a neighborhood setting for orientation and mobility training.

The anticipated *frequency, duration* (including projected starting date), and *location* of the services and modifications must also be included.[29] The addition of location as a requirement provides a way to monitor whether related services are being provided in the regular education setting. It probably increases the pressure to provide related services in a location that does not significantly reduce the child's ability to participate in the regular classroom and the general curriculum.

Under the 1997 Amendments, a statement of *transition service "needs"* must be included in the IEP when the child reaches the age of 14.[30] The needs should focus on the student's course of study and indicate whether or how the student will participate in advanced placement courses, vocational education courses, and so forth.

[†]School personnel and parents should be aware that IDEA defines instruction in a resource room as a *supplementary service* provided in conjunction with regular class placement. 34 C.F.R. § 300.551(a)(2). This language indicates that a resource room placement that accompanies a regular classroom placement does not constitute a removal from the regular educational environment. See 34 C.F.R. § 300.550(b)(2) and chapter 17.

If the student has reached the age of 16, the IEP must contain a statement of necessary *transition services* to facilitate the child's entry into the postschool world.[31] Postschool outcomes, although improving, are still poor for many children with disabilities, and IDEA '97 expects schools to do a better job of preparing these children for postschool life.† The postschool world includes a range of possible pursuits, such as postsecondary education, vocational training, integrated employment (including supported employment), continuing and adult education, adult services, independent living, and community participation. In developing an individualized and coordinated set of transition activities for each student, the IEP team, including the student, should consider the student's full range of potential needs for (a) instruction and related services, (b) community experiences, (c) the development of employment and postschool adult living objectives, and (d) if appropriate, the acquisition of daily living skills and a functional vocational evaluation. Linkages with, or responsibilities to be assumed by, noneducational agencies should be specified.[32]

Finally, because students with disabilities are expected to be included in state and districtwide assessments of achievement, any *modifications in the administration of the tests necessary for a student to participate must be specified in the IEP.*[33] If the IEP team determines that the student cannot participate in an assessment, the IEP must explain why the assessment is inappropriate and how the child will be assessed instead. Alternate assessments must be developed by July 2000 for the small number of students who may not be able to participate in regular standardized achievement testing. The intent of these provisions is to ensure that schools are accountable for the achievement levels of all their students, not solely regular education students.

†Interagency agreements must be in effect to facilitate the delivery of transition services. If a noneducational agency fails to provide the transition services to which it committed itself in the IEP, the IEP team must reconvene to identify alternative strategies for providing the needed services. The LEA must implement the IEP but can claim reimbursement from the nonperforming agency. *See* 34 C.F.R. § 300.348 and § 300.142.

Appendix A Guidance

Appendix A expands on the above IEP components and attempts to explain the reasons for the new requirements. It makes the following points, among others:

1. A child's IEP must address involvement in the general curriculum regardless of the severity of the dis-

ability and the setting in which the child is educated.[34] Students in special schools, as well as those in regular classrooms, should be accessing the general curriculum.

2. The IEP need not include annual goals related to parts of the general curriculum in which the child's disability does not affect participation.[35] For instance, if the child needs no program modifications, supportive services, or specialized instruction during social studies, then social studies does not have to be mentioned in the IEP.

3. All services specified in the IEP must be provided, either directly through local school district resources or indirectly by contracting with another agency or making other arrangements. The district may use whatever sources of public and private support are available, but the services must be at no cost to the parent.[36]

4. A single meeting may be used to determine eligibility, develop the IEP, and determine placement,[†] as long as the required team participants are present and proper notification has been given.[37]

5. The IEP must precede a placement decision, not follow it.[38] Of all the mistakes that OSEP has uncovered while monitoring state compliance with IDEA, premature placement continues to be one of the most difficult to eradicate. School officials tend to "slot" students by classification into one of the district's existing service delivery options, whereas IDEA requires an individualized assessment of the nature and extent of special services required for each child. The placement decision should be based on how close to the instructional mainstream those services can be appropriately delivered. Until the IEP is developed and services are specified, any placement decision is premature.[‡]

Special Factors

IDEA '97 includes a whole section telling the IEP team what to "consider" when developing the IEP.[39] The first three among many considerations are the strengths of

[†]Many experienced special educators advise caution in proceeding with a single meeting for eligibility, IEP, and placement decisions because the lengthy agenda can overwhelm parents. In most situations, parents need time to digest evaluation data before addressing IEP goals, services, and placement options.

[‡]The decision in *Spielberg v. Henrico County Public Schools,* 853 F.2d 256 (4th Cir. 1988), is instructive. The court held that FAPE was denied because the public school had proposed a transfer to a private school placement prior to development of a new IEP.

the child, the results of the last evaluation, and the parents' concerns. If the child's behaviors impede learning, then behavioral strategies and supports also must be considered. If the child has limited English proficiency and is IDEA eligible, then the language needs of the child must be considered. If the child is blind or visually impaired, the IEP must provide for instruction in and use of Braille, unless inappropriate. The IEP team must also consider the child's communication needs, and if the child is deaf or hard of hearing, the team must consider the child's opportunity to communicate directly with peers and staff in the child's language and communication mode and the opportunity to receive direct instruction in that mode. Finally, the team must consider whether a child needs assistive technology devices and services.

These statutory additions may be a response to criticism that too often a student's IEP goals and objectives did not directly address the child's presenting problems. In requiring attention to overlooked problem areas, Congress appears to be softening its position that instructional methods do not have to be included in the IEP. Positive behavior strategies can be viewed as instructional methods. So, perhaps, can instruction in Braille and instruction in a deaf child's communication mode (e.g., American Sign Language), although they can also be seen as adaptations to facilitate communication.

The 1999 regulations support the interpretation that instructional methods may need to be specified in some IEPs. First, they state that if, in considering the above factors, the IEP team determines that a child needs a particular device, service, intervention, accommodation, or modification, then the team must say so in the IEP.[40] Second, for the first time the regulations define the meaning of "specially designed instruction," and it includes adapting instructional methods.[41] Third, the analysis accompanying the 1999 regulations states that for some children, selection of a particular instructional method is necessary to individualize their education. The analysis provides two examples: (a) cued speech that could be the basis for the goals, objectives, and other elements of a particular student's IEP, and (b) the selection of a specific reading method for a student with a learning disability who has not learned to read using traditional instructional methods. If no specific method is required to enable a student to receive FAPE, the methodology is left in the hands of those who are actually instructing the student. The decision about methodology rests with the IEP team.[42]

The Expanded Definition of Special Education

IDEA defines *special education* as "specially designed instruction, at no cost to the parents, to meet the unique needs of a child with a disability, including (A) instruction conducted in the classroom, in the home, in hospitals and institutions, and in other settings, and (B) instruction in physical education." 20 U.S.C.S. § 1401(25).

The 1999 regulations define *specially designed instruction* as:

"adapting, as appropriate to the needs of an eligible child under [Part B], the content, *methodology*, or delivery of instruction (i) [t]o address the unique needs of the child that result from the child's disability; and (ii) [t]o ensure access of the child to the general curriculum, so that he or she can meet the educational standards within the jurisdiction of the public agency that apply to all children" (emphasis added).

34 C.F.R. § 300.26(b)(3).

---

† Don't forget about surrogate parents. In *Abney v. District of Columbia*, 849 F.2d 1491 (D.C. Cir. 1988), the court ruled that the IDEA procedural safeguards had been violated because of a failure to notify the child's surrogate parent that the child's special education program had been curtailed for a period of time.

‡ If your state requires parental *consent* for new IEP services, it must make sure that a school district has procedures (e.g., to override lack of consent) to ensure that lack of consent does not result in the failure to provide FAPE.

Is an Agreed-Upon IEP Binding?

Yes and no. The school district must implement the IEP as written. Failure to provide the listed services will constitute a denial of FAPE. Sometimes, however, school team members decide later that an IEP should be modified.[†] Under these circumstances, the parents must be notified and allowed input into any revised IEP.[43] Lack of parental approval does not excuse the school district from delivering any new services that it sees as necessary for FAPE.[44] If the parent remains adamantly opposed to new services or activities, the parent's recourse is to request a hearing or file a state complaint.[‡]

Faithfully implementing the IEP does not require that all IEP goals be realized. If that were the case, the goals would be set lower than otherwise necessary, but the school must make a good-faith effort to enable the child to make progress toward the specified goals. When lack of expected progress toward IEP goals occurs, the IEP should be revised.[45]

Although school districts are obligated to implement the services in an agreed-upon IEP, the parents are entitled to change their minds about the effectiveness of that IEP. They can request a new meeting to revise the IEP. If the school declines to introduce services that the parent believes have become necessary, the parent may seek a hearing, enter into mediation, or file a complaint with the state Office of Education.

IEPs When Public Agencies Place a Child in a Private School

IEPs are not limited to special education students at public schools but are required as well for students receiving publicly financed special education and related services at private schools. When the private placement is made by a public agency, the IEP must be developed prior to the placement, and participation at the IEP meeting by a representative of the private school is mandatory.[46]

After the child has begun to attend a private school, meetings to review and revise the IEP may be conducted by the private school, if the public agency is willing. Nonetheless, the LEA must make sure that the parents and the LEA representative are involved in IEP decisions and that they agree to any proposed changes before such changes are made.[47]

Judicial Interpretation of IEP Requirements

Curiously, prior to IDEA '97, courts were slow to utilize the goals, objectives, and older measurement provisions of the IEP as a means of determining whether a student was receiving benefit, in the sense of making meaningful educational progress. Although many cases analyzed the nature and extent of special education and related services in the IEP and whether they met the student's needs, too seldom did one see evidence of whether there was meaningful progress toward achievement of the goals and objectives specified in the IEP. The Supreme Court's decision in *Hendrick Hudson Central School District Board of Education v. Rowley*[48] is illustrative. The Court used evidence of Amy Rowley's regular classroom achievement rather than measures of progress toward meeting her own IEP goals and objectives in determining whether she was receiving FAPE.

A clear understanding of the need for a fully developed IEP was reflected by the New Jersey Supreme Court in *Lascari v. Board of Education*.[49] The *Lascari* court determined that a student was not receiving FAPE because of inadequacies in his IEP, rendering it incapable of review. Specifically, current levels of performance were not indicated in the IEP, and the goals and objectives were "so vague that they were meaningless."[50] For instance, the first of two contested IEPs specified that the student was to strengthen his reading skills in a phonetic-linguistic program, develop practical math skills and vocational skills, "develop" a language arts program, and build self-esteem. The IEP contained no indication of how progress toward the goals and objectives was to be measured, nor any rationale for the proposed placement. For these reasons, the court ruled that the IEP was inappropriate.[51]

Because of the increased attention to measurable goals, regular progress reports, and the desire for improved outcomes in IDEA '97, the door has been opened to increasing opportunities to litigate IEP goals and the extent of progress. When the IEP fails to produce meaningful progress toward achievement of the student's IEP goals, parents have more leverage under IDEA '97 than they had before. Therefore, one can anticipate that court decisions may increasingly have to pay more attention to goals and measures of progress.

Implications

Because the IEP is at the core of the substantive requirements under IDEA, all teachers should be trained to understand its purpose and function. In addition, all of a child's teachers must have access to the IEP if they have any responsibility for its implementation, and they must be informed of their responsibilities.[52] This is particularly relevant to secondary school teachers because one teacher can represent all the others and can obligate them to various program modifications and supplementary aids and services.

The increased role of the regular educator should be seen as an opportunity to solicit the program supports needed to make the regular education classroom appropriate for a child with a disability. "Dumping" a child into a regular classroom without the necessary program supports and supplementary services is unacceptable under IDEA.

IEP team members should carefully consider when to use benchmarks and when to use objectives to measure progress toward IEP annual goals. Sometimes benchmarks may be simpler but equally effective in measuring progress. At other times, objectives may be more appropriate.

Teachers will need to work more closely than ever with parents. The requirement to share progress reports with parents and to revise IEPs to address lack of progress encourages more parental involvement on a regular and continuing basis.

Special and regular education teachers must balance IDEA students' need for achievement in appropriate areas of the general curriculum with their need for a specialized curriculum in other areas. Neither kind of curricular need should be sacrificed for the other.

Finally, school officials should be aware that if they commit serious procedural violations in the development of an IEP, courts will consider such violations to constitute the denial of FAPE if they produce harm.[53†]

†Occasionally, a potentially serious procedural omission may be considered harmless, as in *Doe v. Defendant I,* 898 F.2d 1186 (6th Cir. 1990), in which the court found no IDEA violation for IEP omissions because both parties knew the missing information, and the spirit of the law was honored.

Review

1. What must be included in an IEP?

    An IEP must include the following: (a) the child's present levels of educational performance; (b) measurable annual goals that address the child's special education needs relating to both the general curriculum and areas independent of the general curriculum; the goals should address both academic and nonacademic goals, as appropriate; (c) how progress toward the goals will be measured and how parents will be informed of the extent of that progress; (d) the specific special education and related services, supplementary aids and services, and program modifications or supports to be provided; (e) the extent to which the student will not be participating with nondisabled children in the regular class and in extracurricular and nonacademic activities; (f) the anticipated frequency, duration, and location of services and modifications; (g) transition service needs when the child reaches 14 and transition services when the child reaches 16; and (h) modifications, if any, in the administration of schoolwide or districtwide assessments of achievement.

2.   Who should be on the IEP team?

The IEP team should comprise the parent(s), the special educator (or provider of special education, such as a speech-language pathologist), and, in most instances, the regular educator. An official representative of the LEA and someone who can interpret the instructional implications of evaluation results must also be on the team, but the special or regular educator might also serve in those positions. Others who have "knowledge or special expertise" regarding the child may also be on the team.

3.   What are some of the reasons that development of an IEP is so crucial to the effective implementation of IDEA?

It is the best means of developing home-school cooperation in the education of a child with a disability, it is the basis for determining the appropriate placement, and it is the primary mechanism for determining whether FAPE is being provided.

Notes

[1] 20 U.S.C.S. § 1414(d)(2)(1998).

[2] 34 C.F.R. § 300.344(1999).

[3] *Id.* Part 300, app. A at questions 23 and 27.

[4] 20 U.S.C.S. § 1414(d)(1)(B).

[5] *Id.* § 1414(d)(3)(C).

[6] *Id.* § 1414(d)(4)(B).

[7] 34 C.F.R. Part 300, app. A at question 24.

[8] 20 U.S.C.S. § 1414(d)(1)(B).

[9] *Id.*

[10] 34 C.F.R. § 300.344(c).

[11] *Id.* § 300.344(b).

[12] *Id.*

[13] 34 C.F.R. Part 300, app. A at question 28.

[14] *Id.* § 300.345(d).

[15] *Id.* § 300.345(f).

[16] *Id.* § 300.345(e).

[17] *Id.* Part 300, app. A at question 5.

[18] *Id.* at question 32.

[19] *Id.,* app. A at subsec. II: Involvement of Parents and Students.

[20] 20 U.S.C.S. § 1414(d)(1)(A). *See also* 34 C.F.R. § 300.347.

[21] 20 U.S.C.S. § 1414(d)(1)(A)(i).

[22] 34 C.F.R. § 300.347(a)(1)(i).

[23] 20 U.S.C.S. § 1414(d)(1)(A)(ii).

[24] *Id.*

[25] 34 C.F.R. Part 300, app. A at question 1.

[26] 20 U.S.C.S. § 1414(d)(1)(A)(iii).

[27] *Id.* § 1414(d)(1)(A)(iv).

[28] 20 U.S.C. § 1401(20) (1995).

[29] 20 U.S.C.S. § 1414(d)(1)(A)(vi).

[30] *Id.* § 1414(d)(1)(A)(vii)(I).

[31] *Id.* § 1414(d)(1)(A)(vii)(II)

[32] 34 C.F.R. §§ 300.29 and 300.347.

[33] 20 U.S.C.S. § 1414(d)(1)(A)(v).

[34] 34 C.F.R. Part 300, app. A at question 2.

[35] *Id.* at question 4.

[36] *Id.* at question 28.

[37] *Id.* at question 19.

[38] *Id.* at question 14.

[39] 20 U.S.C.S. § 1414(d)(3).

[40] 34 C.F.R. § 300.346(c).

[41] *See id.* § 300.26(b)(3).

[42] See 64 Fed. Reg. 12552 (March 12, 1999).

[43] *See* 34 C.F.R. § 300.350.

[44] *See* 34 C.F.R. § 300.505(d).

[45] *Id.* § 300.343(c).

[46] *Id.* § 300.349(a).

[47] *Id.* § 300.349(b).

[48] 458 U.S. 176 (1982).

[49] 560 A.2d 1180 (N.J. 1989).

[50] *Id.* at 1190.

[51] *Id. See also* County of San Diego v. California Special Educ. Hearing Office, 93 F.3d 1458 (9th Cir. 1996).

[52] 34 C.F.R. § 300.342(b).

[53] *See, e.g.*, Blackmon v. Springfield R-XII Sch. Dist., 29 IDELR 855 (W.D. Mo. 1998); Amanda S. v. Webster City Community Sch. Dist. 27 IDELR 698 (N.D. Iowa 1998); Gerstmyer v. Howard County Pub. Schs., 850 F. Supp.361 (D. Md.1994); W.G. v. Board of Trustees of Target Range Sch. Dist. No. 23, 960 F.2d 1479 (9th Cir. 1992).

Selected Supplementary Resources

Bateman, B., & Linden, M. A. (1998). *Better IEPs* (3rd ed.). Longmont, CO: Sopris West.

Kukik, S., & Schrag, J. (1998). *IEP connections*. Longmont, CO: Sopris West.

Turnbull, A. P., & Turnbull, H. R. (1997). *Families, professionals, and exceptionality: A special partnership* (3rd ed.). Upper Saddle River, NJ: Merrill/Prentice-Hall.

Chapter 13

Due Process Protections Under IDEA

Constitutional Due Process

Overview

The origin of the due process protections for public school students is the due process clause in the Fifth and Fourteenth Amendments to the U.S. Constitution.[†] Both amendments provide, among other things, that no person shall be deprived of life, liberty, or property, without due process of law. The Fifth Amendment restrains the power of the federal government, while the Fourteenth Amendment restrains the power of individual states. The federal courts have inter-

preted the due process clause to contain two kinds of rights: substantive due process and procedural due process. Substantive due process has not been of primary importance in special education matters; in contrast, procedural due process has been central to the whole body of special education law. Therefore, this chapter focuses on procedural due process.

Procedural Due Process

Procedural due process requires the use of fair procedures in restricting someone's right to life, liberty, or property. In this country, an individual's right to life, liberty, and property is not absolute; restrictions are placed on the exercise of these personal rights so that the rights of the community as a whole may be protected. In restricting these rights, however, federal and state governments are not allowed to operate in a manner unrestrained by law. What this means is that certain procedures are owed to persons protected by the U.S. legal system before those rights can be seriously abridged.

In the context of public education, procedural due process requires that students receive the process they are due before government restricts their property rights or

†The relevant portion of the Fifth Amendment reads: "No person shall be . . . deprived of life, liberty, or property, without due process of law. . . ." The comparable portion of the Fourteenth Amendment reads: "No State shall . . . deprive any person of life, liberty, or property, without due process of law. . . ."

liberty interests. Schools are not proposing to take student lives, so their right to life is not a due process issue. Just what is the process that is due—namely, proper or fitting? The basic elements of procedural due process, common across varying circumstances, are as follows: (a) notice—informing the person of the contemplated governmental action to restrict one's life, liberty, or property and the reason for the action, and (b) a chance to respond—allowing the person to tell his or her side of the story at some kind of hearing, informal or formal. The less serious the contemplated governmental action against the person, the more informal the procedures. When more is at stake, more extensive procedures are required.

Legislation sometimes goes beyond constitutionally required minimums and specifies additional procedures to assure parents that school decisions affecting a student's property and liberty interests are fair. One such statute is IDEA, which specifies extensive procedural safeguards when identification, evaluation, placement, and provision of FAPE to a student with disabilities are at stake.

Procedural Due Process Under IDEA

Background

In the 1960s and early 1970s, prior to the passage of IDEA, advocates for students with disabilities sought to remedy what they perceived as unfair treatment of those students by invoking the due process protections of the Constitution, among other things. For students to be entitled to due process, they first had to establish that they were being denied a liberty or property right to which they were entitled under the Constitution. The advocates argued that excluding students with disabilities from regular education classrooms and schools was a substantial infringement of their liberty because it restricted their freedom to be educated "like all the other kids" and it was potentially stigmatizing. The advocates also argued that education is a property right, namely, a legal entitlement to an economic interest, because education is important to one's self-sufficiency and income-producing potential and because states undertake to provide it to all children between certain ages. In short, advocates asserted that because the proposed treatment of students with disabilities at the hands of school authorities threatened their "good name" and their future economic interests, they were entitled to procedural due process to ensure that the proposed treatment was not arbitrary or otherwise unfair.

Two landmark lower court cases, *PARC v. Pennsylvania*[1] and *Mills v. District of Columbia Board of Education*,[2] ruled that before being removed from regular education classes or otherwise denied access to regular education, students with disabilities had a constitutional right to procedural due process. In *PARC* and *Mills*, formal (written) notice and a formal hearing were determined to be necessary.[†] In *PARC*, thousands of students with mental retardation had been excluded from public school. Many were placed in institutions that did not provide any educational component. In *Mills*, thousands of students with various kinds of disabilities, ranging from mental retardation to serious emotional disturbance, had been denied entrance to or expelled from public schools. In both situations, the parents of those students had not been provided with prior notice of the pending expulsion or exclusion, nor were they given any kind of hearing at which to protest the intended action.

[†]Both *PARC* and *Mills* also concluded that students with disabilities have a constitutional right to a public school education and their exclusion from school violates the principle of equal educational opportunity for all children of school age.

Goss v. Lopez: Students' Liberty & Property Rights

The procedural due process arguments that were advanced in the *PARC* and *Mills* cases anticipated by several years the Supreme Court's 1975 decision in *Goss v. Lopez*, 419 U.S. 565 (1975). The Court in *Goss* held that all students had a property interest in completing their education and a liberty interest in their good name, that is, their reputation. In *Goss*, a suspension from school, even for only up to 10 days, was determined to involve those interests because students might miss an exam, fail a course, or be stigmatized among their peers as a result of the suspension. The *Goss* decision requires that prior to short-term suspensions from school, students must receive at least a minimal amount of procedural due process—oral notice of the alleged violation and an informal opportunity to present their side of the story. This right applies to all students, including those with disabilities.

Influenced by the *PARC* and *Mills* decisions, Congress incorporated extensive due process safeguards into IDEA. It did so under the authority of section five of the Fourteenth Amendment, which gives Congress the power to enact appropriate legislation to implement the protections of the Fourteenth Amendment. The specific due process safeguards enacted in the statute go beyond the basics of notice and a chance to respond; they detail a set of explicit protections that are enforceable in court. These procedural safeguards are meant to protect students with disabilities from unilateral and possibly ill-advised school decisions and to allow parental involvement and advocacy for their children. The extent to which the statute elaborates on and extends the basic due process requirements of the Constitution is discussed in the next section.

Procedural Safeguards in the Statute and 1999 Regulations

Procedural Safeguards Notice   A full written explanation of the basic due process safeguards of IDEA '97 that are extended to parents on behalf of their children must be given to parents at least on the following occasions: upon initial referral, upon each notification of an IEP meeting, upon reevaluation of their child, and upon receipt of a request for a due process hearing.[†]

†Failure to provide notice to parents can produce adverse decisions for school districts. *See Hall v. Vance County Board of Education,* 774 F.2d 629 (4th Cir. 1985), which held that failure to inform parents of their rights produced failure to provide FAPE, and *Max M. v. Thompson,* 566 F. Supp. 1330 (N.D. Ill. 1983), which held that intentional failure to notify parents of their right to review the psychological evaluations and obtain an independent educational evaluation (IEE), and failure to inform parents of placement meetings, would constitute violations of EHA (IDEA) for which reimbursement for private treatment would be available.

Although districts are used to giving parents a formal, written statement of their due process safeguards, frequently parents have not understand their importance. Often the required statement has been lengthy and legalistic, to the dissatisfaction of parents and teachers alike. To address this problem, IDEA '97 requires that the notice be written in "an easily understandable manner" and in the native language of the parents, unless it is clearly not feasible to do so.[3] Despite this requirement, communicating intelligibly in the right form and at the right time to parents remains a challenge.

The Procedural Safeguards Notice to parents must contain the following explanation of their rights to[4]:

1. Written prior notice before an education agency proposes (or refuses) to initiate or change the child's identification, evaluation, educational placement or provision of FAPE

2. Give or withhold consent at specific times

3. Access their child's educational records

4. Obtain an independent educational evaluation (IEE) of their child

5. Present complaints to initiate an impartial due process hearing with respect to any of the items mentioned in number 1

6. Mediation prior to a hearing

7. A due process hearing

8. A second-tier (state-level) hearing-review procedure if the impartial due process hearing is conducted by an LEA rather than the SEA

9. Appeal the final administrative hearing decision to state or federal court

10. Attorney's fees if the parent is the prevailing party

These ten rights are, in effect, an elaboration of the basic elements of due process—notice and some kind of hearing prior to the intended government action. The provisions give the parent (or a guardian or surrogate parent) a chance to have input into or challenge the school's decision making at various points in the process. Even the attorney's fees provision fits within this concept, for it allows parents with modest financial resources a way to obtain their "day in court"; without the provision, many parents with good claims could not attract the services of an attorney.

Additional procedural safeguards must also be explained in the notice:

11. The requirement that the child remain in his or her current placement while administrative or judicial proceedings are pending, unless the parents and the educational agency agree otherwise (also known as the stay-put provision)

12. The procedures allowing an exception to the stay-put provision for students who are subject to a disciplinary placement in an interim alternative educational setting

13. The requirement for prior notification from parents if they unilaterally seek a private school placement at public expense for a child with a disability

14. The right to file a complaint with the SEA on any matter mentioned in number 1 above. (Others besides parents also have a right to file such a complaint—for example, teachers.)

These last four safeguards have purposes that extend beyond the basic elements of due process. They are directed at the welfare of students—those subject to placement changes and other students as well. They also obligate parents to give notice to schools (a basic fairness issue from the school's standpoint), and they inform parents of a separate mechanism for dispute resolution outside the mediation and hearing processes. Each of these 14 safeguards will be explained more fully in turn. A 15th safeguard, parental right to participate in decision-making meetings, will also be discussed.

Written Prior Notice Written prior notice is meant to keep parents informed about the school's action or inaction with respect to their child's identification as a special education student, evaluation, placement, or provision of FAPE. The written prior notice must contain a description of what the education agency proposes or refuses to do, an explanation of its position, and a description of the various options considered.[5] If evaluation is the topic, then each evaluation procedure or evaluation report used by the district must be described. In other words, parents are to understand the reasons for agency positions. All this information must be conveyed in lay language and provided in the native language or mode of communication (e.g., American Sign Language) of the parent, "unless it is clearly not feasible to do so."[6] This notice must also tell parents how to obtain assistance in understanding its contents and how to obtain a copy of the Procedural Safeguards Notice.

Consent IDEA requires that school districts seek written consent from parents at three points in time: prior to an initial evaluation for eligibility, prior to initial provision of special education and related services, and prior to reevaluation.[7] The consent must be both informed and voluntary. If such consent is not forthcoming, the district cannot act on its own but must either follow state procedures governing consent, if there are any, or invoke the IDEA hearing procedures to attempt to override a parent's refusal to consent. An attempt at mediation may also be appropriate at this point. In the case of reevaluation, written consent can be bypassed if the school district can demonstrate that it took reasonable measures to obtain consent and the parent never responded.[8]

A state may choose to require that parental consent be sought at stages other than those mentioned above, provided that a parent's refusal to consent does not result in a failure to provide FAPE to a child who has already been receiving IDEA services.[9] For instance, states often require that parents sign IEPs as an indication of consent to their content. Nonetheless, refusal to sign the IEP may not be used as an excuse by the school district to refuse to provide appropriate services. Although a signed IEP is protection for a school and may provide evidence that the parent attended an IEP meeting and agreed to the IEP at a given point in time, it neither obligates the parent to continue to agree with the IEP until the development of the next one nor allows a district to withhold services if the signature is not obtained.

Why does IDEA require that parental consent be sought at three specific times and not at others? The concept of due process provides an explanation. The student's liberty interests are most vulnerable at the stages of initial evaluation and initial placement into a special education program because these are the stages at which the student is first identified and treated as a student with different, "special" education needs. Misclassification and misplacement at these stages would seriously infringe on a student's liberty interests. The parent should understand the implications of the process at these stages above all. If the parent consents to the initial evaluation and initial provision of special education services, then, arguably, subsequent changes in the student's individualized services or placement involve the child's property and liberty interests less than the first time the child is labeled and served as a "special education" student.

Access to Records   The IDEA regulations incorporate the parents' right to access their child's education records that is found in the Family Educational Rights and Privacy Act of 1974 (FERPA).[10] Access to the education records means the right to "inspect and review" them. Except for the IEP, it does not include a right to receive copies of them, unless failure to provide copies would prevent the parent from being able to inspect and review them.[11] This might be the case for someone who was physically unable to come to the record site. The education agency may charge a fee for any copies made for the parents, as long as the fee itself does not prevent the parents from inspecting and reviewing the record.[12] (More detailed information on access rights is provided in chapter 14.)

Independent Educational Evaluation   School districts view the IEE as one of the more problematic due process protections because of the cost implications. The regulations state that parents are entitled to such an evaluation at public expense if they disagree with the education agency's evaluation.[13] If the parents obtain an IEE at their own expense and follow agency criteria, the education agency must consider the independent evaluation in making decisions about the provision of FAPE to the child.

A school district may ask but not require parents to explain why they want an IEE.[14] Additionally, if parents request an IEE, the school district must provide information about where to obtain one and must share its evaluation criteria with the parents, "including the location of the evaluation and the qualifications of the examiner. . . ."[15] This cryptic phrase has been interpreted to mean that the district can set geographic limits, as long as those restrictions do not prevent parents from obtaining an appropriate IEE for their child. Similarly, a district can designate which kinds of examiners are qualified to make an educational diagnosis of disability. In the past, OSEP has allowed school districts to establish cost caps, as long as they were reasonable and did not prevent a given student from obtaining an appropriate outside evaluation,[16] The 1999 IDEA regulations, however, indicate that the school district may not impose conditions or timelines other than the criteria it uses in initiating an evaluation of its own,[17] so the future of cost caps is a bit uncertain.

To overcome a request for reimbursement from parents, the district must initiate a due process hearing and prove either that its own evaluation was appropriate or that the parents did not follow district criteria.[18] Often the cost of the hearing is more than the cost of the IEE, so districts sometimes choose not to exercise this option.

Parental Participation at Meetings   Although not required to be included in the Procedural Safeguards Notice, parental participation in meetings at which key decisions are made is specified in IDEA '97 and is included in the due process regulations.[19] Parental input is consistent with the concept of due process and gives the parents an important chance to be heard at critical stages in the development of their child's special education program. Failure to require explanation of this right in the Procedural Safeguards Notice seems to be a serious oversight.

Parents have a right to provide input into the evaluation process and to participate in meetings at which eligibility is determined, the IEP is developed, and placement is determined[20]—all key points at which disagreements can arise. The importance of parental input on the IEP is explained in Appendix A of the IDEA regulations; in a nutshell, parents are to be coequal participants.[21] The IEP team includes them, and their input must be considered in developing the IEP, which is not to be written in advance of the IEP meeting.[22] Parents are in a particularly good position to contribute to the annual goals and to articulate their view of the necessary kinds of special education and related services. When their input is solicited and respected, it furthers the IDEA goal of cooperation between home and school. When it is not sought or is ignored, the likelihood of parental distrust at some future time increases. Failure to involve parents in the development of their child's IEP has produced a number of court decisions adverse to school districts.[23] Conversely, parental refusal to participate in the IEP process may defeat their claim to the right to a procedurally correct IEP process. For instance, in *Cordrey v. Euckert*,[24] the court ruled that the parents had forfeited their right to a procedurally correct IEP meeting because they had refused the school district's offer to convene a properly constituted IEP meeting subsequent to an improperly constituted meeting.

Initiating a Due Process Hearing   The due process safeguards already mentioned are meant to place parents on something of an equal footing with school districts. If the safeguards fail to satisfy the parents that the school is acting in the student's interests, and if the parents believe that their child's rights are being denied, they have the right to request an administrative hearing (the so-called due process hearing). Issues subject to the hearing process include identification, evaluation, placement, and the provision of FAPE. The provision of FAPE includes both procedural and substantive rights.[25] Requesting a hearing prevents the school district from acting unilaterally despite the objection of the parent.

IDEA '97 requires that parents who request a hearing provide or have their attorney provide the following information to the education agency when requesting a hearing: the child's name, address, and name of the school the child is attending; a description of the nature of the presenting problem (including relevant facts); and a proposed resolution of the problem, if possible.[26] In the past, some of this basic information was not always available until close to the hearing itself, thereby impeding the ability of the school district to prepare its defense or pursue mediation or a settlement agreement.

Mediation[†]   IDEA '97 requires SEAs and LEAs to provide a mediation option prior to a due process hearing.[27] Most but not all states were already doing so. The procedures themselves must be voluntary and may not be used to deny or delay a parent's right to a hearing. The mediator must be impartial and trained. The SEA must pay for the mediation. If an agreement is reached, it must be set forth in writing, but "discussions" during the mediation process are confidential and cannot be used in subsequent hearings or court cases. This is to protect the parties from having their verbal comments used against them if the mediation ultimately fails. Attorneys may represent the parties at mediation proceedings, but if they do so, costs will escalate.

Due Process Hearing   The due process hearing is a formal hearing, and both parties have the right to examine, cross-examine, and subpoena witnesses; to use the services of an attorney and others with special knowl-

†Mediation is a dispute resolution procedure in which a third party recommends but cannot impose a solution. Mediation is less adversarial than a hearing or court case, but it is important that both parties voluntarily agree to mediate their dispute. If both do not really want to settle the dispute, mediation is likely to fail.

edge or training with respect to the problems of children with disabilities; to obtain a verbatim transcript of the hearing; and to obtain a written decision, including findings of fact.[28] In addition, each party has the right to know of each other's evidence, including evaluations and recommendations based on those evaluations, at least 5 business days before the hearing.[29] The regulations add that parents have the right to decide whether to open the hearing to the public and whether to have the child present at the hearing.[30] This provision respects the privacy rights of the family.

The hearing is conducted by an impartial hearing officer, not by an employee of a public agency involved in the education or care of the student nor by anyone with any other personal or professional conflict of interest.[31] Unlike a mediator, the hearing officer has the right to impose a solution on the parties. A decision must be written and mailed to the parties within 45 days of the education agency's receipt of the request for the hearing.[32] If the decision of the hearing officer is not appealed, it is final.[33]

State-Level Review   As the statute itself makes clear, states have the option of establishing a one-tier or two-tier administrative hearing system.[34] If a one-tier, state-level due process hearing is established, appeal of the hearing decision is to a court. If a two-tier hearing system is established, then a state-level review of the local hearing decision precedes any appeal to a court. The review of the local hearing must be conducted impartially, and the reviewing officer(s) must make an independent decision after completion of the review.

Litigation (Civil Action)   At the end of the administrative hearing process, the losing party may appeal the decision to state or federal court. The court receives the records of the administrative proceedings, hears additional evidence at the request of a party, and bases its decision on the preponderance of the evidence, granting "such relief as the court determines is appropriate"[35] (see chapter 20). Preponderance means that the weight of the evidence favors one side more than the other—namely, the evidence on one side is more convincing than the evidence on the other side.

Technical issues arise at both the hearing stage and in court—issues as to which party has the burden of proof and what the appellate standard of review is. Because IDEA is silent on these matters, these standards vary across state and federal jurisdictions.[36]

Attorney's Fees   Although attorney's fees are listed in IDEA as one of the due process safeguards for parents,[37] they are discussed in this book under the topic of remedies (see chapter 20). The reason for this is that school districts, perhaps incorrectly, tend to see attorney's fees as an additional remedy for a prevailing parent rather than as a means of parental access to the hearing system and the courts.

Stay-Put Provision   While administrative or judicial proceedings are pending regarding a complaint brought under IDEA, IDEA provides that the child is to remain in the then-current placement, unless the parents and the SEA or LEA agree otherwise.[38] Congress enacted this provision to ensure that a student is not buffeted back and forth or uprooted based on who is winning a placement argument after any given stage in the proceedings. Until the issue is resolved, the child is to stay put. If the child is applying for initial admission to public school, then, with the parent's consent, the child is to be "placed in the public school program" until all the proceedings are completed.[39]

Although the stay-put provision obligates school districts to keep a student in the current placement while proceedings are pending, it does not prevent parents from removing a child from what they see as an inappropriate placement and placing the child in private school. The Supreme Court so ruled in *Burlington School Committee v. Massachusetts Department of Education*.[40] Of course, parents remove a child at their own financial risk, but as the Court observed, parents cannot be at the mercy of a school district that is violating IDEA. In short, the stay-put provision binds school districts but not parents.

The 1999 regulations go one step further than the statutory stay-put provision and interpret a state-level hearing decision that supports a parent's placement request to be an agreement between the parents and the SEA or LEA.[41] The result can be to allow the parents to be reimbursed for a unilateral private school placement from the time of the favorable state hearing decision until the time of a court decision reversing the state hearing officer. This interpretation of the statute may create a disincentive for a school district to appeal an adverse state hearing decision because the district will be responsible for the costs of a private school placement throughout the litigative process, even if it ultimately wins.

Special Disciplinary Stay-Put Provisions   In response to safety considerations, IDEA '97 allows an alternative stay-put setting for students who bring a weapon to school, possess or use illegal drugs, sell or solicit the sale of controlled substances, or otherwise are dangerous to themselves and others. These provisions are discussed in chapter 19.

Notice by Parents Seeking Reimbursement for Unilateral Private School Placement   Most of the procedural safeguards are meant as protections for parents and their children with disabilities. This one, however, is a safeguard for the school. It obligates parents to notify the public school when they plan to remove their child from the school and then seek reimbursement for a private school placement. If they do not do so, any reimbursement for which they might become eligible can be reduced. This provision is explained in more detail in chapter 18.

State Complaint Procedures   Since its inception, IDEA has had state complaint procedures that could be used by an organization or individual willing to submit a signed written complaint to the SEA alleging a violation of IDEA. For many years, the procedures were lost from view because they were moved to the DOE General Administrative Regulations. Since 1992, the procedures have been back in the IDEA regulations. They have been strengthened and formalized over the years. OSEP believes that the State Complaint Procedures are an increasingly important component of an SEA's role in monitoring compliance with IDEA. As a result, the procedures are being given increased visibility as an alternative to mediation and due process hearings.

The 1999 regulations are the fullest expression yet of the State Complaint Procedures.[42] The complaint must include facts supporting an alleged violation of IDEA. It can be about systemic noncompliance or any individual matter that could be subject to a due process hearing. Generally speaking, the complaint must allege a violation that is no more than a year old. The SEA must investigate the complaint and issue a written decision within 60 days of its receipt, except under exceptional circumstances. The SEA, if it chooses, can require that the complaint be filed with the LEA, subject to SEA review. It can also encourage mediation if appropriate.

If the SEA determines that there has been a failure to provide appropriate services, the SEA must determine how to remedy the failure, including taking such corrective action as monetary reimbursement where appropriate. It also must address the appropriate future provision of services for all children with disabilities. In other words, it must take corrective action with regard to both individual and systemic denials of FAPE.

If a written complaint is filed that contains one or more issues that are or have been subject to a due process hearing, the state must defer to the hearing decision. Any issues that are not part of the hearing, however, must proceed within the 60-day time limit. If the complaint alleges an agency's failure to implement a due process hearing decision, the SEA must resolve the complaint.

The state's procedures must be widely disseminated—not just by incorporating a description of them in the Procedural Safeguards Notice but also by disseminating them to various advocacy groups within the state. The person or group filing a complaint does not have to have been directly affected by the school district's actions or inactions; therefore, a bystander or a teacher's association can be among those filing the complaint. Complaints can also come from out of state.

One of the major advantages of filing an SEA complaint instead of seeking a due process hearing is that an attorney is not required. The savings can be significant for the individual or group bringing the complaint. In addition, the procedures allow an investigation rather than an adversarial hearing. A 1995 survey of how state complaint managers rated the comparative effectiveness of hearings, mediation, and complaint procedures found that mediation was the preferred option, with complaint procedures next. Due process hearings were seen as the least desirable alternative for dispute resolution, in terms of either parent or LEA satisfaction and in terms of cost effectiveness and effective results for the students involved.[43]

Surrogate Parent   When a "parent" of a student with an IDEA disability cannot be identified or cannot be located after reasonable efforts, or when the student is a ward of the state, the IDEA regulations require that a surrogate parent be appointed.[44] The regulatory definition of *parent* is broad, however, so appointments of surrogate parents are infrequent. In addition to natural or adoptive parents, the regulatory definition of a parent includes a guardian or a person acting in place of a parent, such as a grandmother or stepparent with whom the child lives, or a person who is legally responsible for the child's welfare. At the state's discretion, it can also include a foster parent, as long as the foster parent is willing to serve, has a long-term parental relationship with the child, and has no interest that would conflict with the interests of the child. The natural parents' authority to make educational decisions on the child's behalf, however, must have been extinguished under state law.[45]

The regulations give SEAs the freedom to select a surrogate in any way permitted by state law, as long as the surrogate (a) is not an employee of a public agency that is involved in the education or care of the student, (b) has no interests that conflict with the student's interest, and (c) has sufficient knowledge and skills to adequately represent the student.[46] Whether the education agency pays the surrogate to represent the student is a matter of state law.

The surrogate is to ensure that the student's rights are protected and to represent the child in matters of identification, evaluation, placement, and the provision of FAPE—in short, the same matters that are the subject of a due process hearing. Issues of surrogacy, though rare, occasionally have been litigated in federal court. Failure to appoint a surrogate parent, for instance, has resulted in the denial of a motion to dismiss a case.[47]

Explanation of the surrogate provision is not required in the Procedural Safeguards Notice. Presumably, this is because a surrogate will be appointed if necessary, and the Notice will be given to the surrogate instead of the parent.

Tips for Parents

In working with your child's school, it may help you to remember the following:

1. *Ask for what you think your child needs. Share your expectations for your child.* Put your hopes and requests in writing, if necessary.

2. *Be courteous and civil.* Educators are people like everyone else; they appreciate being treated nicely. Assertiveness, combined with a cooperative attitude, is more persuasive than aggressiveness or hostility.

3. *Know your rights and responsibilities.* If you do not have information on your rights and responsibilities under federal and state law when you need it, ask the school district for the information and study it.

4. *Ask for explanations of what you don't understand.* You should not feel that you are "in the dark." For instance, you should understand your child's evaluation data, current levels of educational performance, and progress under the IEP.

5. *Be willing to share information about your child with the school.* Keep important medical records, past school records, and so on.

6. *Understand the school's challenges and burdens. Realize that sometimes your request may not be realistic.* In general, educators are overworked and underpaid. They get tired like parents. Funds are limited. IDEA does not require schools to fulfill a child's potential but rather to meet the child's special needs in a way that provides meaningful progress toward IEP goals.

7. *Be willing to participate in meetings that determine your child's eligibility, IEP, and placement under IDEA. Also be willing to help your child at home and in school, if appropriate.* Never forget that you are an important teacher of your child.

8. *Be willing to "brainstorm" various options to meet your child's needs.* "There is more than one way to skin a cat."

9. *Work for "win-win" solutions to problems.* Education is not like competitive athletics. No one should have to lose.

10. *Know where to turn for help.* Resources include your child's teacher and principal, school district special education director, school district Section 504 coordinator, State Office of Special Education complaint officer, state parent learning center, parent advocacy group, state protection and advocacy center, and public library.

Transfer of Parental Rights to Students

Students with IDEA disabilities who have not left the public school system are eligible for services up to the age of 22, unless state law establishes a younger age ceiling. At the age of majority established by state law (usually 18), IDEA '97 allows states to transfer parental rights to the student unless he or she has been judged incompetent under state law.[48] If a state exercises this option, it must still provide parents with all the notices that it would provide to students, but other IDEA rights will shift to the student. Notice of the transfer must be given to both the student and the parents.

If your state has a mechanism for determining that a student who has not been declared incompetent nonetheless does not have the ability to give informed consent about his or her educational program, procedures must be established to allow the parent to continue to represent the educational interests of the student. If the parent is not available, then another appropriate individual must be selected.[49]

Implications

Because due process of law is a constitutional concept with statutory protection under IDEA, it deserves utmost respect by school personnel. If school personnel extend basic courtesy and respect to parents, they honor the concept of due process. If they provide notice and a chance to be heard, they will save themselves a great deal of trouble. Keeping parents "in the dark" has led to many court cases. Showing respect helps to create a co-operative learning environment and helps parents to assume their responsibilities to their children with disabilities.

Review

1. What are the two basic requirements of procedural due process under the Constitution of the United States?

    They are notice of the alleged violation and a chance to respond.

2. Name two kinds of notice provisions in IDEA.

    One is written notice prior to taking action or refusing to act in a matter concerning the child's identification, evaluation, placement, or provision of FAPE. The other is notice of the procedural safeguards available under IDEA.

3. Name the ways in which parents "can be heard" on behalf of their child.

    They can give or withhold consent at key stages. They can obtain an IEE if they disagree with the school district's evaluation. They can have access to their child's educational records and can place information in the record under certain conditions. They can participate in the evaluation process and in eligibility, IEP, and placement decisions. They can utilize a number of mechanisms, including mediation, hearings, and litigation to resolve disputes, formally or informally. They can receive attorney's fees under certain conditions. They can use the State Complaint Procedures when they believe IDEA is being violated. Finally, a surrogate can be appointed to speak in lieu of the parent under certain conditions.

Notes

[1] 343 F. Supp. 279 (E.D. Pa. 1972).

[2] 348 F. Supp. 866 (D.D.C. 1972).

[3] 20 U.S.C.S. § 1415(d)(2) (1998); 34 C.F.R. § 500.504(c)(1999).

[4] *See* 20 U.S.C.S. § 1415(d); 34 C.F.R. §§ 300.500–.517.

[5] 20 U.S.C.S. § 1415(b)(3); 34 C.F.R. § 300.503.

[6] 20 U.S.C.S. § 1415 (b)(4); 34 C.F.R. § 300.503(c)(i).

[7] 20 U.S.C.S. § 1414(a)(1)(C); 34 C.F.R. § 300.505(a).

[8] 20 U.S.C.S. § 1414(c)(3); 34 C.F.R. § 300.505(c).

[9] 34 C.F.R. § 300.505(d).

[10] 20 U.S.C.S. § 1232g (1995).

[11] 34 C.F.R. § 300.562(a)(2).

[12] *Id.* § 300.566(a).

[13] *Id.* § 300.502(b).

[14] *Id.* § 300.502(b)(4).

[15] *Id.* § 300.502(a)(2) and (e).

[16] See Letter to Anonymous, 22 IDELR 537 (OSEP 1995); Letter to Aldine, 16 EHLR 606 (OSEP 1990).

[17] 34 C.F.R. § 300.502(e)(2).

[18] *Id.* § 300.502(b).

[19] *Id.* § 300.501(b) and (c).

[20] *See id.*(participation in meetings, including meetings at which placement decisions are made). *See also id.* § 300.532 (input into evaluation), § 300.534 (participation in eligibility determination), and § 300.345 (participation at IEP meetings).

[21] *Id.* Part 300, app. A.

[22] *Id.*

[23] *See, e.g.*, Board of Educ. of County of Cabell v. Dienelt, 843 F.2d 813 (4th Cir. 1988); Greer v. Rome City Sch. Dist., 950 F.2d 688 (11th Cir. 1991).

[24] 917 F.2d 1460 (6th Cir. 1990).

[25] *See* Board of Educ. of Hendrick Hudson Central Sch. Dist. v. Rowley, 458 U.S. 176 (1982).

[26] 20 U.S.C.S. 1415(b)(7); 34 C.F.R. § 300.507(c)(2).

[27] 20 U.S.C.S. 1415(e)(2); 34 C.F.R. § 300.506.

[28] 20 U.S.C.S. § 1415(h).

[29] *Id.* § 1415(f)(2).

[30] 34 C.F.R. § 300.509(c).

[31] *Id.* § 300.508.

[32] *Id.* § 300.511.

[33] 20 U.S.C.S. § 1415(i)(1)(A); 34 C.F.R. § 300.510.

[34] 20 U.S.C.S. § 1415(g).

[35] *Id.* § 1415(i)(2)(B).

[36] For further information on these matters, see D. S. Huefner & P. A. Zirkel. (1993). *Burden of proof under the Individuals With Disabilities Education Act* (Special Report No. 9). Horsham, PA: LRP.

[37] 20 U.S.C.S. § 1415(i)(3)(B).

[38] *Id.* § 1415(j).

[39] *Id.*

[40] 471 U.S. 359 (1985).

[41] 34 C.F.R. § 300.514.

[42] *Id.* §§ 300.660–.661.

[43] N. Suchey, & D. S. Huefner. (1998). The state complaint procedure under the Individuals With Disabilities Education Act. *Exceptional Children, 64,* 529–542.

[44] 34 C.F.R. § 300.515.

[45] *Id.* § 300.20.

[46] *Id.* § 300.515.

[47] Ramon H. v. Illinois State Bd. of Educ., 1992 U.S. Dist. LEXIS 11798 (N.D. Ill. 1992).

[48] 34 C.F.R. § 300.517.

[49] *Id.*

Selected Supplementary Resources

Dobbs, R., Primm, E., & Primm, B. (1991). Mediation: A common sense approach for resolving conflicts in education. *Focus on Exceptional Children, 24,* 3.

Edmister, P., & Ekstrand, R. E. (1987, Spring). Lessening the trauma of due process. *Teaching Exceptional Children,* 213–217.

Huefner, D. S. (1999). A model for explaining the procedural safeguards of the Individuals With Disabilities Education Act (IDEA '97). *Education Law Reporter, 134,* 445–451.

Chapter 14

Student Records and Privacy Issues Under FERPA and IDEA

Background

Since the 1970s, both federal and state governments have developed heightened awareness of the need for public access to many kinds of government documents, as a check on their accuracy and so that government officials do not act in secrecy when secrecy is not justified. Simultaneously, privacy issues have grown in importance as the potential for the unwarranted dissemination of personal information has increased because of the rapid enlargement of computerized data banks. The issues of access to information and privacy of information are reflected in laws that apply to students in general and special education students in particular.

Two federal statutes have particular importance for the access and privacy

rights of students with disabilities and their parents. The first is the Family Educational Rights and Privacy Act (FERPA). The second is IDEA, which incorporates and expands the FERPA rights specifically for students with disabilities. Of course, state laws and regulations—such as health codes and state freedom of information acts—may extend beyond the federal protections and become additional sources of privacy or access rights. This chapter, however, is limited to federal protections and access rights.

The Family Educational Rights and Privacy Act

FERPA[1] applies to all education agencies that receive federal funds; failure to comply risks loss of the federal funds. FERPA[†] was enacted at a time when parents had been

†FERPA is also known as the "Buckley Amendment."

‡Any form of notice to parents that is reasonable under the circumstances may be selected, such as mailed notices, published notices, or distribution of the student handbook.

routinely denied access to their children's school records, usually on grounds that the records were written by and for professionals and would not be understood by parents. In a climate encouraging greater access to public documents, advocates argued successfully that the school should be willing to share information with parents about their child's performance and needs, especially information that might adversely affect their child.

FERPA provides two basic kinds of rights to parents of public school students: (a) the right to inspect and review their child's educational records, and (b) the right to prevent unauthorized persons from seeing that same information. Every year parents must be notified‡ of these rights.[2] The rights transfer to students when students reach 18 years of age or attend an institution of postsecondary education.[3]

What Is an Educational Record?

To understand the scope of FERPA's access and privacy rights, one must understand what information is considered to be a part of a student's "educational record." The Act defines educational records as "those records, files, documents, and other materials which (i) contain information directly related to a student; and (ii) are maintained by an educational agency or institution or by a person acting for such agency or institution."[4]

Files that are likely to be educational records include reports of attendance, academic performance, and behavior at school; results of standardized tests and psychological examinations; disability classifications, evaluations, and program and placement decisions; teacher and counselor observations; and health information.

Excluded from the definition of educational records are anecdotal notes and memoranda of instructional, supervisory, and administrative personnel that are in the sole possession of the maker and not accessible to or revealed to anyone else except a substitute.[5] To allow such private notes to be accessible would not only be seen as an invasion of privacy but might inhibit certain necessary professional activities (such as a teacher's maintenance of notes in a grade book or a psychologist's notes of a counseling session with a student). Of course, even these records could be discoverable if subpoenaed by a court; short of that, they remain private files.

Also excluded from the definition of educational records are a student's police files maintained by the law enforcement unit of the school district, if they were created for law enforcement purposes.[6] If information from these police files is part of a student's educational file, however, it becomes an educational record.

When Are Juvenile Court Records Educational Records?

Daniel Belanger was an adolescent who was placed in a residential school pursuant to a court order under the New Hampshire juvenile delinquency statute. He was also a child with a disability under IDEA. His mother wanted access to all his educational records to help her contest his placement. She also was seeking reimbursement for the sums she had to pay for his residential placement.

The attorney who worked for the school district kept files on Daniel separate from the cumulative educational file. She was a member of the team evaluating Daniel's IEP and placement. Because her records related to the juvenile court action, the LEA refused to give the mother access to them, arguing that they were not educational records but juvenile records.

The court determined that the attorney's files on Daniel met the definition of an educational record because they contained information directly related to Daniel and were used by the LEA in making decisions that affected Daniel's life. The clincher was that the records were being maintained by an educational agency rather than a law enforcement agency. The source of the records was immaterial. *Belanger v. Nashua New Hampshire School District*, 856 F. Supp. 40 (D.N.H. 1994).

Employee records are also excluded from the definition unless the employee is also a student at the institution and is employed because of his or her student status.[7] Finally, medical records of students 18 years of age and older are generally excluded from FERPA coverage.[8]

Access Rights

When parents request information from their child's educational record, school districts must produce it for inspection within a reasonable time, and in any event within

45 days of the request.[9] Either parent, even one who is not living with the student, may inspect the records unless the agency has been informed that under state law one parent has been denied parental rights.[10] Making the child's educational record available to parents serves several purposes: (a) it allows parents to catch errors in their child's records, (b) it recognizes the role of parents as partners with the school in addressing a child's school-related issues, and (c) it discourages undocumented, stigmatizing, and possibly defamatory remarks about a child in the record.

If a parent believes that information in the education record is inaccurate, misleading, or a violation of the child's privacy rights, the parent may request its removal or amendment.[11] If the request is denied, the parent may request a hearing to challenge the information. If the hearing officer determines that the information should remain in the record, then the parent is entitled to place a statement in the record commenting on the retained information.

If a hearing is held, the FERPA regulations specify that (a) it must occur within a reasonable period of time after the institution has received the request; (b) parents must be afforded an opportunity to present all relevant evidence and to use an attorney; and (c) the agency must render a written decision within a reasonable period of time.[12] This hearing is different from an IDEA due process hearing in key respects; it may be conducted by an official of the educational agency, as long as the official has no direct interest in the outcome, and it lacks many of the formal procedures established for IDEA due process hearings.

Privacy Rights

Of equal importance to the access provisions in FERPA are the provisions prohibiting dissemination of student record information to unauthorized third parties. Only "directory information" may be released to unauthorized persons without the prior written consent of parents (or eligible students).[13]

In general, those who are authorized to see the educational records include school personnel with a legitimate need to know, and they must be designated as such

Directory Information

"Directory information" is defined as the student's name, address, phone number, date and place of birth, major field of study, participation in school activities, dates of attendance at school, honors, awards, and other similar information. 20 U.S.C.S. § 1232g(a)(5)(A). Unless the school district complies with procedures for the release of directory information, FERPA does not allow public access to the information. For instance, in *Brent v. Paquette*, 567 A.2d 976 (N.H. 1989), the court permitted no access to student directory information connected to a "Special Education Plan" because the parents were neither given proper notice nor provided a sufficient comment period. Also, schools must provide an opportunity for a parent to request that all or part of such information be withheld. 20 U.S.C.S. § 1232g (a)(5)(B). To avoid administrative headaches, some public schools choose not to publish directory information.

by their respective school districts.[14] Typically, teachers, building administrators, other school professionals, and even student teachers will be authorized to see a student's records. If a student moves to a new district, the new district is also automatically entitled to receive the child's educational records, as long as notice is provided to the parents.[15]

Others authorized to see the educational records under limited circumstances include the following:[16] (a) federal and state officials, for the purpose of evaluating or auditing a program receiving federal and state support, (b) organizations or persons conducting certain types of educational research, (c) official accrediting organizations in conjunction with the accreditation process, (d) appropriate parties who need information to deal with health or safety emergencies, (e) court officials pursuant to judicial order or subpoena, and (f) state and local officials, if the disclosure is allowed by a state statute and concerns the juvenile justice system's ability to serve the student effectively prior to adjudication, and if further disclosure will not occur without parental consent.

The above exceptions to the general prohibition of release of student information to third parties are narrow and specific. If the request for student information does not fall within one of these exceptions, written consent from the parent must be obtained. For instance, if an employer, medical doctor, or noneducation agency social worker seeks information from a student's record, written parental consent is necessary. To be effective, the consent must be specific, designating the information to be released and to whom the information is to be given.[17] Furthermore, persons receiving the information may not redisclose it to others without additional parental consent. The school district must also keep a record of which persons or institutions have requested information on the student if such requests come from outside the school system.[18] This list is available only to parents, school officials with custodial responsibilities for the records, and auditors of the system.

Controversies

Some of the more troublesome privacy issues under FERPA have concerned the disclosure of psychological records, health records, and law enforcement records kept at school. Sometimes reports of child abuse enter a student's records, in which case school officials usually should protect the anonymity of the reporter by keeping that person's name out of the records. Health records would seem to fall under the definition of an educational record, yet a school nurse might wish to keep certain sensitive information out of the child's file, lest it be seen by other school personnel when disclosure could be harmful to the student. The health or medical record of a student with AIDS is one example of information that should be available to only a few people. How to protect the confidentiality of health records may depend on state law but may also depend on the record-keeping procedures of a given school district. Nurses should carefully consider what information to maintain in school files and what to maintain in their own personal records, which are available only to a substitute nurse.

Another problematic situation may arise if the police are called to a school to quell a disturbance. Some school officials in past years have declined to provide specific information about the students lest the disclosure violate FERPA rights. This would seem to be an unnecessary response because FERPA allows disclosure to noneducation officials when necessary to protect the health or safety of the student or others. Moreover, FERPA allows release of records to state or local officials, if disclosure is required by state law and concerns the ability of the juvenile justice system to effectively serve a student prior to adjudication.[19] For example, information that the student is a special education student with certain kinds of behaviors and special needs might be valuable to a juvenile detention center in determining how to manage an unruly student.

Finally, a 1994 FERPA amendment specifies that an education agency is not prohibited from placing appropriate information in the student's file about disciplinary actions for misconduct that posed "a significant risk to the safety or well-being" of the student or other members of the school community.[20] Nor does FERPA prohibit the disclosure of that information to school personnel with "legitimate educational interests in the behavior of the student."[21] That these clarifications were even necessary indicates just how uncertain some school officials had become about what would violate a student's privacy rights.

Remedies for FERPA Violations

The sanction for a FERPA violation is termination of federal funds after a hearing by a review board. In other words, FERPA itself establishes no private right of action in court by an aggrieved parent or student.[22] However, DOE is unlikely to terminate federal funds for a limited violation of the law, so the question arises as to whether an individual harmed by a violation lacks a remedy. Several recent cases have established a private right to sue under another statute, 42 U.S.C. Section 1983 (referred to as Section 1983), to enforce FERPA or seek damages to compensate for actual injury for FERPA violations.[†] (See chapter 20 for a longer explanation of lawsuits under Section 1983.) Other cases, however, have ruled to the contrary, so you will need to consult an attorney for up-to-date advice on the law in your jurisdiction.

†In *Fay v. South Colonie Central School District,* 802 F.2d 21 (2d Cir. 1986), the court allowed a Section 1983 action while disallowing a suit under FERPA in a situation where a father, with joint custody of his children, had been denied access to his children's school records while the children were living with their mother. Compare *Sean R. v. Board of Education,* 794 F. Supp. 467 (D. Conn. 1992), in which the court allowed a damage suit under Section 1983 for public release of information about a child's special education placement.

Incorporation of and
Additions to FERPA in IDEA

Parental access to a student's educational records is especially important to parents of special education students because the risk of stigmatization of these students is great. If the educational records contain errors or prejudicial information, a student's instructional program or placement can be affected adversely. In order to stress the importance of the basic FERPA rights for students with disabilities, OSEP included the provisions already mentioned and elaborated on several of them in IDEA's implementing regulations.[23]

Among the elaborations, the IDEA regulations require *any* agency that maintains or uses personally identifiable information on an IDEA student to give access to that information to the parents. For instance, a private provider of related services with whom the school has contracted must also comply with the FERPA requirements incorporated into IDEA.

The IDEA regulations also go beyond FERPA in specifying that, "without unnecessary delay and before any meeting regarding an IEP or any [due process] hearing . . .", the education agency must comply with parental requests to inspect and review their child's education records.[24] This may result in a foreshortening of the 45-day time limit for responding to a request. The regulations also require that an actual copy of the IEP be provided to parents at no cost,[25] creating an exception to the general rule that inspection is sufficient and that if copies are needed, a reasonable fee may be charged.

Special educators have sometimes worried that a parent will gain access to confidential test protocols, particularly standardized IQ test protocols, in a child's file. Test protocols are not necessarily educational records.[26] If possible, only the answer sheet should be placed in the file; and the protocols should be retained elsewhere to protect the confidentiality of the questions themselves. The LEA should be prepared, however, to respond to reasonable requests for explanations and interpretations of standardized test results and other material in the file.[27]

Under IDEA, whether the FERPA rights extend to students over the age of majority depends on state law. IDEA '97 indicates that a state may transfer parental rights under IDEA to the child at the age of majority if the child has not been deemed incompetent under state law.[28] These rights include access to the educational record. The parents must be notified of the transfer, although an exception to the transfer can be created if a student is determined not to have the ability to provide informed consent with respect to his or her educational program. Furthermore, the 1999 regulations provide that each SEA must determine the extent to which children are given privacy rights similar to those given to their parents, "taking into consideration the age of the child and type or severity of disability."[29]

Under FERPA, students over the age of majority or enrolled in a postsecondary institution can be denied access to records "created, maintained, or used only in connection with the provision of treatment" by a physician, psychiatrist, psychologist, or other recognized professional or paraprofessional.[30] In contrast, under IDEA, parents will be able to see their child's treatment records if they are forwarded to the school by a physician or mental health therapist and placed in the child's educational record. This fact has particular relevance in the case of special education students with emotional disturbance. School officials should be alert to the need to return extraneous, sensitive material to the sender, who should be made aware that parents may access all the information in the child's educational record.

Finally, the 1999 IDEA regulations go beyond FERPA in permitting a state to *require* a school district to place disciplinary information in a child's educational record. If the child subsequently transfers to another school, any records that follow the child to the new school must include the disciplinary action as well as the IEP.[31]

Destruction of Records
Under FERPA and IDEA

No provision in FERPA stops an education agency from destroying educational records, as long as there is no outstanding request to inspect and review them and as long as the agency does not single out for destruction a parent's written explanation of challenged information that remains in the file.[32] Under IDEA, however, if a school district no longer needs a student's educational records to provide educational services, it must notify the parents.[33] The parents may then request destruction of the information, and the district must honor the request. At its discretion, however, the school district may permanently retain the following information: name, address, telephone number, grades, attendance record, classes attended, grade level completed, and year completed.

Because the preservation of some kinds of information may prove helpful in establishing eligibility for adult disability benefits, parents should be aware of the possible disadvantages of destroying assessment information in their child's file. Moreover, the district should transfer records whenever possible when a student moves out of the district, so that the new school has access to information that is necessary to provide services.

Miscellaneous Privacy Rights

Occasionally, other student privacy rights requiring interpretation or application of FERPA and IDEA to new situations have been litigated. One such case raised the issue of the extent of courtroom privacy for a special education student.[34] IDEA provides that the parent controls whether a due process hearing is open or closed to the public. Both IDEA and FERPA require parental consent prior to disclosure of a student's educational record to unauthorized persons. Applying these requirements, the court held that the privacy rights of students under IDEA and FERPA extended to the court setting. The school district was seeking a court injunction to allow expulsion of a student for carrying a loaded handgun to school, and the press wanted to cover the proceedings. The court granted the student's motion for a closed courtroom and sealed records because it concluded that the privacy rights of the minor outweighed any qualified common law or First Amendment right of courtroom access by the press.

Another case addressed the right of privacy in re-evaluation procedures. In *Andress v. Cleveland Independent School District*,[35] a federal district court found that a 3-year public school reevaluation under IDEA, as applied, constituted a violation of a child's constitutional right to privacy because it generated test anxiety for the student, who had difficulty relating to unfamiliar school personnel. The parents had argued for an independent evaluation of their son, who had both a learning disability and a serious emotional disturbance. The court held that the school had no absolute right to reevaluate the student under IDEA but must consider the child's health and welfare when performing evaluations. On appeal, the U.S. Court of Appeals for the Fifth Circuit reversed the lower court, holding that IDEA provided no exception to the school district's right to reevaluate a student if the parents wanted publicly funded special education services.[36]

Perhaps in response to the Fifth Circuit's ruling, Congress added a requirement in IDEA '97 that parental consent must be sought prior to "conducting any re-evaluation."[37] If the parents fail to respond to reasonable attempts to obtain consent, the school district may proceed without the actual consent of the parents. If, on the other hand, the parents actually refuse their consent, the school district presumably can stop serving a child it believes is no longer eligible under IDEA. If the district wishes to override the parental refusal, it must obtain permission from a due process hearing officer or court, depending on state standards.[†]

[†]The 1999 regulations clarify the statutory parental consent provision by indicating that consent is not required for a reevaluation if all that is needed is a review of existing data. Consent is also not required to administer a test that can be given to nondisabled children without parental consent. See 34 C.F.R. § 300.505(a)(3). Privacy issues do not arise in these contexts.

Implications

The statutes and court cases described above all indicate that a public school should be careful about releasing personally identifiable student information to the general public or putting its own interests in disclosure of information ahead of the privacy interests of the child. It is easy for educators with good intentions to "talk too much." Therefore, chief among the implications is the need to train staff to prevent "leaks." In fact, IDEA requires training or instruction regarding both the FERPA and IDEA confidentiality procedures.[38]

As a part of the training procedures, the staff should also be instructed about what to put in a student's file in the first place. Information with no educational implication should be omitted, as should undocumented characterizations of a student's behavior or performance.

Review

1. What are the two primary concerns of FERPA?

    They are parental access—providing access to the information in their child's educational record—and privacy—restricting access so that only authorized persons can see the records.

2. In what ways does IDEA go beyond FERPA in providing for access and privacy?

    It requires access to the educational record prior to IEP meetings and due process hearings, which may require a school district to respond more quickly than the 45-day maximum allowed under FERPA. It also requires that parents be given an actual copy of their child's IEP at no cost, it allows states to decide whether to transfer parental rights to the child at the age of majority, and it allows states to require that disciplinary information be placed in the child's educational record.

Notes

[1] 20 U.S.C.S. § 1232g (1995). FERPA was enacted in 1974 as Public Law 93-380, tit. V § 513(a), 88 Stat. 571.

[2] 34 C.F.R. § 99.7 (1998).

[3] 20 U.S.C.S. § 1232g(d).

[4] *Id.* § 1232g(a)(4)(A).

[5] *Id.* § 1232g(a)(4)(B)(i).

[6] *Id.* § 1232g(a)(4)(B)(ii).

[7] *Id.* § 1232g(a)(4)(B)(iii).

[8] *Id.* § 1232g(a)(4)(B)(iv).

[9] *Id.* § 1232g(a)(1)(A).

[10] *See* 34 C.F.R. § 99.3.

[11] 20 U.S.C.S. 1232g(a)(2).

[12] 34 C.F.R. § 99.22.

[13] 20 U.S.C.S. § 1232g(b)(1).

[14] 20 U.S.C.S. § 1232g (b)(1)(A).

[15] *Id.* § 1232g(b)(1)(B).

[16] *See* 20 U.S.C. § 1232g(b)(1)(C)-(J). Two omitted exceptions pertain only to the higher education context. *See* 20 U.S.C. § 1232g(b)(1)(D) and (H).

[17] *Id.* § 1232g(b)(2)(A).

[18] *Id.* § 1232g(b)(4)(A).

[19] *Id.* § 1232g(b)(1)(E).

[20] *Id.* § 1232g(h)(1).

[21] *Id.* § 1232g(h)(2).

[22] *See* Klein Indep. Sch. Dist. v. Mattox, 830 F.2d 576 (5th Cir. 1987); Fay v. South Colonie Cent. Sch. Dist., 802 F.2d 21 (2d Cir. 1986); Smith v. Duquesne Univ., 787 F.2d 583 (3d Cir. 1986); Girardier v. Webster College, 563 F.2d 1267 (8th Cir. 1977).

[23] 34 C.F.R. §§ 300.560–.577(1999).

[24] *Id.* § 300.562(a).

[25] *Id.* § 300.345(f).

[26] *See* Letter to MacDonald, 20 IDELR 1159 (OSEP 1993).

[27] 34 C.F.R. § 300. 562 (b)(1).

[28] 20 U.S.C.S. § 1415(m); *see also* 34 C.F.R. § 300.517.

[29] 34 C.F.R. § 300.574.

[30] 20 U.S.C. § 1232g(a)(4)(B)(iv).

[31] 34 C.F.R. § 300.576.

[32] *Id.* § 99.10(e).

[33] *Id.* § 300.573.

[34] Webster Groves Sch. Dist. v. Pulitzer Publishing Co., 898 F.2d 1371 (8th Cir. 1990).

[35] 832 F. Supp. 1086 (E.D. Tex. 1993).

[36] Andress v. Cleveland Indep. Sch. Dist., 64 F.3d 176 (5th Cir. 1995).

[37] 20 U.S.C.S. § 1414(c)(3).

[38] 34 C.F.R. § 300.572(c).

Selected Supplementary Resources

Daggett, L. M. (1997). Bucking up Buckley I: Making the federal student records statute work. *Catholic University Law Review, 46,* 617–670.

Gelfman, M., & Schwab, N. (1991). School health services and educational records: Conflicts in the law. *Education Law Reporter, 64,* 319–338.

Johnson, T. P. (1993). Managing student records: The courts and the family educational rights and privacy act of 1974. *Education Law Reporter, 79,* 1–18.

Chapter 15

Free Appropriate Public Education Under IDEA

Statutory Definition

The most important right given to students with disabilities under IDEA is the right to a free appropriate public education (FAPE). Under IDEA, FAPE is not just a privilege bestowed at the convenience of school districts but rather a right that must be made available to all eligible students. Therefore, it is particularly important for educators and parents to understand what is meant by FAPE. This is easier said than done because the definition of FAPE in the statute is cryptic. According to IDEA, FAPE is "special education and related services" that (a) are provided at public expense, under public supervision and direction, and without charge, (b) meet standards of the state educational agency, (c) include an appropriate education at the preschool, elementary, and secondary school levels, and (d) are delivered in conformity with the child's IEP.[1] Item (a) addresses the "free" and "public" portion of FAPE. Items (b) through (d) address the "appropriate" portion of FAPE.

Because this definition does not establish any particular level of educational quality, its meaning has been subject to dispute. In 1982, the U.S. Supreme Court provided a definitive interpretation of the statutory language. Its decision remains the Court's most important pronouncement on IDEA, and its interpretation has been the binding precedent for all FAPE cases in all the courts in the country.

The *Rowley* Case

The case providing the opportunity for the Supreme Court to interpret the FAPE definition was *Hendrick Hudson Central School District Board of Education v. Rowley*.[2]

Amy Rowley was an academically able first grader with a severe hearing impairment. Amy's school had developed an IEP in consultation with her parents, who themselves were deaf. The Rowleys were satisfied with parts of Amy's IEP but also wanted the services of a qualified sign language interpreter for all of Amy's academic classes. Amy's IEP called for her education in the regular classroom with support services from a tutor for the deaf 1 hour per day and a speech therapist 3 hours per week, along with the provision of an FM wireless hearing aid in her classroom. During Amy's kindergarten year she had received the services of an interpreter for a 2-week trial period, services which the interpreter stated Amy did not need or use. Based on that assessment and Amy's academic and social achievement without the interpreter, the school declined to provide an interpreter during Amy's first-grade year.

The primary argument in favor of an interpreter was that although Amy was an excellent lip reader, she was nonetheless able to decode only approximately 60% of the oral language available to her classmates. Her parents argued, and the lower courts agreed, that this denied Amy an opportunity to learn that was equivalent to that provided to her classmates. As the federal district court put it, Amy was denied an opportunity to achieve her full potential at a level "commensurate with the opportunity provided to other children."[3]

The "commensurate opportunity" standard was borrowed from the public education regulations for Section 504 of the Rehabilitation Act. The Section 504 regulations define an "appropriate" public education as regular or special education and related aids and services designed to meet the student's individual needs "as adequately as the needs of the nonhandicapped" are met.[4] Presumably, if Amy's classmates had the opportunity to access 100% of what was being said, then Amy should have commensurate or equivalent access.

The Supreme Court declined to apply the Section 504 definition, concluding that IDEA had its own operative definition of FAPE and there was no need to borrow one. After studying both the statute and the legislative history leading to its passage, the Court held that Congress intended the necessary "special education and related services" to be personalized (through the IEP) and of "some educational benefit" to the student.[5] In determining that more was not required, the Court drew on landmark federal court cases leading up to IDEA, which had established the constitutional principle that all students with disabilities must be given access to a public education that addressed their needs.[6] Accordingly, the Court concluded that meaningful access, rather than any particular substantive level of educational benefit, was the primary purpose of FAPE.

In so ruling, the Court addressed the argument that Congress intended FAPE to provide "full educational opportunity"[7] to implement the equal protection clause of the Fourteenth Amendment.[†] The Court interpreted the concept of equal or full educational opportunity to require meaningful access rather than commensurate services or the same services that are provided to the nondisabled. On the one hand, it said, to provide special instruction and related services that would maximize one's potential in a manner commensurate with the opportunity provided to regular education students would entail difficult measurements that would be entirely unworkable. On the other hand, providing exactly the same services, it said, would be insufficient in some situations and too much in others and would not meet the individualization requirement.

The Court's translation of "meaningful access" into personalized instruction designed to provide "some educational benefit" came directly from the IDEA definitions of special education and related services. Special education is defined as "specially designed instruction . . . to meet the unique needs of a child with a disability. . . ."[8] Related services are defined as various types of supportive services necessary "to assist a child with a disability to benefit from special education. . . ."[9] In other words, the Court deduced that if the purpose of related services is to help the child benefit from special education, then logically, benefit must be the purpose of special education as well. Therefore, according to the Court, if (a) the four items on the statutory FAPE checklist definition are met, (b) the IEP is properly designed to address the student's unique (individual) needs, and (c) the IEP is reasonably calculated to produce educational benefit, then that is all the statute requires for FAPE.

[†]The "full educational opportunity" language appears in IDEA '97 at 20 U.S.C.S. § 1412(a)(2) (1998).

What the Court did not decide was how much benefit would be enough for any student other than Amy. Instead it simply said that the benefit must be "meaningful." In Amy's case, the Court determined that because she was receiving "substantial specialized instruction" and related services and was at the same time making academic progress in her regular classroom and advancing from grade to grade, she was receiving FAPE.

It is important to understand what the *Rowley* decision does and does not stand for. First of all, although the FAPE standards of "some educational benefit" and "meaningful access" are modest, they are real. FAPE is a legitimate legal right with accompanying obligations for educators. By interpreting the meaning of FAPE under IDEA, the Supreme Court established the legal standard for all subsequent FAPE cases in the courts. This is not to say, however, that some child other than Amy might not need a sign language interpreter in order to receive some educational benefit from her or his IEP. The facts of each individual situation must be weighed on their own terms. In some situations, some educational benefit or meaningful access might require an interpreter (or some other service or program), and in other situations it might not.

The *Rowley* decision does not stand for the proposition that every child who is advancing from grade to grade is receiving FAPE. The Court was not addressing what are referred to as "social promotions." At the time of the decision, the Court also did not anticipate the fact that many children with severe disabilities would be included in the regular classroom with supplementary aids and services. Many of these children receive social promotions so that they remain with their age-appropriate peer group. To clarify the point, the 1999 regulations stipulate that FAPE must be available to any child with a disability who needs special education and related services, "even though the child is advancing from grade to grade."[10]

The *Rowley* standard was criticized by the three dissenting justices, who asserted that it failed to go far enough to provide an equal and full educational opportunity. They worried that in Amy's case a teacher with a loud voice might be deemed of some benefit and thereby meet the FAPE standard. It is difficult to imagine, however, that Amy's instruction would be viewed as specially designed, and her IEP as properly developed, if it did not provide individualized services that went beyond a teacher with a loud voice. In any event, subsequent cases have elaborated on the meaning of some educational benefit.

Subsequent Interpretations of Benefit Standard

The Third Circuit case of *Polk v. Central Susquehanna Intermediate Unit 16*[11] is one of the most frequently cited post-*Rowley* FAPE cases. In applying *Rowley*, the Third Circuit decided in *Polk* that it needed to interpret the meaning of "some educational benefit." It concluded that the Supreme Court's FAPE standard required more than trivial benefit—namely, meaningful progress towards the achievement of IEP goals.

Similar interpretations of the meaning of "some educational benefit" have been adopted in at least four other circuits of the United States Court of Appeals.[12] In *Burlington School Committee v. Massachusetts Department of Education*, the First Circuit's language is that Congress indubitably desired "effective results" and "demonstrable improvement" for the Act's beneficiaries.[13]

While interpreting the *Rowley* standard to require more than trivial benefit, courts remain clear that it does not require an ideal education or the best that money can buy, nor does it guarantee the achievement of the goals and objectives specified in the IEP. Rather it requires a school district to implement the IEP as written and, in effect, make a good faith attempt to enable the student to make good progress toward the goals therein. The 1999 IDEA regulations embody the same standard.[14]

Extended School Year Services

The first case to apply the Supreme Court's interpretation of FAPE to an extended school year (ESY) context was *Battle v. Pennsylvania*.[15] In *Battle*, the Third Circuit decided that Pennsylvania's statutory 180-day school year would have to yield when IDEA students could demonstrate that failure to provide summer services meant failure to individualize an education to meet their unique needs. Otherwise, the state limit on school days would conflict with the FAPE requirement of IDEA. The case generated the now well-known concept of "regression-recoupment" analysis, that is, analysis of whether failure to provide certain summer school services would produce such substantial regression in educational benefits that a student could not recoup the loss, either at all or in any reasonable period of time.

Two important cases have refined the contours of the *Battle* decision and have been generally viewed as providing appropriate standards for ESY. In *Alamo Heights Independent School District v. State Board of Education*,[16] the Fifth Circuit rejected an argument that a student would have to suffer severe regression from the absence of summer programming in order to be eligible for it. Instead the court concluded that if the benefits that accrued during the regular school year would be "significantly jeopardized," then the district must provide an ESY program. In *Johnson v. Independent School District No. 4*,[17] the Tenth Circuit applied the *Alamo Heights* standard and made the specific point that a decision on ESY cannot be based on past evidence of regression-recoupment alone but also must consider various factors that address the likelihood of future regression.

Johnson was applied in the case of *Reusch v. Fountain*,[18] in which Maryland's Montgomery County Schools' ESY policies were found to be full of IDEA violations. The court ruled that the school district was using an illegal substantive standard for eligibility because the standard was limited to a regression-recoupment analysis. Additionally, procedural defects included inadequate notice to parents, delayed or untimely decisions, and failure to annually assess the need for ESY. The court ordered an extensive set of affirmative remedies, including distribution of a summer school brochure about ESY to parents before IEP reviews, an ESY timeline plan, and staff training.

In general, the ESY court decisions have stood for the proposition that school districts may not establish policies that eliminate any given disability or level of disability from potential eligibility for ESY services; all decisions must be individualized. On the other hand, school officials need not offer ESY services merely to advance or enrich educational progress over the summer or simply to thwart the typical summer regression of students in their educational performance. Instead, refusal to provide an ESY program must result in the denial of FAPE.

The judicial mandate for ESY services has been incorporated into the 1999 IDEA regulations, along with the requirement that the decision to provide ESY services must be made by the IEP team.[19] The exact standards to determine ESY eligibility are left to the SEA, but eligibility cannot be limited to specific categories of disability. In addition, the type, amount, and duration of services cannot be limited unilaterally by a school district. If a court case rather than the SEA has already set specific standards in your jurisdiction, you will need to follow them unless they conflict with the 1999 regulations.

Methodological Disputes

The *Rowley* decision has also been helpful to lower courts in situations where parents have argued that a certain teaching method was superior to the one being used with their child by a school district. *Rowley* cautions that methodological disputes are best left to educational authorities because such disputes exceed the expertise of judicial officials. Prior to IDEA '97, this view was consistent with the fact that the IEP did not require inclusion of instructional methods but left them in the hands of professional educators. Unless parents could demonstrate that the method being used by a school resulted in the denial of FAPE, courts generally did not intervene to solve methodological disputes.

One of the leading cases making this point was *Lachman v. Illinois State Board of Education*.[20] In *Lachman*, a student with a profound hearing impairment sought the services of a cued-speech instructor in his neighborhood high school, while the school district proposed to provide a total communication approach in another school. The dispute was judged to be a methodological dispute rather than a placement dispute, and the judge deferred to the judgment of school officials.

Other examples of methodological disputes have concerned requests for such specific methodologies as the Lindamood-Bell and Orton-Gillingham reading programs for students with learning disabilities or oral communication programs for students with hearing impairments. In the past, these requests have been consistently rejected when the district's program was resulting in student progress.[21]

On the other hand, a number of cases have ascertained that the methods selected by given school districts failed to produce any meaningful progress and therefore resulted in a denial of FAPE. One of the first post-*Rowley* cases was *Adams v. Hansen*,[22] in which the parent of a student with a learning disability was dissatisfied with her son's progress and placed him in a private school. In determining that the public school program had denied FAPE to the boy, the court highlighted his minimal 4-month progress in reading achievement and 8-month progress in math achievement after 2 years of instruction, along with his inability to achieve passing marks and advance from grade to grade.

A more recent case is also illustrative. In *Delaware County Intermediate Unit No. 25 v. Martin K.*,[23] the parental choice of the Lovaas teaching method (a behavioral management approach using discrete trial training) for a student with Pervasive Developmental Disorder was upheld over the district's proposed shift to TEACCH (a cognitive approach). The court concluded that TEACCH was inappropriate for the particular student and was likely to produce regression. Even an enhanced TEACCH program was judged inappropriate, given its late introduction and the fact that the Lovaas program had only 1 more year to run.

IDEA '97 and the 1999 regulations indicate that Congress and DOE have shifted their interpretation with respect to the incorporation of instructional methods in the IEP. New language requires consideration of methods and, in some cases, their inclusion in an IEP. One example is the mandate to include "positive behavioral interventions [and] strategies" for a child whose behavior impedes his or her learning or that of others.[24] The regulations make clear that when this has occurred or is likely to occur, a statement of the required intervention or a behavioral intervention plan (BIP) must be included in the IEP.[25] This apparently must happen even though some of the interventions or management "strategies" are likely to involve methods of reducing misbehaviors and teaching new, substitute behaviors.

In addition to the BIP clarification, the regulations expand the definition of special education to include "adapting the content, *methodology,* or delivery of instruction [emphasis added]."[26] Furthermore, the analysis accompanying the regulations includes a discussion of the appropriateness of selecting particular teaching methods and approaches when needed to produce educational benefit.[27] It states that although day-to-day adjustments and lesson plans normally do not require IEP team consideration, overall approaches to instruction may. For instance, cued speech is singled out as an example of a "mode of instruction" that might need to be reflected in a child's IEP. Similarly, for a student with learning disabilities who has not learned to read using traditional reading methods, the analysis states that a particular instructional strategy might need to be selected and would be integral to a child's IEP.[28]

These changes suggest that educators need to be more careful to select teaching methods that match a child's unique instructional needs. They also seem to invite increasing judicial involvement in the assessment of various teaching methods.

Procedural Errors

It is important to remember that significant procedural errors can be grounds for ruling that FAPE was denied. Errors such as failure to meet timelines for evaluation and IEPs, IEP meetings that fail to consider the parents' requests, absence of key personnel (like parents) at IEP meetings, IEPs that are completed prior to the IEP meeting, evaluation without involvement of persons knowledgeable about the particular disability, and delivery of services by untrained personnel have all resulted in judicial decisions holding that FAPE had been denied. Furthermore, IDEA hearing officers have granted a number of parental requests for intensive Lovaas-style training for their young children with autism because of the above kinds of procedural errors by school districts.[29]

State FAPE Standards

One of the four items in the statutory FAPE definition is the delivery of special education and related services that "meet the standards of the state educational agency." This item takes on particular significance when states have FAPE definitions that provide a higher standard than the federal government's, because then the state standard will override the federal standard. In FAPE cases, it is important to know whether the state in which the case arises has a higher standard than the "some educational benefit" standard established by the Supreme Court in the *Rowley* case.

Massachusetts, Michigan, Tennessee, California, North Carolina, Maryland, and Arizona have FAPE standards that on their face appear higher than the federal standard established under *Rowley*.[30] New Jersey, Iowa, and Arkansas used to have language suggesting a higher standard, but each state has now changed its statute or regulations to conform to the federal standard.[31] Comparably, a federal court has interpreted Tennessee's statutory language ("maximize the capabilities") to establish a FAPE standard no higher than the federal standard.[32] In contrast, North Carolina and California cases have ruled that the commensurate opportunity (Section 504) standard is their state's FAPE standard under IDEA.[33] Moreover, federal court cases in Michigan and Massachusetts have ruled that FAPE standards in those states ("maximum potential" and "maximum possible development," respectively) are higher than the IDEA FAPE standard.[34] In some situations, this could mean that services must be more intensive or extensive that those required under the federal standard alone. You will want to keep up to date on your state's current FAPE standard.

FAPE for Suspended or Expelled Students

IDEA '97 makes explicit that all age-eligible children with disabilities, including those suspended or expelled from school, have a right to FAPE. 20 U.S.C.S. § 1412(a)(1). This provision prevents school districts from totally excluding a disruptive or dangerous child with a disability from educational services addressing his or her needs. Although placements can be changed for the safety and welfare of the child and other children, services cannot cease. If they could, we would be back to the pre-1975 days when school districts excluded children from school whom they did not want or did not know how to serve. (More information about the nature and extent of required services is provided in chapter 19.)

Provision of FAPE
in the Correctional System

The IDEA regulations specify that IDEA applies to education in state correctional facilities.[35] This provision has been applied in several juvenile court cases, including one in which the court ordered evaluation of a juvenile for special education eligibility and possible placement.[36] Another application of this policy resulted in a ruling that pretrial detainees could not be denied access to regular and special education during detention.[37]

Under IDEA '97, a state may choose not to provide special education to students from ages 18 through 21 if, in the student's educational placement prior to incarceration in an adult correctional facility, the student was not identified as having an IDEA disability or[†] did not have an IEP.[38] The implication is that if the student had been declassified and terminated from or properly rejected for IDEA services, then the right to FAPE does not exist. Apparently, under this provision, an incarcerated 18- to 21-year-old disabled student who mistakenly was never identified as having an IDEA disability could not claim eligibility for services in jail or prison, even if the student had not graduated from high school.[‡]

In addition, the governor of the state, if permitted to do so under state law, may assign to an agency other than the SEA the responsibility for meeting IDEA requirements for children who are convicted as adults under state law and incarcerated in adult prisons.[39] Note

[†]The federal regulations change the "or" to "and." See 34 C.F.R. § 300.311. The difference clarifies that a student is not eligible for services simply by virtue of having an IEP under Section 504. But see 34 C.F.R. § 300.122(a)(2)(ii) (adding that an identified IDEA student has a right to special education in a correctional facility if the IEP has not yet been developed or has lapsed because the student left school).

[‡]Remember that inmates with a disability could bring a claim of discrimination under Title II of the ADA if they believed that the educational services (or other services) in prison discriminated against them on the basis of their disability. In *Pennsylvania Department of Corrections v. Yeskey*, 524 U.S. 206 (1998), the Supreme Court held that the nondiscrimination requirements of Title II of the ADA apply to state prisons. An earlier case in federal district court concluded that Section 504 applied to educational services for inmates in North Carolina state prison because the Department of Corrections was an LEA and therefore covered under Section 504. *Anthony v. Freeman*, 24 IDELR 929 (E.D.N.C. 1996).

that this potential discretion does not extend to convictions under federal law because states have no obligation to individuals assigned to federal correctional facilities for a federal offense.

If a student with a disability is convicted as an adult under state law and placed in an adult prison, the basic FAPE requirement continues—namely, meaningful access to special education and related services designed to provide some educational benefit. The student, however, no longer must participate in state or districtwide assessments of achievement. In addition, if the student will "age out" of IDEA eligibility before he or she is released from prison, then the transition planning and transition service portions of the IEP no longer are required. Finally, the IEP team may modify the student's IEP or placement "if the State has demonstrated a bona fide security or compelling penological interest that cannot otherwise be accommodated."[40] In other words, safety concerns and other overriding prison interests take precedence over IDEA placement preferences and some of the IEP content requirements.

Implications of IDEA '97 for Future Court Interpretations of FAPE

Given the new focus on results in IDEA '97, educators and academics have begun to speculate that lower court interpretations of *Rowley* that require meaningful progress toward IEP goals will become the standard followed across the country and not just within the circuits in which these interpretations appear. You will recall that IDEA '97 requires regular reports to parents that evaluate the sufficiency of a child's progress toward his or her annual IEP goals. Congress also expects revisions in the IEP if progress toward the annual goals is inadequate.

With the increased emphasis on student outcomes and progress in the general curriculum, more courts can be expected to evaluate FAPE in the context of measurable progress toward annual goals. Instead of limiting their analysis of benefit to whether a student is receiving special education services and achieving passing grades or whether IEPs were "reasonably calculated" to produce progress (i.e., looked good on paper), courts can be expected to carefully scrutinize implemented IEPs to evaluate the student's actual progress toward specified IEP goals. For members of IEP teams, this means that if progress is not occurring at the expected rates, the team should be prepared either to defend and explain the gap or to revise the IEP. Also, when a dispute arises over methods, the educators on the IEP team must be prepared to defend the appropriateness of the instructional method selected.

Food for Thought

Notwithstanding the legal standards that guide the delivery of FAPE and the expectation of meaningful progress for students with disabilities, educators and IEP teams enjoy considerable discretion in designing appropriate services and programs for these students. Neither IDEA nor its regulations can know what services and settings are appropriate for each of the country's nearly 6 million students with disabilities. Moreover, what happens for the vast majority of these students is never challenged in the courts. The law establishes principles and standards to guide decision making, but for the most part the decisions remain with teachers and parents. This means that the law relies on your knowledge and good judgment. It means that, in most circumstances, only you and your teammates can answer the question: What is FAPE for *this* child?

Review

1. In your own words, describe the Supreme Court's interpretation of FAPE in the *Rowley* case.

   In one way or another, you should express the view that the student's education should be at no cost to the parents, meet state standards, be individualized for the student, and conform to the IEP. In addition, you should include the fact that special education (and related services, where appropriate) should provide meaningful access, measured in terms of "some educational benefit."

2. How has the Court's interpretation of FAPE been refined and expanded by a number of circuits of the U.S. Court of Appeals?

   A number of circuits have interpreted "some educational benefit" to mean meaningful, good, or satisfactory progress toward IEP goals.

3.   What aspects of the IDEA '97 IEP requirements seem to support the judicial interpretation of FAPE as requiring meaningful progress toward IEP goals? (You may want to review the IEP chapter.)

The IEP must describe how the disability affects *progress* in the general curriculum. The goals must relate to meeting the child's needs resulting from the disability so as to enable progress in the general curriculum. The IEP must include a statement of special education and related services, program modifications, and supports for school personnel to allow the child to *advance appropriately* toward the annual goals and to *progress* in the general curriculum. The IEP must contain a statement of how the child's parents will be informed of their child's progress toward the annual goals and the extent to which the progress is sufficient to enable the child to achieve the goals by the end of the year.

Notes

[1] *See* 20 U.S.C.S. § 1401(8) (1998).

[2] 458 U.S. 176 (1982).

[3] *Id.* at 186.

[4] 34 C.F.R. § 104.33 (1995).

[5] *Rowley*, 458 U.S. at 200–201.

[6] *See* the discussion *id.* at 192–194 of *Mills v. District of Columbia Bd. of Educ.*, 348 F. Supp. 866 (D.D.C. 1972), and *PARC v. Pennsylvania*, 343 F. Supp. 279 (E.D. Pa. 1972).

[7] *See* 20 U.S.C. § 1412(2)(A)(i) (1980).

[8] 20 U.S.C. § 1401(16)(1980). The same language is in the current version of the statute at 20 U.S.C.S. § 1401(25) (1998).

[9] 20 U.S.C. § 1401(17) (1980), now 20 U.S.C.S. § 1401(22).

[10] 34 C.F.R. § 300.121(e) (1999).

[11] 853 F.2d 171 (3d Cir. 1988).

[12] *See, e.g.*, Burke County Bd. of Educ. v. Denton, 895 F.2d 973 (4th Cir. 1990); Doe v. Smith, 879 F.2d 1340, 1341 (6th Cir. 1989); Evans v. District No. 17, 841 F.2d 824 (8th Cir. 1988); Abrahamson v. Hershman, 701 F.2d 223 (1st Cir. 1983). Cf. County of San Diego v. California Special Educ. Hearing Office, 93 F.3d 1458 (9th Cir. 1996).

[13] 736 F.2d 773, at 788 (1st Cir. 1984) (Burlington II), *aff'd*, 471 U.S. 359 (1985). *Cf.* JSK v. Hendry County Sch. Bd., 941 F.2d 1563 (11th Cir. 1991) (holding that meaningful benefit equals measurable and adequate gains, not meaningful gains generalized across settings).

[14] 34 C.F.R. § 300.350.

[15] 629 F.2d 269 (3d Cir. 1980). *See also* GARC v. McDaniel, 716 F.2d 1565 (11th Cir. 1983); Crawford v. Pittman, 708 F.2d 1028 (5th Cir. 1983).

[16] 790 F.2d 1153 (5th Cir. 1986).

[17] 921 F.2d 1022 (10th Cir. 1990). *See also* Cordrey v. Euckert, 917 F.2d 1460 (6th Cir. 1990).

[18] 872 F. Supp. 1421 (D. Md. 1994).

[19] 34 C.F.R. § 300.309.

[20] 852 F.2d 290 (7th Cir. 1988). *See also* Bonnie Ann F. v. Calallen Indep. Sch. Dist., 835 F. Supp 340 (S.D. Tex. 1993); Brougham v. Town of Yarmouth, 823 F. Supp. 9 (D. Me. 1993).

[21] *See, e.g.*, E.S. v. Independent Sch. Dist. No. 196, 135 F.3d 566 (8th Cir. 1996); Logue v. Shawnee Mission Pub. Sch. Unified Sch. Dist., 959 F.Supp 1338.

[22] 632 F. Supp. 858 (N.D. Cal. 1985).

[23] 831 F. Supp. 1206 (E.D. Pa. 1993).

[24] 20 U.S.C.S. § 1414(d)(3)(B)(i).

[25] 34 C.F.R. § 300.346(c) and accompanying analysis at 64 Fed. Reg. 12589 (1999).

[26] 34 C.F.R. § 300.26.

[27] *See* analysis accompanying 34 C.F.R. § 300.347 at 64 Fed. Reg. 12595 (1999).

[28] *See* analysis accompanying 34 C.F.R. § 300.26 at 64 Fed. Reg. 12552 (1999).

[29] *See, e.g.,* Board of Educ. of Ann Arbor Pub. Schs., 24 IDELR 621 (SEA MI 1996); Capistrano Unified Sch. Dist., 23 IDELR 1209 (SEA CA 1995); Calaveras Unified Sch. Dist., 21 IDELR 211 (SEA CA 1994).

[30] *See In re* Conklin, 946 F.2d 306 (4th Cir. 1991) for a thorough discussion of state standards.

[31] *See* Lascari v. Board of Educ., 560 A.2d 1180, 1189 (N.J. 1989); *In re* Conklin, 946 F.2d 306 (4th Cir. 1991).

[32] Doe v. Board of Educ., 9 F.3d 455 (6th Cir. 1993). *But see* Krichinsky v. Knox County Schs., 17 EHLR 725 (E.D. Tenn. 1991).

[33] *See* Burke County Bd. of Educ. v. Denton, 895 F.2d 973, 983 (4th Cir. 1990); Pink v. Mt. Diablo Unified Sch. Dist., 738 F. Supp. 345, 347 (N.D. Cal. 1990).

[34] David D. v. Dartmouth Sch. Comm., 775 F.2d 411, 423 (1st Cir. 1985); Barwacz v. Michigan Dep't of Educ., 681 F. Supp. 427 (W.D. Mich. 1988). *But see* Roland M. v. Concord Sch. Comm., 910 F.2d 983 (1st Cir. 1990) (balancing Massachusetts' maximum possible development standard against IDEA's preference for mainstreaming in arriving at FAPE determination).

[35] *See* 34 C.F.R. 300.2(b)(1)(iv).

[36] Matter of Jackson, 352 S.E.2d 449 (1987).

[37] *See* Donnell C. v. Illinois State Bd. of Educ., 829 F. Supp. 1016 (N.D. Ill. 1993) (allowing the claim to proceed on the merits).

[38] 20 U.S.C.S. § 1412(a)(1)(B)(ii).

[39] *Id.* § 1412(a)(11)(C).

[40] 34 C.F.R. § 300.311(b) and (c).

Selected Supplementary Resources

Eyer, T. L. (1998). Greater expectations: How the 1997 IDEA Amendments raise the basic floor of opportunity for children with disabilities. *Education Law Reporter, 126,* 1–19.

Huefner, D. S. (1991). Judicial review of the special educational program requirements under the Education for All Handicapped Children Act: Where have we been and where should we be going? *Harvard Journal of Law & Public Policy, 14,* 483–516.

McKinney, J. R. (1998). Charter schools' legal responsibilities toward children with disabilities. *Education Law Reporter, 126,* 565–576.

Osborne, A. (1992). Legal standards for an appropriate education in the post-Rowley era. *Exceptional Children, 58,* 488–494.

Chapter 16

Related Services, Nonacademic Services, and Supplementary Services Under IDEA

"Related Services" Definition and Examples

Under IDEA, education agencies are to make both special education and related services available to eligible students. The definition of *related services* is "transportation and such developmental, corrective, and other supportive services as are required to assist a child with a disability to benefit from special education. . . ."[1] In other words, if the service is not necessary for the student to benefit from special education, then it is not a related service under IDEA.[2] A service basically for enrichment purposes but that need not be part of a student's IEP will not qualify. Similarly, if a student with a disability needs an audiology test or counseling services but does not need special education, then the service is not a related service under IDEA.[†] Therefore, the federal government does not contribute IDEA funds toward the cost of such a service. The service might be a related service under Section 504, however.

A service admittedly "required" or "needed" for some purpose, but not for the student to benefit from special education, is also not a related service. For instance, a substance abuse program was judged not to be a related service for a special education student placed by a public school district into a private school and later expelled from the private school until he underwent drug rehabilitation.[3] The particular drug rehabilitation program treated drug dependency as a disease, and the court viewed the treatment as separate from the student's learning needs, even though it was obviously needed by and was beneficial to the student.

Many kinds of services can be related services. In addition to transportation, the list in IDEA includes the following:[4]

- Speech-language pathology and audiology services

- Psychological services
- Physical and occupational therapy
- Recreation, including therapeutic recreation
- Social work services
- Counseling services, including rehabilitation counseling
- Orientation and mobility services
- Medical services for diagnostic and evaluation purposes
- Early identification and assessment of disabilities in children.

The regulations define the above services and others (see Table 16-1). They add (and then define) parent counseling and training‡ and school health services, and they limit social work services to "social work services in schools."[5] The regulations define medical services as "services provided by a licensed physician to determine a child's medically related disability that results in the child's need for special education and related services."[6] In other words, medical services, at least "to determine a medically related disability," are those provided by a licensed physician rather than by another kind of health care provider.

The 1999 regulations indicate that the list is illustrative and does not exhaust the possibilities.[7] For example, under some circumstances, art, music, and dance therapy might be related services. Also, the room and board costs of a residential placement can be considered a related service needed to assist a student to benefit from special education. Transition services and assistive technology devices and services can be seen as related services, special education, or supplementary aids and services. Extracurricular activities and participation in competitive sports may occasionally be related services but, as is true of the other possibilities, only if deemed necessary for the student to benefit from special education.

At this juncture, it is worth remembering what the definition of *special education* is, because it is not a place. It is "specially designed instruction ... to meet the unique needs of a child with a disability. . . ."[8] The settings in

---

Assistive Technology Devices (ATD's) and Services

ATDs and services are provided when required for FAPE in the LRE. They encompass personal needs (e.g., for a speech synthesizer) and access to technology used by all students. Medication is not an ATD. ATDs or services can be provided in the home if necessary. See 34 C.F. R. § 300.308 and 64 Fed. Reg. 12540 (1999). Table 16-2 defines and illustrates ATDs and services.

---

which special education can be delivered are not restricted and can include the regular classroom, at one end of the placement continuum, or a hospital, at the other end. Moreover, special education is not necessarily limited to education delivered by special educators. It can include instructional services provided by a speech pathologist or other related service provider if the services also are considered special education under state standards.[9] Physical education instruction is included within the definition of special education.[10] Vocational education instruction and travel training to help a student move around effectively and safely in the school and community also can be included if they otherwise meet the definition.

If the parents provide a related service themselves because the education agency refused to provide it, the parents can be reimbursed.[11] The reasoning is analogous to the situation in which a parent enrolls a child in private school because of the failure of a school district to provide FAPE in the public setting (see chapter 18).

Controversial Related Services

Although any desired auxiliary service can become controversial if the education agency and parents disagree over whether it constitutes a related service, some kinds of supportive services have generated more dispute than others. Among the more controversial have been transportation services, psychotherapy, extensive health services of an arguably medical nature, and services (including room and board) in a residential setting.

Transportation   School districts across the country already have transportation policies covering a host of situ-

Table 16-1. Definitions of Related Services in the 1999 IDEA Regulations

Audiology
(i) Identification of children with hearing loss;
(ii) Determination of the range, nature, and degree of hearing loss, including referral for medical or other professional attention for the habilitation of hearing;
(iii) Provision of habilitative activities, such as language habilitation, auditory training, speech reading (lip-reading), hearing evaluation, and speech conservation;
(iv) Creation and administration of programs for prevention of hearing loss;
(v) Counseling and guidance of children, parents, and teachers regarding hearing loss;
(vi) Determination of children's needs for group and individual amplification, selecting and fitting an appropriate aid, and evaluating the effectiveness of amplification.

Counseling Services
Services provided by qualified social workers psychologists, guidance counselors, or other qualified personnel.

Early Identification and Assessment of Disabilities in Children
The implementation of a formal plan for identifying a disability as early as possible in a child's life.

Medical Services
Services provided by a licensed physician to determine a child's medically related disability that results in the child's need for special education and related services.

Occupational Therapy
(i) Services provided by a qualified occupational therapist;
(ii) Includes (A) improving, developing, or restoring functions impaired or lost through illness, injury, or deprivation; (B) Improving ability to perform tasks for independent functioning if functions are impaired or lost; (C) Preventing, through early intervention, initial or further impairment or loss of function.

Orientation and Mobility Services
(i) Services provided to blind or visually impaired students by qualified personnel to enable those students to attain systematic orientation to and safe movement within their environments in school, home, and community;
(ii) Includes teaching students the following, as appropriate: (A) Spatial and environmental concepts and use of information received by the senses (such as sound, temperature, and vibrations) to establish, maintain, or regain orientation and line of travel (e.g., using sound at a traffic light to cross a street); (B) To use a long cane to supplement visual travel skills or as a tool for safely negotiating the environment for students with no available travel vision; (C) To understand and use remaining vision and distance low vision aids; (D) Other concepts, techniques, and tools.

Parent Counseling and Training
(i) Assisting parents in understanding the special needs of their child;
(ii) Providing parents with information about child development;
(iii) Helping parents to acquire the necessary skills that will allow them to support the implementation of their child's IEP or IFSP [Individual Family Service Plan].

Physical Therapy
Services provided by a qualified physical therapist.

Psychological Services

(i) Administering psychological and educational tests, and other assessment procedures;

(ii) Interpreting assessment results;

(iii) Obtaining, integrating, and interpreting information about child behavior and conditions relating to learning;

(iv) Consulting with other staff members in planning school programs to meet the special needs of children as indicated by psychological tests, interviews, and behavioral evaluations;

(v) Planning and managing a program of psychological services, including psychological counseling for children and parents;

(vi) Assisting in developing positive behavioral intervention strategies.

Recreation

(i) Assessment of leisure function;

(ii) Therapeutic recreation services;

(iii) Recreation programs in schools and community agencies;

(iv) Leisure education.

Rehabilitation Counseling Services

Services provided by qualified personnel in individual or group sessions that focus specifically on career development, employment preparation, achieving independence, and integration in the workplace and community of a student with a disability. The term also includes vocational rehabilitation services provided to a student with disabilities by vocational rehabilitation programs funded under the Rehabilitation Act of 1973, as amended.

School Health Services

Services provided by a qualified school nurse or other qualified person.

Social Work Services in Schools

(i) Preparing a social or developmental history on a child with a disability;

(ii) Group and individual counseling with the child and family;

(iii) Working in partnership with parents and others on those problems in a child's living situation (home, school, and community) that affect the child's adjustment in school;

(iv) Mobilizing school and community resources to enable the child to learn as effectively as possible in his or her educational program;

(v) Assisting in developing positive behavioral intervention strategies.

Speech-Language Pathology Services

(i) Identification of children with speech or language impairments;

(ii) Diagnosis and appraisal of specific speech or language impairments;

(iii) Referral for medical or other professional attention necessary for the habilitation of speech or language impairments;

(iv) Provision of speech and language services for the habilitation or prevention of communicative impairments;

(v) Counseling and guidance of parents, children, and teachers regarding speech and language impairments.

Transportation

(i) Travel to and from school and between schools;

(ii) Travel in and around school buildings;

(iii) Specialized equipment (such as special or adapted buses, lifts, and ramps), if required to provide special transportation for a child with a disability.

Source: 34 C.F.R. § 300.24.

Table 16–2. Definition and Examples of Assistive Technology Devices and Services

Assistive Technology Device: Any item, piece of equipment, or product system, whether acquired commercially off the shelf, modified, or customized, that is used to increase, maintain, or improve functional capabilities of individuals with disabilities. 20 U.S.C.S. 1401(1).

Examples:

Computer Assisted Instruction & Computer Access

Educational software
Interactive video discs
Talking word processors

Wrist rests
Adapted keyboards
Head pointers
Mouse alternatives

Augmentative Communication Devices

Looptapes
Communication boards
Link, Speaking Language Master (text-
   to-speech devices)

DynaVox, Speak Easy, Delta Talker,
   Superhawk (voice-output communication aids)

Visual Aids or Substitutes

Magnifying devices and screen magnifica-
   tion software
Large-print books
Braille materials

Large-font xeroxed or word-processed
   materials
Large-screen TV or computer monitors
Audiotapes
Reading machines and reading software

Listening Aids

Hearing aids
Personal FM units
Closed captioning devices on TV

TDD (talking text) and TTY (teletype-
   writer) devices
Vibrating "beepers"

Mobility and Positioning Aids

Stand-up desks
Scooters
Laser Canes
Adaptive driving controls

Wheelchairs
Walkers
Chair inserts
Cushions

Physical Education & Recreation Aids

Adapted puzzles
Beeping balls and goalposts

Stencils, adapted pencils, and drawing
   software
Game instructions in Braille or on audiotape

Self-Care Aids / Environmental Control

Air-filtering and air-conditioning
Adapted utensils
Electric feeders

Adapted on/off switches
Pointer sticks, head pointers
Remote control switches

Assistive Technology Service: Any service that directly assists an individual with a disability in the selection, acquisition, or use of an assistive technology device. 20 U.S.C.S. § 1401(2).

Examples:

Evaluating an individual's need for an assistive technology device (ATD)

Coordinating and using other therapies, interventions, and services with ATDs

Training or technical assistance for children with disabilities, their families

(if appropriate), and the professionals who work with them

Purchasing, leasing, or otherwise providing for the acquisition of an ATD by a child with a disability

Selecting, designing, fitting, customizing, adapting, applying, maintaining, repairing, or replacing an ATD

---

ations, such as when a child lives too far from school to walk, when busing is used to transport children to other than their neighborhood school (e.g., for racial desegregation purposes), or when dangerous traffic or other environmental hazards necessitate special transportation. The transportation needs of some special education students are an additional subset that must be accommodated within the district's overall transportation policy and services. The determination of whether transportation (beyond that available to children without disabilities) is a related service is made by the IEP team as part of the development of the IEP.

According to the IDEA regulations, transportation includes both travel to and from school and between schools as well as travel in and around school buildings. It also incorporates specialized equipment such as ramps and bus lifts, if necessary to provide special transportation for a student with a disability.[12]

The basic question in determining the need for transportation is whether the student requires it to access special education or related services. The decision is made on a case-by-case basis. The provision of transportation as a related service is not limited to those who cannot walk. It can also be required when, because of a child's disability, the child is unable to get to school safely and independently. For instance, in addition to a mobility impairment, cognitive, emotional, sensory, or health disabilities can produce such a need.[†] Vulnerability based on age alone can also necessitate transportation in order

[†]The frequently miscited case of *McNair v. Oak Hills Local School District*, 872 F.2d 153 (6th Cir. 1989), seems to stand for a restrictive interpretation of when transportation is required. The court in *McNair* ruled that transportation should be deemed a related service when it is designed to "meet the unique needs of the child caused by the handicap." *Id.* at 156. It then determined that the deaf plaintiff had no special transportation needs "caused by" her deafness, something to which the parties had stipulated in the case—a fact ignored by other courts citing *McNair*.

to access special education, as the transportation needs of preschoolers eligible for coverage under IDEA help to make clear. Finally, if a school district makes a placement at a distant school in order to provide FAPE, it has obligated itself to pay the transportation costs. If the placement is at a distant residential school, transportation may only be required at the beginning and end of the school year and at holiday times, unless the student needs to be able to return home more often.†

After the IEP team has decided to provide transportation, other decisions can arise: how to discipline the student on the bus, how to load and unload the student, whether to provide door-to-door transportation, and when to provide an aide or special equipment on the bus to protect the safety of the student or others. All of these issues have been subject to both IDEA hearing decisions and Section 504 rulings from OCR. Each decision is made on a case-by-case basis.

Door-to-Door Transportation

In *Hurry v. Jones*, 734 F.2d 879 (1st Cir. 1984), the court ordered that parents be reimbursed for the cost of transporting their severely disabled son to his special education program after the school declined to continue door-to-door transportation service. A state regulation seemed to call only for public assistance to and from the street level of a dwelling, and the school was concerned about the safety of carrying the overweight boy to and from his front door, which was 12 steep steps above street level. The parties eventually reached an agreement, but not before the parents had incurred $5,750 in reimbursable transportation expenses.

In general, a district must remember that, under the logic of the Supreme Court's decision in *Honig v. Doe* (see chapter 19), suspensions from transportation for more than 10 school days can constitute a change of placement just as readily as can suspension from a classroom, if transportation has been designated a related service in the child's IEP.[13] Under some circumstances, a day of bus suspension would count as a day of school suspension if the school does not provide the child with access to the setting in which IEP services are delivered. With respect to door-to-door transportation, physician documentation can be helpful in determining whether such assistance is required.[14] Furthermore, training school-bus drivers and/or aides to manage the behavior of special education students with behavior problems is a wise measure to prevent injuries on the bus that might open the district to liability. Finally, those who transport children with disabilities should be knowledgeable about specific conditions so that they are in a position to determine what might constitute a medical emergency.

School Health Services   Two Supreme Court cases address the need for health services as a related service. The first is *Irving Independent School District v. Tatro*.[15] The second is *Cedar Rapids Community School District v. Garret F.*[16] The cases are 15 years apart, and the Supreme Court's ruling in *Garret F.* was necessary to resolve conflicting applications of *Tatro* in the lower courts.

Amber Tatro, a young student with spina bifida and a neurogenic bladder, required catheterization in order to attend a regular class, which had been determined to be the LRE. The school subsequently declined to pay for the clean intermittent catheterization (CIC) that she needed during the school day. The Supreme Court held that CIC met the definition of related services and, like transportation, was needed to enable access to FAPE in what was Amber's LRE. Then it held that CIC was not excluded as medical treatment but rather was a school health service, primarily because it did not need to be performed by a licensed physician and also because the nature and extent of the service was consistent with the type of service provided by school nurses. The Court also observed that the IDEA regulations limited medical services to diagnostic and evaluation purposes, apparently in order to contain costs, thereby arguably introducing a cost factor into the determination of what constituted a related service.

Subsequent to *Tatro*, determinations in the courts of what constituted a related health service became more complex, as increasing numbers of medically fragile students entered the school system. One judicial view held that the key question was not whether a service was provided by a physician but rather whether the nature and extent of the required care resembled medical care more than it resembled school health services, even if the care was provided by a nurse rather than a doctor. Applying this view, a series of cases determined that continuous, one-on-one nursing care was not required as a related service.[17]

On the other hand, another series of decisions held that *Tatro* established a "bright-line" test—namely, that if the service was not provided by a licensed physician, it was not a medical service, no matter how extensive the health care.[18] Because of the split of opinion in the circuits and the cost implications of the issue, the Supreme Court agreed to review the Eighth Circuit's decision in the *Garret F.* case and resolved the issue during its 1998–99 term.

The *Garret F.* case concerned a boy whose spinal cord was severed in a motorcycle accident at the age of 4, leaving him paralyzed from the neck down and dependent on a ventilator to breathe. Garret's thinking abilities were unimpaired, and he performed successfully in his regular education classrooms with the assistance of a personal care attendant throughout his school day. The attendant performed such duties as urinary catheterization, monitoring his ventilator and blood pressure, suctioning his tracheostomy tube, positioning him in his wheelchair, helping with eating and drinking, and other tasks.

Private insurance and a settlement from the motorcycle company provided for the in-school services of a licensed practical nurse until Garret was in the fifth grade. His mother then asked the school district to pay for the continuous, one-on-one care that Garret needed. It refused, arguing that the extent and costly nature of the care qualified the service as medical care rather than school health services.

In a straightforward and succinct decision, the Supreme Court held that the definition of related services under IDEA required the school district to provide Garret with the continuous, one-on-one health care services he needed to remain in regular classes. According to the Court, Garret's nursing services did not fall within the medical services exemption. It interpreted its earlier decision in *Tatro* as establishing a bright-line test for distinguishing between medical and school health services:

a nurse is not a physician. It concluded that although cost may be relevant in construing IDEA, it cannot be the determining factor when a related service is needed to integrate a student like Garret into the public schools.

The impact of the ruling could be significant. The lower court cases that conflict with the Supreme Court decision are no longer good law. How many students will require services like Garret's can only be estimated. Some who are in separate schools already have access to both a nurse and a doctor on staff. The financial impact will be greatest in school districts with medically fragile students in regular classrooms. In large school districts, it may be possible to cluster some of these children in the same school for economies of scale and still include them in classes and activities with their nondisabled peers.

The implications are harder to predict for LEAs with disabled children who are not medically fragile but whose parents seek one-on-one aides in the regular classroom

---

Nursing Practice Acts

School officials should be careful not to ask teachers, paraprofessionals, and health aides to perform services that, under their state's nursing practices act, can be performed only by a registered nurse (RN) or a licensed practical nurse (LPN). Nursing practice acts usually differentiate the services that can be performed by RNs, LPNs, and health aides, based on the level of training and risk attached. In addition, guidelines often limit teachers and nonhealth care staff to routine and common health and safety procedures. Of course, teachers and other nonhealth care staff do not wish to perform health procedures for which they are untrained and that carry liability risks, but sometimes school officials ask them to. In *Stamps v. Jefferson County Board of Education*, 642 So.2d 941 (Ala. 1994), special education teachers sued the school board for allegedly requiring them to practice nursing without a license. The Alabama Supreme Court dismissed the case for failure to involve the state nursing association as a party in the suit. If professional nursing associations monitor school district practices and conclude that school districts are requiring school employees to practice nursing without a license, lawsuits from the nursing associations could follow.

---

to enable their children to benefit from their involvement in the general curriculum and with nondisabled children (see chapter 17). On the one hand, court watchers are wondering if personal aides might be required for some of these children as an extension of the *Garret F.* decision. On the other hand, some speculation has arisen that, as a result of the Supreme Court's interpretation of the statute, Congress may want to amend IDEA '97 to incorporate a definition of medical services that includes extensive nursing care.

The alternative, forcing children like Garret out of a regular school and into a hospital or similarly restrictive setting away from their peers, is not an attractive option. His situation reveals the complexity and difficulty of the decisions required under IDEA.

Psychotherapy   The term *psychotherapy* does not appear among the examples of related services specified in the IDEA regulations. Nonetheless, counseling services, psychological services, and social work services in schools are among the listed examples, and each arguably incorporates the concept of mental health therapy for an individual student or group of students. Additionally, even the complete absence of any terms incorporating the concept of psychotherapy would not exclude it from falling within the definition of related services because the list of examples is not inclusive.

Two problems arise with respect to psychotherapy: its general unavailability in schools, and who can be reimbursed for providing it. If provided by someone such as a clinical social worker, licensed family therapist, or clinical or counseling psychologist, it need not be excluded as medical treatment. On the other hand, if provided by a psychiatrist or psychoanalyst (i.e., physicians), then under the Supreme Court's ruling in *Garret F.,* it would fall within the medical services exclusion, resolving what was a judicial split in the lower courts.

Curiously, the issue has cooled down as the health care issue has heated up. Inclusion of behavioral intervention plans (BIPs) and positive behavioral strategies in the IEP may or may not relieve the pressure for more mental health services to individual students.

Residential Placement   Residential placement, including room and board costs, can be viewed as a supportive service necessary to assist a student to benefit from spe-

---

Psychotherapy in Hospital and Private Settings

In *Clovis Unified School District v. California Office of Administrative Hearings*, 903 F. 2d 635 (9th Cir. 1990), although both parties agreed that Michelle Shorey needed a residential placement, the school district asserted that the need was primarily medical. The Ninth Circuit agreed that Michelle's psychiatric hospitalization was not for educational reasons and that therefore her extended psychotherapy, even though provided by nonphysicians, was not a related service. Rather, it was part of the attempt to treat her mental illness, which had reached a crisis stage.

In contrast, when a placement is made for special educational reasons, then services such as psychotherapy, at least if delivered by nonphysicians, can be viewed as related services. See, for example, *Babb v. Knox County School System*, 965 F. 2d 104 (6th Cir. 1992). The court concluded in *Babb* that psychological and counseling services at a psychiatric hospital were related services because hospitalization was necessary to provide FAPE. Similarly, *T.G. v. Board of Education of Piscataway*, 576 F. Supp. 420 (D.N.J. 1983), held that psychotherapy by a social worker at a private day school was a related service.

---

cial education. When the placement is made by the public agency, no issue arises over the viability of paying for the room and board costs. What does arouse controversy is when the parents make the placement and the LEA challenges the need for it (see chapter 18).

Cost Issues

Lurking behind virtually all related services disputes is the issue of cost. Although the cost of providing special education instruction is more expensive than regular education, it is the cost of related services that is particularly troublesome to many school districts. Under fiscal stress, many school districts have reduced the availability of auxiliary service providers used by both regular and special education students—personnel such as school psychologists, school social workers, and school nurses. Even more difficult to fund (and find) are services provided by qualified occupational and physical therapists, sign language interpreters, and psychotherapists.

The IDEA regulations demonstrate awareness of cost issues by stating that funds to pay for related services may come from third party sources, both public and private, and that insurers are not relieved of otherwise valid obligations to provide or pay for services for a child with a disability.[19] Interagency agreements are encouraged, but turf battles often arise when social service and mental health agencies are invited to help pay for the cost of various related services, such as room and board at private residential placements, and mental health services. Among the problems are differences in funding mechanisms and regulations, such as the requirement under IDEA that all related services be at no cost to the parent, while social service and health agencies typically can use a sliding scale and charge for services based on the ability to pay.

Private insurance may be available to pay for related services, but effectively tapping this source requires considerable bureaucratic expertise and coordination. OSEP has made clear that parents may not be asked to spend their deductibles, nor may the insurance be used if it results in a reduction in lifetime coverage† or an increase in premiums.[20] In other words, using the insurance must not result in any cost to the parent. Moreover, if insurance payouts become too large under IDEA, or if the insurance company realizes that government agencies can also be obligated to pay for the same service, the insurance company can amend or cancel future coverage.‡

Medicaid is also a source of payment for related services. In 1988 Congress amended IDEA to clarify that Medicaid was available to pay for related services that fell within any given state's list of Medicaid-covered services.[21] Prior to the amendment, Medicaid administrators had taken the position that related services incorporated into a student's IEP could not be paid for with Medicaid funds. Two years after the congressional amendment, a federal appeals court affirmed a lower court ruling that the Secretary of Health and Human Services (HHS) was interpreting HHS regulations in an obsolete fashion by paying for private duty nursing only if provided at home or in a hospital rather than in an educational setting.[22] As a result, HHS reinterpreted its regulations to allow private duty nurses in school settings.

---

†In *Seals v. Loftis,* 614 F. Supp. 302 (E.D. Tenn. 1985), the court ruled that parents were not required to use their insurance for their child's psychological evaluation because of the lifetime cap on the extent of insurance benefits available for that purpose.

---

‡In *Chester County Intermediate Unit v. Pennsylvania Blue Shield,* 896 F.2d 808 (3d Cir. 1990), the court upheld an insurance company's "exclusionary clause," which excluded from coverage services to which the insured was entitled under federal or state law.

Subsequent to the Medicaid amendment in IDEA, the Health Care Financing Administration, the agency within HHS responsible for Medicaid administration, issued a regulation prohibiting reimbursement from Medicaid funds for "formal educational services or for vocational services."[23] The purpose was to distinguish related services of a rehabilitative nature from traditional academic programs, which remain the responsibility of education agencies.

Medicaid reimbursement, although clearly available, is limited because of state and federal eligibility requirements. Essentially, only children whose families meet poverty guidelines are eligible. In addition, covered services vary by state, as do the reimbursement rates. Related services such as occupational and physical therapy, speech therapy, audiology, and psychological services may or may not be Medicaid-covered services within a given state.

It is fair to conclude that although school districts may solicit funds from a variety of third-party sources, it is difficult to raise substantial sums in this way. The burden of the costs of related services still falls heavily on education agencies.

Nonacademic Services Under IDEA

IDEA requires that students with disabilities be provided an equal opportunity to participate in nonacademic services and extracurricular activities.[24] Such an opportunity encourages interaction between students with disabilities and without disabilities and ensures that students with disabilities are not denied access to various services extended regularly to nondisabled students. Among the nonacademic services listed in the regulations are counseling services, recreational athletics, transportation, health services, recreational activities, special interest groups or clubs sponsored by the school, referrals to appropriate outside agencies, and student employment opportunities. The IDEA provision basically parallels a similar provision under Section 504.[25]

You can see that the above services could become related services under IDEA if written into a student's IEP as necessary to assist the student to benefit from special education. The basic requirement, however, is not that students with disabilities be provided all these services but simply that they be given the opportunity to participate on an equal basis with regular education students.

Supplementary Aids and Services

Under IDEA '97, a category of service entitled "supplementary aids and services" has been given enhanced visibility. Such services are defined for the first time in the statute as "aids, services, and other supports that are provided in regular education classes or other education-related settings to enable children with disabilities to be educated with nondisabled children to the maximum extent appropriate. . . ."[26] Supplementary aids and services are to be included in a student's IEP. They are different from related services in that they are not linked to enabling the child to benefit from special education. Instead, they are linked to enabling the child to participate with nondisabled children in educational activities and extracurricular and other nonacademic activities. Presumably, these types of aids and services will prove less costly than related services, although the only examples of supplementary services provided in the statute or regulations are resource rooms and itinerant instruction to be provided in conjunction with regular class placement.[27]

Implications

School districts constrained by limited budgets sometimes must find innovative ways to provide related services. Training of paraprofessionals is one way and is being systematized and improved in many districts. The use of video technology is another means and may be tapped in creative ways, for instance (a) by use of videotapes of physical therapy and speech therapy instruction for careful follow-through by special educators and (b) by interactive diagnostic and instructional sessions from centralized sites. Moreover, for students with multiple and severe disabilities, sometimes an extended school day combined with parent counseling, or possibly respite care or group home placement, can provide FAPE at less cost than a residential placement with its expensive room and board costs. In general, education agencies should brainstorm nontraditional ways to deliver related services effectively.

The need for nurses and nurses' aides in schools is growing. Many school districts have cut back on the number of school nurses in recent decades as the seriousness of infectious disease outbreaks in schools has declined. Now, with the advent of more children who are medically fragile and more children with noncontagious but serious health conditions, such as asthma, diabetes, orthopedic impairments, neurological impairments, and respiratory impairments, the need for health care in schools is rising sharply. Serving the needs of these children will require increased health care services in school. Education agencies and parent advocacy groups should be prepared to make the case to state legislatures to expand school health services.

School districts also need to gear up to properly evaluate the need of some students with disabilities for assistive technology devices and services. Although these issues for the most part have not yet reached the courts, school districts report growing requests for evaluation and provision of augmentative communication devices and computer hardware and software, along with refined equipment for the visually or hearing impaired and adapted equipment for those with mobility impairments and self-care needs.

Finally, if a school is to meet the needs of the whole child, as is increasingly expected under IDEA, better links with other state agencies must be established. Interagency agreements are frequently nothing more than statements of good intentions, without the resources to facilitate interagency cooperation and collaborative service delivery. Models developed in states such as Utah, to serve the social service, health, and educational needs of a child by also addressing the family's needs, deserve serious consideration.[†]

[†]FACT (Families and Agencies Coming Together) is Utah's state-funded model of service delivery to students at risk, including students with disabilities. The model requires local interagency teams, drawn from education, corrections, social services, and health departments. It provides additional funding for their collaborative projects in pilot schools that involve working with the family as well as the student at risk. See Utah Code Ann. § 63-75-1 *et seq.* (1994).

Review

1.   What is the definition of a related service under IDEA?

It includes transportation or developmental, corrective, or other supportive services that are necessary to assist a child to benefit from special education. Without special education, there can be no related service obligation under IDEA.

2.   What is the difference between a related service and a supplementary aid or service?

A related service is one that is needed to assist the student to benefit from special education. Without it, some of the child's unique educational goals cannot be met. A supplementary aid, on the other hand, helps the child to be included in regular classroom instruction and in extracurricular and other nonacademic activities.

Notes

[1] 34 C.F.R. § 300.24 (1999); *see also* 20 U.S.C.S. § 1401(22)(1998).

[2] 34 C.F.R. § 300.7(a)(2).

[3] Field v. Haddonfield Bd. of Educ., 769 F. Supp. 1313 (D.N.J. 1991).

[4] 20 U.S.C.S. § 1401(22) (1998).

[5] 34 C.F.R. § 300.16.

[6] *Id.* § 300.16(b)(4).

[7] *Id.* § 300.14 and app. A at question 34.

[8] *Id.* § 300.26(a)(1).

[9] *Id.* § 300.26(a)(2)(i) and app. A at question 30.

[10] *Id.*

[11] *See, e.g.*, Hurry v. Jones, 734 F.2d 879 (1st Cir. 1984).

[12] *See* 34 C.F.R. § 300.24(b)(15).

[13] *See* 64 Fed. Reg. 12619 (1999); *see also* Greenbrier County (WV) Sch. Dist., 16 EHLR 616 (OCR 1990).

[14] *See* Duchesne County (UT) Sch. Dist., 16 EHLR 112 (OCR 1989).

[15] 468 U.S. 883 (1984).

[16] 119 S. Ct 992 (1999).

[17] *See, e.g.*, Fulginiti v. Roxbury Township Pub. Sch., 116 F.3d 468 (3d Cir. 1997) (affirming, without opinion, the lower court decision); Neely v. Rutherford County Sch., 68 F.3d 965 (6th Cir. 1995); Detsel v. Board of Educ. of Auburn, 820 F.2d 587 (2d Cir. 1987); Granite Sch. Dist. v. Shannon M., 787 F. Supp. 1020 (D. Utah 1992); Bevin H. v. Wright, 666 F. Supp. 71 (W.D. Pa. 1987).

[18] *See, e.g.,* Cedar Rapids Community Sch. Dist. v. Garret F., 106 F.3d 822 (8th Cir. 1997); Skelly v. Brookfield La Grange Park Sch. Dist., 968 F. Supp. 385 (N.D. Ill. 1997).

[19] 34 C.F.R. § 300.301.

[20] *Id.* § 300.142(b).

[21] 20 U.S.C.S. § 1412(e); *see also* 42 U.S.C. § 1396b(c).

[22] Detsel v. Sullivan, 895 F.2d 58 (2d Cir. 1990).

[23] 42 C.F.R. § 441.13(b).

[24] 34 C.F.R. § 300.306.

[25] Cf. *id.* § 104.37.

[26] 20 U.S.C.S. § 1401(29).

[27] 34 C.F.R. § 300.551(2).

Selected Supplementary Resources

American Federation of Teachers, AFL-CIO. (1997). *The medically fragile child in the school setting.* Washington, DC: Author.

Chambers, A. C. (1997). *Has technology been considered? A guide for IEP teams.* Reston, VA: Council of Administrators of Special Education and the Technology and Media Division of the Council for Exceptional Children.

Colorado State Pupil Transportation Association. (1996). *Guidelines for transporting students with disabilities.* Boulder, CO: Author.

Council for Exceptional Children (1992). *Guidelines for the delineation of roles and responsibilities for the safe delivery of specialized health care in the educational setting.* Reston, VA: Author.

Golden, D. (1998). *Assistive technology in special education: Policy and practice.* Reston, VA: Council of Administrators of Special Education and the Technology and Media Division of the Council for Exceptional Children.

Julnes, R. E., & Brown, S. E. (1993). The legal mandate to provide assistive technology in special education programming. *Education Law Reporter, 82,* 737–748.

Rebore, D. & Zirkel, P. A. (1999). The Supreme Court's latest special education ruling: A costly decision? *Education Law Reporter, 135,* 331–341.

Spaller, K. D., & Thomas, S. B. (1994). A timely idea: Third party billing for related services. *Education Law Reporter, 86,* 581–592.

Thomas, S. B., & Hawke, C. (1999). Health-care services for children with disabilities: Emerging standards and implications. *Journal of Special Education, 32,* 226–237.

Chapter 17

Least Restrictive Environment, Mainstreaming, and Inclusion Under IDEA

Introduction and Definitions

The issue of educational placement of students with disabilities has been controversial over the years. Prior to the 1975 enactment of Public Law 94-142, many school districts denied public school admission to many children with disabilities, especially those with mental retardation, physical disabilities, and behavioral disorders. Other school districts expelled students indefinitely when they did not know how to manage or teach them, sometimes placing students on waiting lists for nonforthcoming tuition grants to private schools. Public Law 94-142 was designed to help school districts pay for the excess costs of providing to *all* children with disabilities— including difficult children—an appropriate public education at no cost to their parents. Excluding children with disabilities from public school education was unacceptable.

Several years before passage of P.L. 94-142, cases such as *PARC v. Pennsylvania*[1] and *Mills v. District of Columbia Board of Education*[2] had established the principle that exclusion of children with disabilities from the public school system was a denial of equal protection of the laws under the Fourteenth Amendment to the U.S. Constitution. Both court cases also had declared a legal preference for the education of nondisabled students with disabled students to the extent to which it could be accomplished appropriately. This preference was labeled the least restrictive placement alternative, or least restrictive environment (LRE), borrowing these terms from cases involving the deinstitutionalization of persons with mental illness.

Over the years the term LRE has been joined by the terms *mainstreaming* and *inclusion,* all of which are used, sometimes indiscriminately, with respect to placement preferences. Treating these three terms as synonyms represents a misunderstanding of the legal meaning of LRE. No reference to "mainstreaming" or "inclusion" appears in IDEA or the IDEA regulations. Prior to 1997, the term LRE appeared only as a subheading in the IDEA regulations.[3] In 1997, it was introduced as a subheading in the statute itself.[4] All three terms need more explanation. To avoid misunderstanding, it is also important to ask each user what these terms mean to him or her.

Mainstreaming

Mainstreaming generally refers to an educational placement that allows students with disabilities and students without disabilities to be integrated for some or all of the school day. *Physical mainstreaming* is sometimes used to refer to integration in the same school building but not in the same classrooms. *Social mainstreaming* refers to integration in the same school settings during times when social interaction is possible—for instance, during lunch and recess. *Instructional mainstreaming* refers to integration in the same regular education classroom during academic instructional time.

When the term *mainstreaming* is used generically, it typically refers to instructional mainstreaming, and the assumption typically has been that a student so mainstreamed should be able to handle the regular education curriculum, with or without modifications. The distinction between types of mainstreaming has been important in certain federal court cases, some of which have dealt with physical and social mainstreaming issues, while others have addressed instructional mainstreaming issues.

Inclusion

Since the late 1980s, the concepts of inclusion, full inclusion, partial inclusion, and supported inclusion have gained visibility. In general, inclusion refers to placement of students with disabilities in regular education classrooms and schools. Broadly speaking, inclusion means integration of children with disabilities and children without disabilities in the same settings. "Integration," however, at least in the school context, is linked with race, and "inclusion" is linked with placement issues affecting students with disabilities.

Usually, *full inclusion* means that all special education services are delivered in regular education classrooms in the school the child would attend if not disabled (hereafter, the "neighborhood school"). Services are brought to the student rather than vice versa. *Partial inclusion,* in contrast, usually indicates some pullout services, with the regular education classroom remaining as the child's home base. *Supported inclusion* emphasizes the need for support services in regular education settings in order for inclusion to be successful.

"Inclusion" has replaced "mainstreaming" for most purposes related to public schooling. Inclusion reflects the view that society is improved by the interaction of school children who have disabilities and those who do not. Arguably, children with disabilities learn better what is expected of them in the neighborhood and in society when they have an opportunity to observe and interact with children without disabilities. Conversely, children without disabilities learn better how to understand and accept children with disabilities when both groups learn and play together.

Least Restrictive Environment

The legal term for special education placement preferences is *least restrictive environment* (LRE). Basically, LRE refers to the educational setting closest to the regular classroom in which FAPE can be delivered to a special education student. LRE captures the balance between the statutory mandate to provide FAPE and the statutory preference for education of disabled students with nondisabled students to the maximum extent appropriate. The LRE is not necessarily the regular education classroom; it must be determined individually for each child. For some students, it may be a self-contained placement in the regular school; for others, it is a separate school or even a residential setting. For most students, the LRE is the regular classroom with supplementary aids and services, including part-time resource room placements.

What Does IDEA Require?

When P.L. 94-142 was enacted in 1975, it adopted the regular classroom placement preference found in the *PARC* and *Mills* cases. The same preference continues today in IDEA, but it has been strengthened. The original provision required states to establish procedures assuring that, "to the maximum extent appropriate," children with disabilities were educated with nondisabled students and that special classes, separate schooling, or other removal of children with disabilities from the regular educational environment occurred only when the nature or severity of the disability was such that education in regular classes with the use of supplementary aids and services could not be achieved satisfactorily.[5]

Although this provision remains intact in IDEA '97,[6] the statutory section dealing with IEPs now requires "an explanation of the extent, if any, to which the child will *not* participate with nondisabled children in the regular class and in [extracurricular and nonacademic] activities. . . . [emphasis added]"[7] Prior to IDEA '97, the IDEA regulations had required a description in the IEP of the extent to which the child *would* be able to participate in regular education programs. In other words, IDEA '97 reverses the expectation: the IEP team must explain any nonparticipation in the regular education setting rather than describing any services delivered within it. The effect of the reversal is to buttress the legal underpinnings of inclusion and create a legal presumption in favor of regular classroom placement.

The new IEP language in IDEA '97 also emphasizes that special education and related services are to be accompanied by supplementary aids and services, program modifications, and supports for school personnel so that students with disabilities can be educated successfully with other children, both with disabilities and without.[8] Moreover, the IEP language also stresses that these same kinds of services are intended to allow children with disabilities to participate in extracurricular and other nonacademic activities, both with children who have disabilities and those who do not.[9] The result of these changes is to focus on the desirability of finding ways to allow children with disabilities to succeed in regular classrooms and schools. Nonetheless, the child's individual needs must come first; not all children can be successfully educated in regular education settings.

In an attempt to more fully involve parents at all stages of decision making and perhaps to reduce the number of placement disputes, IDEA '97 requires that parents be included as members of any group that makes placement decisions.[10]

Because school violence has become an issue in recent years, school officials have sought the authority to suspend or expel all students, regardless of disability, who bring a dangerous weapon to school, use or possess illegal drugs, sell controlled substances, or are otherwise likely to injure themselves or others. This concern has resulted in a set of disciplinary provisions under IDEA '97 that allows removal to an interim placement without the same stay-put safeguard extended with respect to other changes of placement. Placement changes in the context of disciplinary actions are discussed in chapter 19.

Finally, IDEA '97 makes it clear that an education agency may report a crime to appropriate authorities and that IDEA allows state law enforcement agencies to carry out their responsibilities under federal and state criminal law.[11] Nonetheless, when the agency reports the crime, it must also ensure that copies of the child's special education and disciplinary records are transmitted for consideration by the authorities to whom it reports the crime.[12][†]

If the law enforcement authorities decide to take jurisdiction, presumably no violation of IDEA has occurred if a placement change results. The provision does not excuse the school, however, from honoring the procedural safeguards until law enforcement authorities remove the child from school. If there is a meaningful difference between reporting a crime and filing a juvenile court petition or a criminal complaint, then school

[†]The 1999 regulations require that transmission of copies of the child's educational record comply with FERPA. 34 C.F.R. § 300.529(b)(2). Presumably, what this means is that, without written parental consent, the child's record can be shared only (a) pursuant to a state law that allows disclosure if it concerns the juvenile justice system's ability to serve the student effectively prior to adjudication or (b) pursuant to a court order or subpoena for law enforcement purposes (see chapter 14).

†In *Wisconsin v. Trent N.,* 569
N.W.2d 719 (Wis. Ct. App.
1997), juvenile court proceedings were allowed to proceed
independently of IDEA proceedings, because, among other
reasons, only the district
attorney could file delinquency
proceedings.

officials should be careful to allow the judicial or law enforcement authorities to actually file the complaint.[†]

What Do the IDEA Regulations Add to the Statutory Language?

The IDEA implementing regulations flesh out the statutory LRE provisions. The LRE regulations reinforce the requirement that each public agency ensure the availability of a continuum of placement options and supplementary services in conjunction with regular class placement. Placement options include regular classes, special classes, special schools, home instruction, and instruction in hospitals and institutions. Resource rooms and itinerant instruction are viewed as supplementary services provided in conjunction with regular class placement.[13] A separate provision establishes that a public or private residential program, if necessary to provide special education and related services to a child with a disability, must be at no cost to the parents.[14]

In detailing various placement considerations, the regulations emphasize that placement decisions are to be made on an individualized basis. Each placement is to be "determined annually" and "based on the child's IEP." Moreover, each placement is to be "as close as possible to the child's home" and in the school the child would attend if not disabled, unless the IEP "requires some other arrangement."[15] In addition, in selecting the LRE, consideration must be given to "any potential harmful effect on the child or on the quality of services that he or she needs,"[16] a potentially important provision that has been frequently overlooked in the past.

The 1999 regulations contain a new provision that a child with a disability is not to be removed from education in "age-appropriate" regular classrooms solely because of necessary modifications in the general curriculum.[17] This statement was added in response to concerns that some children with cognitive disabilities might be removed from regular classrooms in an attempt to avoid accountability for their educational performance. Inability to function at grade level without modifications is not viewed in and of itself as a legitimate reason for removing special education students from age-appropriate regular classrooms. Instead, modifications to the general curriculum should accommodate the child's needs in this regard. This provision may seem to conflict with the national momentum to end "social promotions," but the term "age-appropriate regular classrooms" allows for classrooms with multiage groupings and may prove to be a more flexible concept than strict chronological age alone. Of course, if students with disabilities are kept in age-appropriate classrooms, their grades should not mask their true performance and progress.

How Do Courts Determine Whether Regular Classroom Placements Are the LRE?

Many school districts and parents alike have been disenchanted with placements for particular children with disabilities, because the settings were viewed either as not able to provide FAPE or as not constituting the LRE. Many parents have sought to have their children placed in private schools, including residential treatment centers, at public expense, not trusting the ability of the public schools to educate their children appropriately. This has been true particularly for students with severe learning disabilities, serious emotional disturbance, autism, and multiple disabilities. Other parents have preferred separate but state-operated programs, such as schools for the deaf and blind. At the same time, still other parents of children with disabilities have tried to close separate schools and institutions, especially separate facilities for students with mental and physical disabilities, and to return their children to regular public school settings. Controversies surrounding the placement of students in private facilities are discussed in chapter 18. Controversies about the placement of students in regular classrooms and neighborhood schools are covered in the material that follows.

Prior to IDEA '97, three different circuits of the U.S. Court of Appeals had established the dominant standards or tests for judging whether a regular education setting constituted the LRE for a given student. As a result of the increased emphasis on regular classroom placements under IDEA '97, courts can be expected to scrutinize disputes over regular classroom placements even more closely than in the past. Nonetheless, nothing in IDEA '97 contradicts the approaches taken in these cases, and it is helpful to understand the specific standard in the circuit in which your school district is located. As of 1999, the U.S. Supreme Court had not agreed to hear a case involving a regular classroom placement dispute, and until it does so, where a student lives could make a difference to the outcome of LRE disputes.

Circuits Without a Judicial Standard

The First, Second, Seventh, Tenth, and District of Columbia Circuits have not adopted a clear, explicit judicial standard for LRE issues involving regular classroom placements. If you live within these circuits, ask your attorney if there is a federal district court case that establishes the regular classroom placement standard for your particular school district. Your attorney should also be able to inform you when new circuit decisions interpret the standards of IDEA '97.

The *Roncker* Standard

In the 1983 case of *Roncker v. Walter*,[18] Neill Roncker's parents wanted him placed in a regular school instead of the special school for children with mental retardation in which the school district proposed to place him. It is important to realize, however, that Neill's parents were not seeking his placement in a regular education classroom. The standard adopted by the Sixth Circuit required the lower court to reexamine the facts and determine whether Neill's educational, physical, or emotional needs required a service that could be provided feasibly in a special education class in a regular education school. Frequently referred to as the *Roncker* "portability" or "feasibility" test, the standard also required a determination of whether the mainstreaming benefits to the child would be far outweighed by the benefits of the separate setting, whether the child would be a disruptive force in the regular setting, or whether the cost of the shift would take away too many funds from other children with disabilities. If the answer to any of these questions was yes, the *Roncker* decision indicated that the placement change would not be feasible.

The standard developed in *Roncker* has been followed in the Fourth, Sixth, and Eighth Circuits. Cases applying the *Roncker* standard have largely upheld services in other than the child's neighborhood school. Several court decisions have supported the cost savings and other efficiencies achieved by centralized services or facilities in nonneighborhood schools, so long as appropriate levels of mainstreaming were provided.[19] Other court decisions applying *Roncker* have upheld pullout placements as the LRE for given students.[20]

The *Daniel R.R.* Standard

In *Daniel R.R. v. State Board of Education*,[21] the parents of a young boy with Down syndrome sought court support for their son's placement in a regular education, half-day prekindergarten class. School officials had placed Daniel there at the parents' request but believed that the placement was failing Daniel. The Fifth Circuit ruled that the class was not Daniel's LRE. The class was found to be too stressful in spite of curriculum modifications and extra attention from Daniel's teacher. Evidence suggested that Daniel was falling asleep and developing a stutter.

Despite the outcome, the two-pronged test established in *Daniel R.R.* has become the basic standard for regular classroom placement in the Third, Fifth, and Eleventh Circuits. The standard asks two major questions when a child with a disability has been placed in a regular classroom:

1. *Has the school attempted to accommodate the student by providing sufficient supplementary aids and services and sufficient program modifications in the regular education setting?*

If the answer is no, IDEA is violated. (This test can be thought of as the "sufficiency" test.) If the answer is yes, the court then asks whether the student is benefiting, both academically and nonacademically, from the accommodations. In considering the question of benefit, the court also considers the student's effect on the regular education teacher and the other students.

In Daniel's situation, the court noted that to meet Daniel's developmental level would have required alterations in 90 to 100 percent of the curriculum. The court concluded that, in spite of the supplementary aids and services, Daniel was not benefiting from the placement, and that the effort to help him was draining the teacher's time and attention away from the other students. Although the parents argued that the opportunity for interaction with nondisabled students was a sufficient ground for mainstreaming him, the court concluded that opportunity for interaction alone was insufficient when balanced against the benefits of a special education placement.

2. *If the student cannot be accommodated in the regular education setting (i.e., is not benefiting despite sufficient efforts), has the public agency mainstreamed the student to the maximum extent appropriate?*

This question, in effect, is addressing the extent of social and physical mainstreaming in cases where instructional mainstreaming is inappropriate. In Daniel's case, the court concluded that mainstreaming Daniel for lunch and recess met the test. Interestingly, in subsequent years, Daniel was able to be successfully mainstreamed into regular classrooms.[22]

The Eleventh Circuit adopted the *Daniel R.R.* standard in *Greer v. Rome City School District*.[23] It applied the standard to a situation in which parents sought regular classroom placement for their daughter Christy, an elementary school student with Down syndrome. The placement had been rejected by the school. The court ordered regular class placement for Christy on the basis that her school district had not given proper consideration to whether regular classroom placement with supplementary aids and services could be accomplished. The school had considered only two limited options: a self-contained classroom with speech therapy as a related service, and a regular classroom with speech therapy. No consideration had been given to the range of supplementary services that Christy would need in the regular classroom, such as resource room services, itinerant instruction by a special educator within her classroom, or curriculum adjustments. In effect, the school "flunked" the first part of the *Daniel R.R.* test. (The school made another major error: it proposed an IEP and placement to the parents at the IEP meeting without having solicited parental input into the IEP.)

The court in *Greer* elaborated on the factors required to ascertain benefit under the *Daniel R.R.* standard. It mentioned that, in weighing the academic and nonacademic benefits of special versus regular class placements, the school board may consider whether regular class placement might cause a child to fall substantially behind peers with disabilities who are being educated in self-contained placements. It also added a cost factor to the *Daniel R.R.* two-pronged test. It specified that if the cost of regular classroom placement for the student with a disability would significantly reduce the money available for the education of other students (presumably including the nondisabled), then the mainstream placement would not be appropriate. Courts following the *Daniel R.R.* two-pronged standard frequently refer to it as the *Daniel R.R./Greer* test.

The *Rachel H.* Standard

The Ninth Circuit used its own test in deciding *Sacramento City Unified School District v. Rachel H.*[24] It upheld regular second-grade classroom placement for Rachel Holland, a young girl with mental retardation and significant speech and language deficits. Rachel had made academic, social, and behavioral progress in a private school classroom with nondisabled students. Her parents sought the same opportunities for her in a public school classroom. The court ruled that Rachel's IEP goals could be implemented satisfactorily in a regular classroom with curriculum modifications and the help of a part-time aide.

The Ninth Circuit said it was adopting the four-factor balancing test employed by the district court, but it paraphrased those factors as follows (district court language is in parentheses):

1. What are the educational benefits of full-time placement in a regular classroom? (How do the educational benefits of full-time placement in a regular

classroom with supplementary aids and services compare with special education placement?)

2. What are the nonacademic benefits of such a placement?

3. What effect does the student with disabilities have on the regular classroom teacher and children?

4. What are the costs of mainstreaming the student? (Do the costs significantly impact upon the education of other students?)

A Comparison of *Roncker, Daniel R.R. / Greer,* and *Rachel H.*

Similarities

1. All three standards consider the potential disruptive effect of a student with disabilities in the regular classroom.

2. All introduce cost factors.

3. All consider the benefits of regular classroom placement and weigh them against the benefits of special class placement.

4. All employ multifactored analyses. None conclude that *all* children with disabilities should be placed in regular education classrooms and allowed or forced to fail there before they can be placed elsewhere.

Differences

1. The standard in *Roncker* measures the costs of serving a student with disabilities against the needs of similar students, while the standards in *Rachel H.* and *Daniel R.R. / Greer* assess the impact of the costs on "other" students, presumably including those without disabilities.

2. Only the *Daniel R.R. / Greer* test includes the need to assess the extent of backup interactions with nondisabled students if instruction in the regular classroom is not appropriate.

3. Only the *Daniel R.R. / Greer* standard requires the school district to prove the sufficiency of its past or proposed efforts to serve a special education student with supplementary aids and services in the regular education classroom.

4. Only the *Daniel R.R. / Greer* and *Rachel H.* standards include assessment of the nonacademic as well as academic benefits of regular class placement. Issues 3 and 4 did not arise in *Roncker* because the plaintiff was not seeking regular class placement.)

Applying Judicial Standards to Differing Factual Situations

The test or standard adopted by a circuit to determine whether a student should be educated in a regular classroom must be applied to a specific set of facts. The standard alone does not dictate the outcome for a given student. A different set of facts can produce a different outcome, as can be seen by reviewing the outcome for Daniel R.R. and Christy Greer.

Applying *Rachel H.* to Different Facts

The case of *Clyde K. v. Puyallup School District*, 35 F. 3d 1396 (9th Cir. 1994) illustrates how the Ninth Circuit applied its *Rachel H.* standard to a student with an emotional disability. Ryan K., the son of Clyde K., had been diagnosed with ADHD and Tourette syndrome. Moreover, he demonstrated severe behavior problems in both his regular and resource classrooms in his high school. In addition to receiving some of his academic instruction in a resource room, he was receiving services from the school's behavioral specialist. He had permission to leave class whenever he needed time to relieve the "tics" that were a manifestation of his Tourette syndrome.

For his most recent school year, his academic tests results showed that his achievement had actually declined. The court decision reports that Ryan taunted other students with name-calling and profanity, insulted his teachers with vulgar comments, directed sexually explicit comments at female students, refused to follow directions, and kicked and hit classroom furniture. He had been suspended briefly on two occasions—the first for punching another student in the face, and the second for pushing another student's head into a door. Teachers and students reported that Ryan's behavior had a negative effect on them and was disrupting the learning process; he was socially ostracized and had few friends.

After Ryan assaulted a teacher, the school sought a court injunction allowing his removal to a self-contained placement called STARS (Students Temporarily Away from Regular School). His IEP could be implemented there, and the school district asserted that Ryan would be in a more structured environment and receive more individual attention at STARS. Ryan's parents argued that he should remain at his junior high school but should have a personal aide.

Apply the *Rachel H.* four-factor test and, on the basis of the facts provided, determine what you think the outcome should be.

Incorporation into IDEA '97 of Aspects of the *Daniel R.R./Greer* Standard

Under the *Daniel R.R./Greer* standard, if a school district has actually placed a student in a regular education classroom, then the district must make available a sufficient or reasonable array of support services rather than "dumping" the student. Also, before refusing to serve a student in a regular education classroom, the school district must consider whether it could serve the student effectively there if it provided a reasonably full set of support services. In effect, these aspects of the *Daniel R.R./Greer* standard have been incorporated into IDEA '97 through the IEP content requirements.

Also incorporated into IDEA '97 is the elaboration of the *Daniel R.R.* standard that was applied in *Oberti v. Board of Education*.[25] In *Oberti*, the Third Circuit upheld a regular classroom placement for Raphael Oberti, a young boy with Down syndrome, because the school did not demonstrate that it had tried to lessen the extent of the child's disruptive effect in his developmental kindergarten.[†] According to the court, the school was required to show that it had tried to reduce Raphael's temper tantrums and other behavioral problems by such supplementary aids and services as training for the regular educator, a behavioral management plan, and program modifications. Reflecting *Oberti*, IDEA '97 specifically requires that, prior to a proposed placement change for disciplinary reasons, hearing officers consider whether a school has made reasonable efforts to minimize the risk of harm to the child or others in the current placement (see chapter 19). Also, in developing the IEP, the IEP team must consider whether positive behavioral supports are required to address a student's behavioral needs.

IDEA '97 makes no mention of cost factors in determining the LRE. It makes no explicit reference to weighing the benefits of special placement versus regular class placement. At the same time, however, the regulatory provision that requires consideration of any harmful effect of a placement on the child or the quality of services needed creates an inference that some weighing of placement benefits may be acceptable. IDEA '97

[†]Despite the court's ruling in favor of a regular education placement, the Obertis decided not to place their son back in the public school system. For a moving account of the emotional tensions accompanying a ground-breaking case of this sort, see L. Schnaiberg, "Educating Raphael," *Education Week,* Jan. 17, 1996, pp. 18–26.

also does not refer to weighing academic and nonacademic benefits but instead relies on individual goal setting in the IEP to guide LRE decisions. (Presumably, some students with disabilities will have nonacademic goals, while others will not.) In any event, the regulatory analysis accompanying the 1999 regulations states that students are not required to fail in regular classrooms before being placed in other settings.[26]

The Neighborhood School Cases

Many parents of children with severe disabilities have sought placement for their children in their neighborhood schools. Court decisions, however, recognize that although IDEA expresses a strong preference for (and now a presumption in favor of) placement in regular *classrooms,* it does not mandate placement in the neighborhood *school.* In other words, although children with disabilities are to be educated with nondisabled children to the maximum extent appropriate, the law does not require that the children live in the same neighborhood.

As you will recall, the regulations specify that children should be educated in the schools they would attend if they were not disabled, but this preference is qualified by "unless the IEP . . . requires some other arrangement." In several cases that apply the *Roncker* standard, financial considerations were important in determining that the appropriate placement for given students was in schools other than their neighborhood schools. Although the courts in those cases were not asked to rule on whether a child has an absolute right to a neighborhood placement under IDEA, the decisions assume that no such right exists.

Several cases in the mid 1990s addressed the neighborhood school issue explicitly. For instance, in *Murray v. Montrose County School District RE-IJ*, the Tenth Circuit ruled that IDEA's LRE mandate neither created a right to placement in the neighborhood school nor a presumption in favor of such a placement. Instead, according to the court, although IDEA "commands schools to include or mainstream disabled children as much as possible, it says nothing about where, within a school district, that inclusion shall take place."[27] At most, the court concluded, IDEA creates a preference for education in the neighborhood school. Other cases have followed suit.[28] A subsequent Tenth Circuit decision in *Urban v. Jefferson County School District R-1* followed the ruling in *Murray* and also held that no greater right to neighborhood placement exists under Section 504 and ADA than exists under IDEA.[29]

Advocates of full inclusion see these recent appellate decisions as setbacks because they do not require a child to be educated with his or her neighborhood friends. Nonetheless, the decisions are complying with IDEA because they honor the requirement that children with disabilities be educated in regular classrooms with nondisabled children when such settings can provide FAPE.

The Politics of Inclusion

The movement to fully include all students with disabilities in regular education classrooms and schools found support in the initial IDEA preference for regular class placement. Inclusionists moved beyond the initial IDEA legal framework, however, by envisioning the elimination of the IDEA continuum of placement options. Although the continuum has been maintained in IDEA '97, the effects of the inclusion movement are reflected in the presumption that all children with disabilities will be placed in regular classrooms with support services and that the IEP team will describe the extent to which this will not occur.

IDEA '97 creates at least a partial paradigm shift for the delivery of services to IDEA students by emphasizing that special education is a set of services, not a particular kind of placement. Not viewing special education as a placement, however, infers that a blanket policy of inclusive placements may be as inappropriate as a blanket policy of pullout placements. The law balances the preference for inclusion with the bedrock belief that the education of children with disabilities must be individualized to meet the special needs of each child. Sometimes that still requires a pullout placement.

For school officials, inclusion continues to create tensions and dilemmas for three primary reasons: (a) parents are split about the value of inclusion for their children with disabilities, (b) special education professionals are also divided, and (c) the regular education community is deeply worried about its ability to meet the needs of students with severe disabilities in regular classrooms without extensive training and support in the classroom. Therefore, whether the IDEA '97 goal of more inclusive education can be successfully implemented is dependent on many factors outside the control of the laws themselves.

Many parents of students with learning disabilities, attention deficit disorders, visual impairments, and hearing impairments support the maintenance of a full continuum of placement options. These parents urge schools to respond to the individual needs of given students, some of whom, in their view, do not or will not benefit either academically or nonacademically from full-time placement in regular classroom settings. Members of the Deaf community (those who use American Sign Language as their primary language and identify themselves as having a Deaf culture) have been especially vocal in urging retention of separate schools and specialized services in pullout settings for some students who are hard of hearing or deaf. The Deaf community fears that inclusion will erode their culture and fail to meet their highly specialized and separate sign language needs.

On the other hand, many parents of students with mental retardation argue equally forcefully that their children are harmed by removal from the regular education environment and benefit from the social and language modeling that is present in that setting. In particular, parents of children with severe mental retardation advocate full inclusion in the belief that it will produce more acceptance of their children in their neighborhoods and communities, especially as they age and prepare for postschool living.

Additionally, the needs of children with severe emotional disturbance and profound multiple disabilities create special dilemmas for both parents and educators. In many instances, the courts have recognized the overwhelming needs of these children and have ordered their placement in residential schools or treatment centers as the only location in which FAPE can be delivered (see chapter 18).

Professionals working with these various groups of children reflect differences in points of view just as parents do. They want good things to happen for children with disabilities, but they differ as to what will produce good outcomes. Then, too, other factors sometimes influence professional outlooks. While some school officials adopt inclusion on the grounds that it enhances the dignity and value of all persons with disabilities, others adopt it because they believe they can save money through a more uniform delivery system. In either event, educators and parents should be aware of two realities: (a) in spite of the IDEA '97 preference for inclusion whenever appropriate, the statute does not support blanket policies of service delivery, nor do court interpretations of the statute, and (b) if children with disabilities are to succeed in regular classrooms, they must be provided with appropriate supplementary aids and services and program modifications. Dumping such children into regular classrooms without the necessary supports serves no one.

Placement Trends

Although placement disputes have generated more litigation than virtually all other IDEA issues, it is important to keep in perspective the fact that most children with disabilities are educated in regular classroom settings for at least part of the day. The heat generated by placement disputes is inversely proportional to the number of children affected.

According to the most recent OSEP statistics, only 4.4% of students with disabilities ages 6–21 did not attend regular education schools. Most of these students were in separate day schools; fewer than 1.5% were in residential facilities or homebound/hospital settings. The disability categories with the highest percentage of children who are not in schools with their nondisabled peers are autism and deaf-blindness.[30]

Of the 95% of students with disabilities who were attending schools with nondisabled peers in 1995–96, more than 45% were being removed for less than 21% of the school day, while close to 30% were receiving resource room services for anywhere from 21%–60% of the school day. About 22% were spending more than 60% of the school day in separate classes. According to OSEP, the figures for the latter group have remained relatively stable during the 1990s. At the same time, the figures for those spending from 21%–60% of their time in resource rooms have been decreasing as the figures in the less than 21% group have been increasing.[31] Nonetheless, the percentage of students in inclusive settings varies considerably by age group, disability group, and state, raising issues that deserve further examination by researchers and policy makers.

Review

1.   Explain the legal meaning of LRE.

LRE refers to the setting closest to the regular education classroom in which FAPE can be delivered. It may or may not be the regular education classroom.

2.   Why does IDEA prefer that children with disabilities be educated with their nondisabled peers?

It helps both sets of children to learn to work and play together, just as they will need to do as adults after they leave school. The IEP chapter provides other reasons: for instance, it encourages higher expectations and better postschool outcomes than have been achieved to date.

3.   Why does IDEA '97 continue to require a continuum of placement options?

Not all children with disabilities can be appropriately educated in one type of setting.

4.   Why are the courts deciding that all children with disabilities do not have to be educated in their neighborhood schools?

Although IDEA specifies that children with disabilities and children without disabilities must be educated together to the maximum extent appropriate, it does not require that the children be neighborhood friends. The IDEA regulations, however, go beyond the statute by adding a preference that children be educated in their neighborhood schools unless their IEP dictates otherwise. The preference has not been elevated to a legal right.

5.   How does IDEA '97 incorporate aspects of the *Daniel R.R./Greer* standard?

It establishes a presumption in favor of regular classroom placement with a full set of supplementary aids and services, including program modifications and supports for school personnel. It encourages the use of positive behavioral interventions in regular classrooms before deciding that a misbehaving child with a disability is too disruptive to remain there. In addition, it requires a hearing officer to consider whether a school district has attempted to reduce a child's misbehaviors before deciding to change the child's placement for disciplinary reasons.

Notes

[1] 343 F. Supp. 279 (E.D. Pa. 1972).

[2] 348 F. Supp. 866 (D.D.C. 1972).

[3] 34 C.F.R. § 300.550 (1995).

[4] 20 U.S.C.S § 1412(a)(5)(1998).

[5] 20 U.S.C. § 1412(5)(B) (1994).

[6] 20 U.S.C.S. § 1412(a)(5)(A)(1998).

[7] *Id.* § 1414(d)(1)(A)(iv).

[8] *Id.* § 1414(d)(1)(A)(iii).

[9] *Id.*

[10] 20 U.S.C.S. § 1414(f)

[11] *Id.* § 1415(k)(9)(A).

[12] *Id.* § 1415(k)(9)(B).

[13] 34 C.F.R. § 300.351.

[14] *Id.* § 300.302.

[15] *Id.* § 300.552(b) and (c).

[16] *Id.* § 300.552(d).

[17] *Id.* § 300.552(e).

[18] 700 F.2d 1058 (6th Cir. 1983).

[19] *See* Hudson v. Bloomfield Hills Pub. Sch., 910 F. Supp. 1291 (E.D. Mich. 1995), aff'd, 108 F.3d 112 (6th Cir. 1997); Schuldt v. Mankato Indep. Sch. Dist., 937 F.2d 1357 (8th Cir. 1991); Barnett v. Fairfax County Sch. Bd., 927 F.2d 146 (4th Cir. 1991); DeVries v. Fairfax County Sch. Bd., 882 F.2d 876 (4th Cir. 1989).

[20] *See, e.g.,* McWhirt v. Williamson County Sch., 28 F.3d 1213 (6th Cir. 1994); Kari H. v. Franklin Special Sch. Dist., 23 IDELR 538 (M.D. Tenn. 1995).

[21] 874 F.2d 1036 (5th Cir. 1989).

[22] Personal conversation with Daniel's attorney, Reed Martin.

[23] 950 F.2d 688 (11th Cir. 1991), *op. withdrawn*, 956 F.2d 1025 (1992), *reinstated*, 967 F.2d 470 (1992).

[24] 14 F.3d 1398 (9th Cir. 1994).

[25] 995 F.2d 1204 (3d Cir. 1993).

[26] *See* analysis accompanying 34 C.F.R. § 300.551 at Fed. Reg. 12638 (1999).

[27] 51 F.3d 921, 928–929 (10th Cir. 1995).

[28] *See* Kevin G. v. Cranston Sch. Comm., 130 F.3d 481 (1st Cir. 1997); Hudson v. Bloomfield Hills Pub. Sch., 108 F.3d 112 (6th Cir. 1997), affirming 910 F. Supp. 1291 (E.D. Mich. 1995); Flour Bluff Indep. Sch. Dist. v. Katherine M., 91 F.3d 689 (5th Cir. 1996).

[29] 89 F.3d 720 (10th Cir. 1996).

[30] U.S. Department of Education. (1998). *Twentieth Annual Report to Congress on the Implementation of IDEA* (Table A2). Washington, DC: U.S. Government Printing Office.

[31] *Id.* at pp. III-34 to III-36.

Selected Supplementary Resources

Bartlett, L., & McLeod, S. (1998). Inclusion and the regular class teacher under the IDEA. *Education Law Reporter, 128,* 1–14.

Ferguson, D. L. (1995). The real challenge of inclusion: Confessions of a 'rabid inclusionist.' *Phi Delta Kappan, 77,* 281–287.

Kauffman, J. M., & Hallahan, D. (1995). *The illusion of full inclusion.* Austin, TX: Pro-ed.

Yell, M. L. (1995). Least restrictive environment, inclusion, and students with disabilities: A legal analysis. *Journal of Special Education, 28,* 389–404.

Chapter 18

Placement of Students in Private Facilities Under IDEA

Overview

IDEA anticipated two kinds of private school placements of students with disabilities: (a) placement by a public agency when necessary for FAPE and (b) placement by parents when, for reasons other than FAPE, they prefer a private school for their child. In the first situation, the statute makes clear that the public agency is responsible for assuring that the placement in the private school is at no cost to the parents. In the second situation, the parents are responsible for tuition costs, but the education agency retains responsibility for the provision of some special education and related services to some private school students. Disputes requiring court resolution have arisen in both kinds of situations, and it is helpful for educators and parents to know something about these disputes so

that they can understand the implications of removing children with disabilities from public school and placing them in private school. These disputes are among the most expensive for school districts and can impact special education budgets heavily.

Placement in Private Facilities for FAPE Purposes

Private Day School Placements by School Districts

Sometimes a school district will choose to place a student with disabilities in a private special education day school at no cost to the parents. This occurs when, for various reasons, the district can neither provide special education and related services to a

261

particular student nor contract with another school district or public agency to provide the services. In such situations, school districts select a private school that meets state standards (the state often maintains such a list), involve the private school in the IEP development, and retain overall responsibility to ensure that the child's rights are honored and that the IEP requirements are met.[1]

Private Day School Placements by Parents

If a conflict arises as to whether a private setting is necessary for the provision of FAPE, parents may request a due process hearing and appeal an adverse decision to court. Numerous cases have arisen in which dissatisfied parents have pulled their children from the public school system and put them in private day schools and then awaited the outcome of administrative proceedings and judicial action. Two Supreme Court cases originally established the applicable reimbursement standards in these situations.

In the first Supreme Court case, *Burlington School Committee v. Massachusetts Department of Education*,[2] the Court held that if the public agency did not make FAPE available to the student and the parental placement was "proper" under IDEA, then parents were entitled to reimbursement for the costs of the private placement. The Court did not elaborate on the factors that would make a parental placement "proper" under IDEA.

In the second case, *Florence County School District Four v. Carter*,[3] the Supreme Court went beyond *Burlington* by holding that reimbursement could be awarded even when a parent selected a private school that did not meet state standards. The school district had argued that because the private school was not approved by the state for this particular placement, the school district should not have to reimburse the parents. The Court rejected this argument, concluding that a private school was not a public agency to whom the FAPE standards applied. In more concrete terms, because a public agency had not made the private placement, the private school was not obligated to develop an IEP or employ only certified teachers.

As in *Burlington*, the Supreme Court concluded in *Carter* that the "appropriate relief" authorized by IDEA gave a court the discretion to fashion an equitable remedy for a school district's denial of FAPE as long as the private school was otherwise "proper." It then stated that courts could determine what level of reimbursement was reasonable and that "[t]otal reimbursement will not be appropriate if the court determines that the cost of the private education was unreasonable."[4] School districts took some comfort in this statement, but the underlying lesson of *Carter* and *Burlington* is that school districts must be certain they are offering FAPE to eligible students lest they be held accountable for private school reimbursement costs (see chapter 20).[†]

In IDEA '97, Congress adopted the underlying rulings of *Burlington* and *Carter* that reimbursement was

[†]In a memorandum providing guidance on the *Carter* case to chief state school officers, OSEP opined that a court might be willing to compare the costs of an unapproved and approved private school in determining the amount of reimbursement. OSEP memorandum 94-14, 20 IDELR 1180 (OSEP 1994).

The Facts in the *Carter* Case

Shannon Carter was not identified as learning disabled until she was in the ninth grade. Her public school had tested her in seventh grade at her parents' request and had failed to identify what was later found to be a fairly severe learning disability. The school proposed regular ninth-grade classes for most of the day, with two periods per day in the resource room. Her parents rejected this IEP because they did not want Shannon instructed in the resource room with children with mental retardation and emotional illnesses. In response, the school proposed that Shannon receive individualized instruction from an itinerant special education teacher for three periods each week. The IEP established a goal of 4 months' progress in reading and math for the entire school year. Her reading was at a fifth-grade level, her math at a sixth-grade level.

Shannon's parents were dissatisfied with this IEP and challenged it at hearings and then in court. In the meantime, they placed her in a private school for children with learning disabilities, where she remained until her high school graduation. The private school evaluated Shannon quarterly and enrolled her in classes with low teacher-student ratios. She made significant progress, received passing marks, and increased her reading comprehension by third grade levels in her 3 years at the school. By the time the case reached the Supreme Court, the public school district had conceded that Shannon's ninth-grade IEP was inappropriate and had set only trivial progress goals. The issue before the Court was whether her parents could select a private school that did not meet state standards.

available to parents when their children were denied FAPE in public settings. It did not, however, speak to the issue of whether the parents' choice of placement must be "proper." The 1999 IDEA regulations filled that gap by specifying that the private placement must be "appropriate." Presumably, this means that the placement is allowing the student to progress appropriately, although the provision does not include a definition of the term. The provision does, however, state that "appropriate" does not mean that the placement must meet state standards.[5]

Congress went further than *Burlington* and *Carter* in certain other respects. For instance, it stated that not only a court but also a hearing officer is authorized to order reimbursement to parents for the cost of private placement when the public agency fails to provide FAPE in a timely manner.[6] The regulations add that an SEA is similarly authorized.[7] These provisions can result in saved court time and costs.

Congress then specified a number of conditions under which the amount of the reimbursement could be limited: (a) if the parents did not inform the IEP team at the most recent meeting they attended that they were rejecting the proposed placement and intended to place their child in private school at public expense, or if the parents did not provide written notice of that intent 10 business days prior to removing their child from public school; (b) if the parents did not make their child available for an evaluation by the public agency after proper notification of the agency's desire to do one; or (c) if a court found that the parents had acted unreasonably.

Prior notice from parents is meant to prevent them from surprising school districts, just as prior notice from school districts to parents is meant to prevent surprises to the parents. It allows the parties another opportunity to understand the seriousness of each other's concerns and see if an agreement can be reached. Also, when the child stops attending public school, the school will know what has happened.

Congress also specified that even if parents did not give the required notice, the amount of their reimbursement could not be reduced if: (a) the school district had prevented the parents from providing the required information, (b) the parents had not received notice of the requirement, (c) the parents were illiterate or could not write in English, or (d) compliance would have been likely to result in physical or serious emotional harm to the child.[8] This kind of detail obviously attempts to foresee various circumstances that would make it unfair to limit reimbursement.

Residential Placements

Another set of cases concerns the need for residential placement, usually for children with severe emotional disturbances or multiple and profound physical and intellectual disabilities. The IDEA regulations provide that when a residential placement, in either a public or a private program, "is necessary to provide special education and related services to a child with a disability, the program, including nonmedical care and room and board, must be at no cost to the parents of the child."[9]

The Supreme Court has not heard a residential placement case, but the same judicial standards established in the day school placement cases have been applied by the lower courts to residential placements. In other words, if the IEP developed for the student by the public agency has been inappropriate and FAPE has been unavailable, and if the private residential placement has been otherwise proper, reimbursement has been available. Numerous lower courts have awarded reimbursement to parents under this reasoning.[†] Now these courts have an explicit statutory basis for their reasoning, because the IDEA '97 reimbursement provisions apply to all private placements.

Other important issues arise in the residential placement cases, such as whether the placement is necessary for special education reasons. In general, courts have ordered residential placements when the students' educational, emotional, and behavioral needs are inseparable and/or when the students require continuous and closely supervised special education and related services throughout their waking hours in order to derive benefit or make progress toward IEP goals. If an LEA does not wish to continue to be obligated for the residential school tuition and room and board, then it needs to make comparable services available within its own system. Among

†It is interesting to compare *Drew P. v. Clarke County School District*, 877 F.2d 927 (11th Cir. 1989), with *Matta v. Board of Education.* 731 F. Supp. 253 (S.D. Ohio 1990). In *Drew P.*, the court concluded that a residential placement in Tokyo and Boston Higashi schools was proper under the *Burlington* standard. A year later, another court ruled, in *Matta*, that parents did not prove that the Tokyo and Boston Higashi schools were proper because the parents failed to investigate a recommended residential placement within the state.

the possibilities for offering comparable services are the provision of group home and day program combinations, respite care, parent training, after-school services, and perhaps even behavioral aides in the home.[10]

Reimbursement of all nonmedical costs, including room and board, is not available if the residential placement is not for special education purposes. Some residential placements of children with disabilities may be necessary for familial reasons (e.g., inability of the family to care for the child) or custodial reasons (e.g., drug addiction). In these situations, the special education needs themselves are not what drives the placement, and the LEA is not responsible for room and board and other nonmedical costs. Instead it should simply provide or pay for the appropriate special education and related services in the institutional setting.

Most courts have viewed hospital placements as medical placements and have held school districts responsible only for any special education instruction and related services.[11] Other courts have occasionally upheld a hospital placement as a special education placement but have attempted to separate the medical from the nonmedical costs by examining the hospital bills closely.[12] Defining nonmedical care by the hospital is not an easy task, because such services as occupational and physical therapy, psychiatric social work, and psychological counseling can be viewed in the hospital setting as either related services necessary for FAPE under IDEA or as excluded services related to the medical care.

Finally, school officials should be aware that the school district could be liable for residential placement costs on the basis of serious procedural failures, such as failure to (a) review a current placement at parental request, (b) develop an IEP in a timely fashion, or (c) review a child's needs and continuing eligibility at least every 3 years.[13]

The Interaction of FAPE and LRE
in Private School Placement Disputes

Private Residential Placements

Because residential placements do not easily mesh with IDEA's preference for educating nondisabled and disabled children together, the outcome of residential placement disputes in the lower courts usually turns on a determination of whether *only* a residential placement can provide FAPE.[14] The usual priority for resolving a FAPE dispute in the residential placement cases is to first determine the availability of FAPE in the public day school. If it is available, then that setting will facilitate more interaction than a residential school or a treatment center and will be the LRE for the student. If, however, FAPE is unavailable in a day school, even with extensive support services, then the need for FAPE will override the preference for more inclusive settings. In other words, the two considerations have not usually been viewed as equal—FAPE has been the first consideration, and the preference for the interaction of disabled and nondisabled children has been second. If FAPE has been available in both or all the alternatives under dispute, however, the setting closest to the regular education environment has been selected (see chapter 17).

Private Day School Placements

The Supreme Court did not factor IDEA's preference for the regular education classroom into its decisions in *Burlington* and *Carter*, but the statutory preference has been reflected in lower court, private day school FAPE cases. A leading example is *Roland M. v. Concord School Committee*.[15]

In *Roland M.*, the First Circuit was asked to rule on whether placement in a public high school provided FAPE. The parents preferred what they saw as an academically superior placement for their son in a private school for students with learning disabilities. They argued that only the private placement met the Massachusetts FAPE standard, which required the student's "maximum possible development"—a standard arguably higher than the federal FAPE standard (see chapter 15).

In ruling that the public placement met both the federal and the state standard, the court considered the nonacademic benefits of the student's public school IEP. Those benefits included the provision of occupational therapy and socialization skills training. The First Circuit also noted the availability of interaction with nondisabled peers in the public school setting.

The court in *Roland M.* concluded that analyzing the appropriateness of an IEP required balancing the LRE requirements with the FAPE determination. The actual language in the decision suggests equal status. If the court's position were interpreted to mean that FAPE has not been provided unless some degree of interaction with nondisabled students is available, it would erode a multitude of private placement decisions under IDEA. In the past, the better interpretation of the *Roland M.* language has been that one should ask how important interaction with the nondisabled is to achieve a student's individualized educational needs and goals. Whether future case law will shift as a result of IDEA '97 language encouraging more inclusive education remains to be seen.

Voluntary Placements in Private Facilities for Non-FAPE Purposes

Many parents voluntarily enroll their children with disabilities in private school because of preferences for religious education, lower teacher-pupil ratios, a particular curriculum or instructional method, and so forth. When parents make a private placement for reasons other than public failure to provide FAPE, IDEA requires that parents accept responsibility for the tuition costs.

Notwithstanding the public agency's lack of obligation to pay for private education in the above circumstances, IDEA requires education agencies to identify, locate, and evaluate all students with suspected disabilities, whether in public or private schools.[16] In other words, IDEA's "child-find" requirements apply to both settings, which was also true prior to IDEA '97. In addition, from its inception IDEA has obligated each SEA to ensure that

[t]o the extent consistent with the number and location of children with disabilities in the State who are enrolled by their parents in private elementary and secondary schools, provision is made for the participation of those children in the program assisted or carried out under [Part B] by providing for such children special education and related services. . . .[17]

Under IDEA '97, these services are to be provided in accordance with certain requirements; chief among them is that the amounts spent by an LEA on these private school students need not exceed an amount equal to the students' proportionate share of federal funds under Part B.[18] If 10% of the students eligible for FAPE are voluntarily enrolled in private schools, then 10% of the state's IDEA allocation under Part B (assistance to states) must be spent to address their needs for special education and related services.

The proportionate expenditure provision resolves a long-standing debate by clearly indicating that only federal IDEA funds must be spent on parentally placed private school children with disabilities. SEAs and LEAs do not have to spend their own money, although IDEA does not prohibit it. On the other hand, another aspect of the meaning of proportionate expenditures is ambiguous. The statute does not clarify whether each student should get his or her proportionate share of the federal funds or whether the total is to be allocated collectively for whichever private school students with disabilities an LEA chooses to serve. The 1999 regulations adopt the latter view. They reiterate OSEP's earlier position that an education agency may elect not to serve every such child[19] and that students voluntarily placed by parents at a private school are not entitled to receive the same special education services or the same amount of services they would have received in the public schools.[20] Nonetheless, the services must be provided by comparably qualified personnel.[21]

This means that when parents opt not to take advantage of FAPE for their children in the public setting, special education services become a privilege offered at the option of the public agency. An LEA can select which private school students to serve, although decisions cannot be made until consultation with "appropriate representatives of private school children with disabilities."[22] Instead of an IEP for the selected students, a "services plan" must be developed. The particular services must comply with the IEP requirements only to the extent appropriate.[23]

On what basis may an LEA, after consulting with representatives of private school children with disabilities, select or reject private school students for receipt of special education and related services? The regulations mention the following factors: the proportionate share of federal funding available to an LEA for private school students "residing" within its jurisdiction,[†] the number of private school students with disabilities, their needs, and their location.[24] This does not make the process absolutely clear, but the final selection rests with the LEA.

In the past, in an attempt to avoid service disputes and to cooperate with parents of private school children with disabilities, many school districts created "dual enrollment" arrangements. Dual enrollment allowed the private school student to attend private school for most classes but attend public school for special education and related services. This model usually required transportation arrangements, but it worked for many children. Other disputes arose, however, when the services were desired or needed at the private school site. These disputes were resolved at due process hearings, subject to court appeal.

The 1999 regulations state that due process hearings do not apply to complaints about the availability and delivery of special services to voluntarily enrolled private school students with disabilities. Instead, complaints must be directed to the SEA, which will use its complaint procedures to investigate compliance with the regulations.[25] The due process hearing procedures do apply, however, to claims that the LEA failed to evaluate a private school student for eligibility under IDEA.[26] The need to identify and evaluate all potential IDEA students is especially important now that an accurate count is needed to generate the proportion of federal funds that must be spent on private school students with disabilities.

[†]"Residing" in a jurisdiction has a technical meaning that does not necessarily extend to all students who have been placed in a private school located within the jurisdiction of the LEA.

Prior to IDEA '97, the court cases that attempted to interpret the meaning of the private school provisions produced conflicting decisions about the extent of LEA obligations to private school students with disabilities. Although the conflict has been partially resolved by IDEA '97, one can anticipate that the 1999 regulations will generate their own set of court challenges, perhaps on the grounds that they exceed the statutory language concerning proportionate spending. Another argument is that denying special education and related services to some private school students with disabilities who need them conflicts with the underlying purposes of IDEA to deliver FAPE to all eligible students with disabilities, arguably regardless of whether they are enrolled in public or private school. How future cases will be decided is of considerable interest to schools and parents alike.

Special Education Services on the Site of Religious Schools

Ever since 1985, when the Supreme Court decided *Aguilar v. Felton*,[27] many school officials have assumed that no special education services could be delivered on the site of religious schools without running counter to the Establishment Clause of the First Amendment to the U.S. Constitution. This assumption has proved incorrect.

The Establishment Clause honors the separation of church and state by prohibiting the U.S. Congress from making any law "respecting the establishment of religion." This clause has generally been interpreted to require governmental agencies to remain neutral toward religion, neither favoring it by sponsoring any form of religious worship nor showing hostility toward it.

Aguilar was a case in which the provision of publicly funded remedial instruction to "educationally deprived" students on the site of religious schools was held to violate the Establishment Clause. The Supreme Court concluded that the instruction unduly entangled the school district in religious matters by requiring excessive monitoring of the remedial teachers and by requiring administrative cooperation with the religious schools. However, the Supreme Court approached the separation issue differently when it subsequently ruled, in *Zobrest v. Catalina Foothills School District*,[28] that the use of a publicly paid sign language interpreter at a religious school was not a violation of the Establishment Clause. In the Court's view, such a related service to a hearing impaired student at a Catholic high school did not have the effect of directly benefiting the religious school nor of inculcating religious beliefs. The interpreter was viewed as a neutral conduit for the messages but not as the one who actually generated the instructional messages.

Although *Zobrest* ruled that the Constitution did not prohibit interpreter services, the case did not address whether IDEA requires the provision of special education or related services on the site of religious schools. IDEA '97 addresses this issue by stating that IDEA services may be provided on the premises of religious schools "to the extent consistent with law."[29] In other words, the statute itself creates neither a mandate for the delivery of such on-site services nor a blanket prohibition of them.[30†]

In 1997, after unusual procedural moves in the lower courts, the Supreme Court agreed to reexamine its decision in *Aguilar v. Felton*. It concluded that, under its evolving standards, *Aguilar* was no longer good law and that on-site remedial services to educationally deprived (Title I) students did not violate the Establishment Clause.[31] The clear inference is that the Constitution does not prevent LEAs from delivering special education instruction on the site of a religious school. Whether the law of a state would prevent it is another matter.

Of course, one should recall that any necessarily on-site related services like sign language interpretation and clean intermittent catheterization would not be IDEA services in the absence of a need for special education itself. Under IDEA, related services are linked to the delivery of special education.[‡] Therefore, if the religious school student declines or is ineligible for special education at the public school or a neutral site, then no related services have to be delivered under IDEA at the religious school.

---

†In *Letter to Moore,* 20 IDELR 1213 (OSEP 1993), OSEP advised that IDEA funds could be used to purchase a personal computer for use at a parochial school if it were required to mitigate the effects of the student's disability and not for religious instruction.

---

‡OSEP indicated in *Letter to Teague,* 20 IDELR 1462 (OSEP 1994), that states could decide on a case-by-case basis whether instructional modifications such as large-print books and interpreter services could be considered specially designed instruction (i.e., special education) for a particular student. The 1999 IDEA regulations also indicate that the determination of whether a specific related service could be considered special education is up to each state. 34 C.F.R. § 300.26(a)(2)(i).

Implications

Many implications arise from the material in this chapter. These are described below.

1. Public school officials can continue to determine when it is necessary to place a student at public expense in a private setting. If they want to avoid costly residential programs, however, they should be prepared to offer a full range of extended services (extended day and extended year) for children with severe disabilities whose needs cannot be met by a regular-length day program.

2. Public school officials should be conscientious about offering appropriate special education and related services to all IDEA students lest they be held accountable for the private school costs of students who have been removed from public school by their parents and enrolled in private school.

3. Parents should remember that they must keep school districts informed when they decide to remove their children with disabilities from public school on the grounds that FAPE is being denied.

4. Given the presumption established in IDEA '97 in favor of regular classroom settings, school districts and parents should give more thought to whether interaction with nondisabled students is important for a given student in a private special education school. In some cases, a child's interaction with other children with the same disabilities may also be important.

5. In determining which voluntarily enrolled private school students to serve and in what locations, public school officials will need to ascertain who should be involved as "appropriate representatives of private school children with disabilities." It is not clear, for instance, whether the representatives should come from the private schools, from associations of parents of private school children, or both.

6. Public school officials need to know whether their state law prohibits the delivery of any publicly funded services to children with disabilities volun-

tarily enrolled by their parents in private schools. If this is the case, IDEA has established a bypass arrangement whereby the Secretary of Education can arrange for the services and pay for them with a proportionate amount of federal funds under Part B of IDEA.

7. School officials and parents need to know if children who are being homeschooled are considered to be private school children under the law of their state. If they are, then the provisions about evaluation and services to voluntarily enrolled private school students must be followed.

Review

1. Who pays when a child with a disability is placed in a private day school or a residential school?

It depends on who makes the placement and on whether FAPE was available in the public setting. If the public agency makes the placement, then it will pay for it. If the parents made the placement because FAPE was not available in the public school, then parents may receive reimbursement for the reasonable nonmedical costs, including tuition and room and board, provided that the parents' choice of the private school was proper or appropriate in the eyes of the court, hearing officer, or SEA.

2. When have residential placements been upheld by the courts?

Generally, this has occurred when such a placement was the only setting in which FAPE could be delivered. Usually the student's educational, emotional, and behavioral needs were intertwined, and/or the student needed continuous and closely supervised special education and related services throughout his or her waking hours.

3. What kind of services can parents expect for their children with disabilities when they place those children in a private school when FAPE is available in the public school?

It depends on the state and the school district. The children may receive a number of special educational services, a few services, or no services. Sometimes the services may be provided at the public school; at other times they may be made available on the site of the private school. Parents have no guarantee that their children will receive the services they would have received in the public school.

Notes

[1] *See* 34 C.F.R. § 300.349(1999).

[2] 471 U.S. 359 (1985).

[3] 510 U.S. 7 (1993).

[4] *Id.* at 16.

[5] 34 C.F.R. § 300.403(c).

[6] 20 U.S.C.S. § 1412(a)(10)(C)(ii) (1998).

[7] 34 C.F.R. § 300.660.

[8] 20 U.S.C.S. § 1412(10)(C)(iv).

[9] 34 C.F.R. § 300.302.

[10] *See, e.g.*, Kerkam v. Superintendent, D.C. Pub. Sch., 931 F.2d 84 (D.C. Cir. 1991); Burke County Bd. of Educ. v. Denton, 895 F.2d 973 (4th Cir. 1990); Abrahamson v. Hershman, 701 F.2d 223 (1st Cir. 1983).

[11] *See, e.g.*, Tice v. Botetourt County Sch. Bd., 908 F.2d 1200 (4th Cir. 1990); Clovis Unified Sch. Dist. v. California Office of Admin. Hearings, 903 F.2d 635 (9th Cir. 1990); McKenzie v. Jefferson, 566 F. Supp. 404 (D.D.C. 1983).

[12] *See* Vander Malle v. Ambach, 667 F. Supp 1015 (S.D.N.Y. 1987). *Cf.* Babb v. Knox County Sch. System, 965 F.2d 104 (6th Cir. 1992)(upholding a hospital placement as necessary for FAPE).

[13] *See* Wirta v. District of Columbia, 859 F. Supp. 1 (D.D.C. 1994).

[14] *See, e.g.*, Matthews v. Davis, 742 F.2d 825 (4th Cir. 1984) (viewing round-the-clock training as necessary for any educational progress); Abrahamson v. Hershman, 701 F.2d 223 (1st Cir. 1983) (same). *See also* Cremeans v. Fairland Local Sch. Dist. Bd. of Educ., 633 N.E.2d 570 (Ohio Ct. App. 1993) (holding that residential placement was the only program that could provide FAPE for a student with autism and severely aggressive and disruptive behaviors).

[15] 910 F.2d 983 (1st Cir. 1990).

[16] 20 U.S.C.S. § 1412(a)(3); 34 C.F.R. § 300.451.

[17] 20 U.S.C.S. § 1412(a)(10)(A)(i).

[18] *Id. See also* 34 C.F.R. § 300.453(a).

[19] 34 C.F.R. § 300.454. *See also* Letter to Schmidt, 20 IDELR 1224 (OSEP 1993); Letter to Peters, 19 IDELR 974 (OSEP 1993); Letter to Mentink, 18 IDELR 276 (OSERS 1991); Letter to Livingston, 17 EHLR 523 (OSERS 1991).

[20] 34 C.F.R. § 300.455.

[21] *Id.*

[22] 34 C.F.R. § 300.454.

[23] *Id.* § 300.455.

[24] *Id.* § 300.454(b).

[25] *Id.* § 300.457.

[26] *Id.*

[27] 473 U.S. 402 (1985).

[28] 509 U.S. 1 (1993).

[29] 20 U.S.C.S. § 1412(a)(10)(A)(i)(II).

[30] *See* a similar position taken earlier in Letter to Orschel, 16 EHLR 1369 (OSERS 1990).

[31] The case was reopened and decided as *Agostini v. Felton*, 521 U.S. 203 (1997).

Suggested Supplementary Resources

Huefner, D. S. (1989). Special education residential placements under the Education for All Handicapped Children Act. *Journal of Law and Education, 18,* 411–440.

Mehfoud, K. S. (1994). *Special education services for private school students.* Horsham, PA: LRP.

Chapter 19

Discipline of Students Under IDEA

Background to IDEA '97

The Stay-Put Provision

Until 1994, IDEA made no mention of measures that could be used to discipline students with disabilities. All it contained was a requirement that while administrative or judicial proceedings were pending, the student was to "remain in the then current educational placement" unless the parents and state or local education agency agreed otherwise.[1] This was and is the "stay-put" provision.[2] It is a mechanism for assuring some stability so that a student is not shuffled back and forth in the course of a placement dispute (see chapter 13). It also has the effect of preventing long-term suspension and expulsion of students with disabilities until an impartial decision maker can determine the correct placement of the student.

In the case of dangerous or unduly disruptive students, many school officials over the years objected to the stay-put provision, arguing that it denied necessary flexibility and prevented school officials from protecting the safety of other students at school. Eventually their objections reached the United States Supreme Court and produced a controversial ruling in *Honig v Doe*.

Honig v. Doe

In *Honig v Doe*,[3] two adolescent boys with serious emotional disturbances were suspended indefinitely, pending their expulsion from two different public schools in Cali-

277

fornia. Both students challenged their suspensions and pending expulsions. Their cases were consolidated, and in 1988 the Supreme Court used the consolidated case to provide a definitive interpretation of the stay-put provision.

Both John Doe and Jack Smith had long records of troublesome behaviors. John Doe was suspended indefinitely when he choked another student and then kicked out a window while being escorted to the principal's office. The behaviors precipitating Jack Smith's indefinite suspension included a number of actions about which he had been warned previously, such as stealing, extorting, and making lewd comments to female classmates. All parties to the lawsuit acknowledged that the misbehaviors of both boys arose from their disabilities.

The Supreme Court ruled that the stay-put provision did not contain a "dangerousness exception." This position superseded lower court rulings in the Fifth and Eleventh Circuits.[4] The Court stated that Congress meant precisely what it said in the stay-put provision, particularly given the history of unwarranted exclusion of students with serious emotional disturbances leading up to the passage of IDEA. In other words, a school district could not automatically and unilaterally expel or indefinitely suspend a student with a disability for dangerous or disruptive behavior arising from the disability. Instead, to make a change of placement even for disciplinary reasons, the procedural safeguards of IDEA had to be honored. This meant that a multidisciplinary placement team had to evaluate the student's needs, judge the appropriateness or inappropriateness of the current placement, and determine the relationship of the misbehavior to the disability. If the team proposed a placement change and the parents challenged the change by requesting a hearing, then the stay-put provision applied until the proceedings (including appeals) were completed.

The Court offered only one way to circumvent the inevitable delay resulting from the hearing process: a court injunction to exclude the offending student from school. Requiring court permission for such an exclusion, the Court observed, would continue to honor the requirement that a school district not act unilaterally, yet it would still provide an opportunity for relief in urgent circumstances. This opportunity, in effect, paralleled the opportunity given to parents to bypass the hearing process when it would be futile or would provide an inadequate remedy for a particular problem.

Furthermore, the Supreme Court in *Honig* noted that an agency could use its normal procedures for dealing with unruly students, including the use of study carrels, time-outs, detention, restriction of privileges, and suspensions of up to 10 school days. Suspensions of that length, it held, did not constitute a change of placement and provided time for the placement team to reconvene and determine a future course of action.

Post-*Honig* Injunctions

If a school did not want to await the outcome of a hearing, *Honig* established that the school must bear the burden of proving in court the need for injunctive relief.[†] *Honig* indicated that when an injunction to keep a student out of school is sought, the stay-put provision creates a "presumption in favor of the child's current educational placement."[5] To overcome the presumption, a school district must prove that the current placement is "substantially likely to result in injury" to self or others.[6]

A number of school districts have successfully obtained post-*Honig* injunctions.[7] The most important case is *Light v. Parkway C-2 School District*,[8] which concerned an adolescent girl with severe, multiple mental and behavioral disabilities and aggressive tendencies. In *Light*, the Eighth Circuit rejected the parents' argument that a student must be "truly dangerous" and "intend" to cause injury before a court injunction could ensue. Instead, the court reiterated the *Honig* standard that the behavior simply must be substantially likely to cause injury, which to the *Light* court meant an "objective likelihood of injury."[9]

Crucially, the court in *Light* also added a requirement not present in *Honig* that, to obtain an injunction, a school district must show that it has made "reasonable efforts to accommodate the child's disabilities so as to minimize the likelihood"[10] that the child will injure self or others. In other words, the school must attempt to mitigate the effect of the misbehavior and the accompa-

[†]The general four-part test for an injunction to keep a student out of school requires a school district to show, (a) a substantial likelihood that it will prevail on the merits and (b) a substantial threat that the school and its students will suffer irreparable injury without the injunction. It must then prove that (c) the threatened injury to the school outweighs the threat of harm to the misbehaving student and (d) the injunction would not be adverse to the public interest. See *Texas City Independent School District v. Jorstad*, 752 F. Supp. 231, 233 (S.D. Tex. 1990).

nying risk of injury. The court deduced this requirement from IDEA's mandate that removal from the regular educational environment is to occur "only when the nature or severity of the disability is such that education in regular classes with the use of supplementary aids and services cannot be achieved satisfactorily."[11]

The school district in *Light* met its burden by carefully documenting both the rate of the student's kicking, hitting, biting, and other aggressive acts and the extensive steps it had taken to try to control them. Those steps included a staff-pupil ratio of 2:1 and assistance of behavior management specialists, inclusion facilitators, special education consultants, and crisis prevention trainers.

The Gun-Free Schools Act of 1994

As the visibility of violent incidents in school escalated in the mid-1990s, Congress and many state legislatures enacted no-tolerance laws that provided severe penalties for those who brought guns to school. The Gun-Free Schools Act of 1994[12] prohibits any state from receiving federal funds under the Improving America's Schools Act unless the state enacts a law requiring expulsion from the current school setting for at least 1 year of any student who brings a firearm, including an unloaded gun, onto the school grounds.[†] Exceptions to the expulsion requirement may be made by the school superintendent on a case-by-case basis. Although this latter provision could be viewed as providing the flexibility needed to ensure that Section 504 and IDEA are not violated, Congress also inserted a provision stating that the Gun-Free Schools Act was to be construed in accord with IDEA.[13] Congress also required school districts to have a policy requiring referral of a student who brings a firearm to school to the state's criminal justice or juvenile delinquency system.[‡]

A more explicit and carefully tailored means of disciplining IDEA students was incorporated into IDEA itself through a provision called the Jeffords Amendment.[14] This provided that a student with a disability who brought a firearm to school could be placed in an "interim alternative educational setting, in accordance with

---

[†]The definition of firearm incorporated into the Act is "(A) any weapon (including a starter gun) which will or is designed to or may readily be converted to expel a projectile by the action of an explosive; (B) the frame or receiver of any such weapon; (C) any firearm muffler or firearm silencer; or (D) any destructive device. Such term does not include an antique firearm." 18 U.S.C. § 921(a)(3).

[‡]The Gun-Free Schools Act of 1994 should not be confused with the Gun-Free School Zones Act of 1990. The latter was a federal criminal statute that prohibited possession of weapons on or within 1000 feet of school grounds. It was struck down by the Supreme Court as an unconstitutional exercise of congressional authority to regulate interstate commerce. (The Court concluded that weapons possession in a school zone was not an activity having a substantial impact on interstate commerce but was properly a matter for state, not federal, control.) *U.S. v. Lopez*, 514 U.S. 549 (1995). The Gun-Free Schools Act is not subject to such a challenge, because its requirements are simply a condition for receipt of federal funds.

State law, for not more than 45 days."[15] This placement was in lieu of being automatically expelled for a year from the current setting. The interim setting was to be determined by the student's IEP team. The 45-day interim placement became the student's stay-put placement for the purpose of any IDEA hearing procedures. This meant that while any administrative and judicial proceedings contesting the placement were ongoing, the student remained in the interim placement rather than being returned to what was the prior current placement.

The Jeffords Amendment obviously strengthened the hand of school districts in dealing with potentially violent students with disabilities while at the same time continuing to offer appropriate services to such students. That did not satisfy all legislators, however, and for the next 3 years, congressional subcommittees, OSEP staffers, and disability advocacy groups spent a great deal of time trying to reach a consensus about discipline under IDEA. OSEP's position and that of parent advocacy groups was that regardless of disciplinary placements, services to a child with a disability could not cease. Others, including many legislators, insisted that children with disabilities should be treated like children without disabilities and totally expelled from the school system if warranted. What emerged in IDEA '97 was a fragile compromise, full of procedural ambiguities.

IDEA '97

After the passage of IDEA '97, DOE took almost 2 years to finalize the IDEA regulations; one reason was disagreement over how key disciplinary provisions of the statute should be interpreted. The statutory and regulatory provisions affecting discipline are lengthy. The regulations clarify many of the ambiguities in the statute and arguably explain what the statute meant to say rather than what it actually said. Because the regulatory interpretation makes better sense than some of the statutory language, it is viewed by educators as a reasonable interpretation of the statute.

Although the statute and the regulations are complex, they both send two distinct, clear messages:

1. School personnel must improve their efforts to manage the misbehavior of disruptive or dangerous students with disabilities.

2. Schools can change the placements of such students quite quickly but must continue to serve them.

Underlying both messages is the importance of safe schools and the value of discipline for all students, including those with disabilities. Also underlying both messages is the importance of FAPE for all students with disabilities and the reality that expulsion would deny that hard-earned right. The need to honor both sets of values has produced the controversial compromise that continues to make many educators and legislators uncomfortable.

Part of the problem is that the disruptive and violent behaviors of children with severe emotional or mental disabilities tend to make the news. Yet there is no evidence that children with disabilities are likelier to be suspended and expelled than other children. Based on available data from the states, estimates are that fewer than 1% of all children with disabilities are involved in serious disciplinary problems, and only about 5% of the nearly six million IDEA students are expected to be suspended once or more during a school year.[16] Nonetheless, an unruly child is an unruly child, and teachers know how time-consuming one child can be. If schools can do a better job of managing misbehavior, then the disciplinary procedures will have to be invoked less often.

The current applied behavior analysis technologies are perhaps better suited to shape the behaviors of children with cognitive disabilities than emotional disorders. There is still much to learn about the factors contributing to emotional illness and how to improve the behaviors of the most difficult children with emotional disabilities. Nonetheless, IDEA '97 expects priority to be given to improving techniques and strategies for dealing with any child with a disability who exhibits harmful or disruptive behaviors.

Basic Standards

With that preface, the actual disciplinary provisions of IDEA '97 must be explained. What follows are the basic standards embodied in the statute, as interpreted and clarified by the 1999 regulations.

Consecutive v. Cumulative Suspension Days

1. Removal from school for up through 10 *consecutive* school days is a disciplinary option that is available for use with all misbehaving students, including students with disabilities. Removal for this length of time is not considered a change of placement and does not require educational services as long as the removal is applied consistently with all students.

   Removal for more than 10 consecutive school days becomes a change of placement.[17] This position reflects prior judicial rulings and the long-standing OSEP position.

2. Removal for a total of more than 10 *cumulative* school days in a given school year does not necessarily constitute a change of placement. Short-term removals of not more than 10 days may occur for separate incidents of misbehavior if they do not create a pattern indicating a disciplinary placement change (e.g., serial suspensions). This position is the same as the OCR position in enforcing Section 504. After removals cumulate to more than 10 school days, some services must continue to be provided to enable the student to appropriately progress in the general curriculum and advance toward achievement of IEP goals. "School personnel" (not the IEP team) in consultation with the special education teacher determine the extent and type of services required.[18]

Interim and Long-Term Placement Changes for Weapon and Drug Use and Other Substantial Risks of Injury

3. All students with disabilities who bring dangerous weapons or illegal drugs to school or school functions, or who use or possess them at school or school functions, can be removed unilaterally by "school personnel" to an interim alternative educational setting (IAES).[19] Students who sell or solicit the sale of a controlled substance at school or a school function can also be removed unilaterally. The regulations do not define "school personnel."

   Services and modifications in the IAES must be determined by the IEP team and must reflect IEP ser-

The definition of *weapon* used in IDEA '97 is the definition of *dangerous weapon* found in 18 U.S.C. § 930, which includes a weapon, device, instrument, material, or substance, animate or inanimate, that is used for or readily capable of causing death or serious bodily injury (except for a pocketknife with a blade less than 2.5 inches long). Given the breadth of this definition, a fist or chair could conceivably be a dangerous weapon under some circumstances. A paintball gun (i.e. a gun that fires paintballs) was not a dangerous weapon, according to the hearing officer in *Independent School District No. 279, Osseo Area Schools*, 30 IDELR 645 (SEA MN 1999).

vices needed to meet IEP goals (including progress in the general curriculum) as well as the misbehavior precipitating the placement change.[20]

This provision establishes a set of "dangerousness" exceptions that the Supreme Court did not find in the statute when it decided *Honig v. Doe*. The provision expands the reach of the former Jeffords Amendment to dangerous weapons other than firearms[†] and to illegal drug use or possession. The provision also allows for immediate disciplinary action against a student who attempts to sell or solicit the sale of a controlled substance such as ritalin, which can be legally prescribed for use with an ADHD student but could have a far different effect on another student.

4. Students who create a substantial risk of injury to themselves or others can also be removed to an IAES if a hearing officer orders the removal. Allowing a hearing officer to make this determination provides an option to going to court for a preliminary injunction or temporary restraining order. In either case, the burden of proving the likelihood of the injury rests with the school district, and the weight of the evidence must clearly favor the district's position. Among the factors to be weighed by the hearing officer are the appropriateness of the current placement and whether or not the school district has made reasonable efforts to minimize the risk of harm in the child's current placement.[21] In effect, this latter factor incorporates the decision in *Light v. Parkway*.

The hearing officer, not the IEP team, decides the IAES. School personnel who have consulted with the child's special education teacher may propose a setting, but the hearing officer determines whether it meets the statutory requirements. If it does not, the hearing officer is responsible for selecting some other placement that does.[22]

5. Ordinarily, placement in an IAES can continue only up to 45 calendar (not school) days.[23] Extensions, however, can be granted by a hearing officer if the school, at an expedited hearing, can demonstrate the continuing dangerousness of returning a child to his or her placement prior to the removal.[24]

More on *Clyde K. v. Puyallup School District*

In chapter 17, you were asked what you thought the Ninth Circuit ruling was in the case of *Clyde K. v. Puyallup School District*. Here is the answer. The court decided that Clyde could be kept in his STARS placement over the objection of his parents. According to the record, Clyde was experiencing few academic and nonacademic benefits from his regular school placement, and his behaviors were highly disruptive to his teachers and the other students. Cost was not a factor in the decision. The case was decided prior to IDEA '97.

If a hearing officer had been asked to rule on this placement dispute under IDEA '97, what else would the hearing officer have had to weigh before making a decision? You may want to reread the facts described in Chapter 17. Would the outcome have been the same, do you think?

---

6. A long-term suspension or expulsion from the prior placement beyond the 45-day period can be imposed as a disciplinary measure if the student's misbehavior is not a manifestation of the disability.[25] The IEP team must determine the extent of the services under these circumstances, but the services must be enough to allow progress in the general curriculum and toward IEP goals and must address the misbehavior precipitating the placement change.[26]

Manifestation Determinations

7. A determination of whether the misbehavior relates to the disability must be performed within 10 school days of the commencement of a disciplinary change of placement. If the student's misbehavior is a manifestation of the disability, then any deficiencies in the IEP or placement of the student must be remedied.[27] (One implication is that the student must be placed in his or her least restrictive environment, which may or may not be the prior placement.)

8. IDEA '97 presumes that the misbehavior is a manifestation of the disability but allows the presumption to be rebutted. Standards for doing so are established in the statute and reiterated in the regulations. First, the IEP team and other qualified personnel must meet and consider all relevant assessment information, classroom observations, the IEP itself, and the placement in which

the misbehavior occurred. Then they must determine that (a) the IEP and placement were appropriate when considered in relationship to the misbehavior and (b) special education, supplementary services, and behavioral interventions were delivered in a manner consistent with the IEP and placement. Finally, they must determine that the child's disability neither impaired his or her ability to understand the "impact and consequences" of the behavior nor the ability to control the misbehavior.[28]

Parental Options

9. If parents agree to a disciplinary placement change, as they often do, then procedures in items 3–8 above need not be invoked. A current or revised IEP can be implemented in the agreed-upon placement, and interim placement changes and team meetings to determine whether the behavior was a manifestation of the disability will not be required.[†]

†Some commentators point out that it may be wise to do a manifestation determination even in situations where parents agree to a change of placement. The reason is that the information gained through the process can be helpful in developing appropriate interventions to address the child's misbehavior.

10. If parents want to challenge any of the disciplinary actions regarding placement changes, they may do so at an "expedited" hearing. Timelines for expedited hearings are to be established by the SEA but must be within the 45-day timeline established for normal due process hearings, without any exceptions or extensions.[29]

In summary, this is how the statutory provisions are clarified in the regulations. Additional guidance about implementation is provided in the regulatory analysis that accompanies the regulations.

Functional Behavioral Assessments and Behavioral Intervention Plans

IDEA '97 requires functional behavioral assessments (FBAs) and behavioral intervention plans (BIPs) for children subject to disciplinary removals of more than 10 school days. In the interest of not overregulating, DOE declined to provide a definition of FBA, leaving its interpretation up to state or local school districts. If such an assessment has not been conducted and if a BIP has not been developed before a child is removed for more than 10 school days or before a change of placement is "commenced," then the IEP team must meet within 10 business days to develop an "assessment plan." (This phrase seems to refer to a plan for the FBA.) If the child already has a BIP, then the IEP team meets to review and modify the BIP and its implementation in whatever ways are necessary to address the misbehavior. If the child does not have a BIP, the school conducts the FBA required by the assessment plan; then, as soon as is practicable, the IEP team develops and implements the BIP.[30]

When Is a Day Not a Day?

The 1999 IDEA regulations differentiate *days*, *school days*, and *business days*. The duration of short-term removals of a child from his or her current placement is measured in school days. The duration of an interim placement (i.e., an IAES) is measured in days (i.e., calendar days). A manifestation determination must be made within 10 school days of the decision to initiate a disciplinary placement change. Functional behavioral assessments (FBAs) must be initiated within 10 business days of commencing a change of placement.

The regulations define school day as any day, including a partial day, that children are in attendance at school for instructional purposes. A business day usually means Monday through Friday, except for federal and state holidays, but if a holiday is specifically included in the designation of business day elsewhere in IDEA, then it's a business day. See 34 C.F.R. § 300.9.

If you are involved in a disciplinary placement change, you'll need your calendar by your side!

The regulatory analysis helps to explain the relationship of the BIP to the IEP. It states that if IEP teams are proactively addressing misbehaviors that impede a child's learning or that of others, then behavioral strategies, interventions, and supports included in the IEP will constitute the BIP.[31] This means that behavioral methods may be introduced into the IEP. (The analysis states that "in some cases, it may be appropriate to include teaching methods and approaches in a child's IEP."[32]) The analysis also states that if the child's IEP includes positive behavioral strategies to address behavior problems, then the appropriate response to misbehavior would almost always be to use the behavioral strategies rather than to implement a disciplinary suspension.[33] Of course, this assumes that the strategies selected by the IEP team are appropriate and will work and that the particular

One Behavioral Specialist's Approach to Functional Behavioral Assessment

Rob O'Neill, Associate Professor, Department of Special Education, University of Utah

What Is Functional Behavioral Assessment?

Functional behavioral assessment (FBA) is a process of gathering information about the things or events that influence a person's problem behaviors. These could either be *external* events in the person's environment (e.g., interactions with others, work demands), or *internal* things (e.g., illness, fatigue, depression).

Why Do We Do an FBA?

An FBA gathers information that is used to guide the development of a treatment or intervention plan. This plan should focus both on reducing or eliminating the problem behaviors and increasing appropriate desired behaviors.

How Do We Carry Out an FBA?

There are three major strategies for collecting FBA information.

Indirect / informant methods. This involves collecting information from teachers, parents, or other relevant persons through interviews or the use of checklists, rating scales, or questionnaires.

Systematic observation in typical settings. This involves conducting structured observations to collect data on the occurrence of the behavior and things that may be related to it. These observations are usually done during the person's typical routine or activities (e.g., during classroom work periods, on the playground).

Experimental manipulations (functional analysis). This involves setting up situations in which different events are directly manipulated (i.e., presented and withdrawn) to assess their effects on the person's problem behaviors. Data on the behavior are systematically collected to allow for comparisons of the effects of different manipulations.

What Should Be the Outcomes of a Good FBA?

1. A thorough description of all of the problem behaviors of concern, including how often they occur, how long, and how intense or potentially damaging they are. Also, it is important to identify behaviors that seem to typically occur together (e.g., the student yells, then throws things).

2. Identification of the general and more specific things and events that seem to "set off" or predict when and where the behaviors are going to occur (e.g., when the student is not getting attention, is asked to do particular activities, is ill, tired, or hungry).

3. Identification of the outcomes or consequences that the behavior receives that may be reinforcing and maintaining it (e.g., getting attention, getting help with work, avoiding or escaping work demands or activities).

4. Summarization of this information into statements or hypotheses about the behavior (e.g., "When Janna gets little sleep the night before and is asked to do math problems that are difficult for her, she will put her head down, refuse, and/or throw or destroy her books to escape having to do the task").

5. Some level of systematic observational data that supports the statements or hypotheses you've developed. This could be either the systematic observations or experimental manipulations mentioned above.

The whole purpose of conducting a FBA is to guide the development of a plan. Such a plan should include a comprehensive array of strategies, such as changing curriculum and instruction, teaching new alternative skills, and rewarding appropriate behaviors.

misbehavior was predictable. Most teachers will tell you that sometimes this is not the case and that nothing works at a given period of time with a given child. The analysis seems to recognize this possibility by acknowledging that an appropriate placement change may be implemented, subject to the parent's right to request a due process hearing.[34]

In-School Suspension and Bus Suspension

Other clarifications that may be of special interest relate to in-school suspension and bus suspension. The analysis indicates that OSEP will not count in-school suspension days as removal days as long as the suspension gives the child the opportunity to progress appropriately in the general curriculum, receive IEP services, and continue to participate with nondisabled children to the same extent as before the removal. Bus suspension would count as a day of suspension if transportation is a part of the child's IEP because unless the school district provides transportation in some other way, lack of transportation would deny the child access to the setting in which other necessary services are delivered.[35]

Protections for Children Not Yet Eligible

Under some circumstances, a child subject to disciplinary actions who has not been determined eligible under

IDEA can assert the protections of IDEA '97. The regulations clarify these circumstances. An LEA will be deemed to know of the child's disability and be required to offer IDEA protections if: (a) the parents requested an IDEA evaluation or expressed concern to school personnel that their child needs special education, (b) the child's behavior or performance has demonstrated the need for special education and was tied explicitly to characteristics associated with the IDEA definitions of the disabilities, or (c) a teacher or other district staff member has expressed concern to the director of special education or "other personnel in accordance with the agency's established child find or special education referral system (see chapter 11)."[36] In other words, the teacher's concern must have been expressed to someone in a position to act on that concern.

The school district will not be deemed to know that a child has a disability if, after receiving any of the above information, it concluded that an evaluation was unnecessary or it conducted an appropriate evaluation and determined that the child was not eligible. The LEA, however, must have provided parents with a notice and an explanation of its actions.[37]

Implications

The final regulations have attempted to provide flexibility that appeared to be lacking in the statute. The most important challenges and major issues surrounding disciplinary placements come from the extensive statutory requirements, not the final regulations.

In many ways, the disciplinary placement (IAES) options are not as limited as one might assume. Alternative settings to the current placement do not require districts to establish alternative schools. Many options remain open: self-contained settings, home instruction, self-contained placements within resource rooms, separate schools for students with disabilities, alternative schools, in-school suspensions, and so forth.

On the other hand, the service requirements in an IAES are quite formidable, even though 10-day removals and 45-day interim placements buy time for school officials to assess the needs of misbehaving students.

IEP teams must ensure that a student's services, regardless of the disciplinary placement, address progress in the general curriculum, implementation of IEP goals, and elimination of the misbehaviors triggering the disciplinary placement. IEP teams must also know how to conduct functional behavioral assessments and manifestation determinations and to develop behavioral intervention plans.

Everyone, including regular educators, special educators, paraprofessionals, school psychologists, social workers, and administrators, needs to receive training and develop skills to manage the behavior of difficult children with disabilities. This is the underlying message of the disciplinary provisions.

What Does the Future Hold?

Many members of the U.S. Congress remain dissatisfied with the IDEA '97 disciplinary provisions. A number of amendments have been referred to congressional committees for study, the most pointed of which would eliminate any federally imposed "dual system of discipline" and allow state and local school officials to discipline all students in the same manner if they so choose. The General Accounting Office has been charged with conducting a study of the discipline provisions to ascertain how they affect the ability of LEAs to maintain safe school environments. The report is due before the end of 1999. Of all the additions made by IDEA '97, the discipline section remains the most vulnerable. If the provisions are weakened, however, the problem of addressing the needs of difficult children will remain. Being allowed to exclude a child with disabilities from all educational services hardly seems to be a realistic, long-term solution.

Review

1. Can students with disabilities be removed from their current placements for at least 10 school days without invoking special IDEA placement procedures?

    Yes, if nondisabled students are treated similarly. Such a removal is considered an ordinary disciplinary action that can be applied to all students. (Remember that notice and a chance to defend oneself should be provided prior to the removal, however. This is a constitutional due process right of all students.)

2. Does IDEA '97 allow students with disabilities to be suspended or expelled from their current placement?

    Yes, for specified reasons, but IDEA procedures must be followed and time limits are imposed. Generally speaking, the student can be placed in an interim setting for up to 45 days, allowing time for the school to conduct behavioral assessments and develop behavioral interventions to address the misbehavior.

3. When can a long-term suspension or expulsion from the current setting be imposed?

    It can be imposed if the misbehavior is not a manifestation of the student's disability and when such a suspension or expulsion would be imposed on nondisabled students for the same misbehavior.

4. Can an IDEA student be disciplined by exclusion from all school district services?

    No. Cessation of services would be a denial of FAPE. Nonetheless, the student can be removed from the setting in which the misbehavior occurred.

Notes

[1] 20 U.S.C. § 1415(e)(3)(A)(1994).

[2] Now 20 U.S.C.S. § 1415(j) (1998).

[3] 484 U.S. 305 (1988).

[4] Jackson v. Franklin County Sch. Bd., 765 F.2d 535 (5th Cir. 1985); Victoria L. v. District Sch. Bd., 741 F.2d 369 (11th Cir. 1984).

[5] *Honig*, 484 U.S. at 328.

[6] *Id.*

[7] *See, e.g.*, East Islip Union Free Sch. Dist. v. Andersen *ex rel.* Chappel, 615 N.Y.S.2d 852 (N.Y. Sup. Ct. 1994).

[8] 41 F.3d 1223 (8th Cir. 1994).

[9] *Id.* at 1228.

[10] *Id.*

[11] *Id.* (quoting what was then 20 U.S.C. § 1412(5)(B)).

[12] 20 U.S.C. § 8921.

[13] 20 U.S.C.S. § 8921(c)(1995).

[14] 20 U.S.C.S § 1415(e)(3)(B)(1995).

[15] *Id.*

[16] Transcript of Judith Heumann's remarks at the live DOE broadcast on the IDEA '97 Regulations, March 18, 1999.

[17] 34 C.F.R. § 300.519.

[18] *Id.* and also § 300.121(d).

[19] *Id.* § 300.520(a)(2) and accompanying analysis at 64 Fed. Reg. 12619 (1999).

[20] 34 C.F.R. § 300.522.

[21] 34 C.F.R. § 300.521.

[22] *Id.* and accompanying analysis at 64 Fed. Reg. 12621 (1999).

[23] 34 C.F.R. § 300.520(a)(2) and § 300.9.

[24] *Id.* § 300.526(c)(4).

[25] *Id.* § 300.524 and accompanying analysis at 64 Fed. Reg. 12626–12627 (1999).

[26] 34 C.F.R. § 300.520 and analysis accompanying § 300.522 at 64 Fed. Reg. at 12622 (1999).

[27] 34 C.F.R. § 300.523(f).

[28] *Id.* § 300.523(c).

[29] *Id.* § 300.528 and accompanying analysis at 64 Fed. Reg. 12630 (1999).

[30] 34 C.F.R. § 300.520 and accompanying analysis at 64 Fed. Reg. 12618–12619 (1999).

[31] *See* analysis at 64 Fed. Reg. 12618–12619 (1999).

[32] Analysis accompanying 34 C.F.R. 300.347 at 64 Fed. Reg. 12595 (1999).

[33] *See* the analysis accompanying 34 C.F.R. § 300.523 at 64 Fed. Reg. 12626 (1999).

[34] *Id.*

[35] *See* the analysis accompanying 34 C.F.R. § 300.520 at 64 Fed. Reg. 12619 (1999).

[36] 34 C.F.R. § 300.527(b).

[37] *Id.* § 300.527 and accompanying analysis at 64 Fed. Reg. 12628–12629 (1999).

Selected Supplementary Resources

Evans, C. (1999). *Navigating the dual system of discipline: A guide for school site administrators and teachers.* Bloomington, IN: Indiana University Forum on Education.

Mead, J. F. (1998). Expressions of congressional intent: Examining the 1997 amendments to the IDEA. *Education Law Reporter, 127,* 511–531.

O'Neill, R. E., Horner, R. H., Albin, R. W., Sprague, J. R., Storey, K., & Newton, J. S. (1997). *Functional assessment and program development for problem behaviors: A practical handbook* (2nd ed.). Pacific Grove, CA: Brooks/Cole.

Rhode, G., Jensen, W. R., & Reavis, H. K. (1997). *The tough kid book*. Longmont, CO: Sopris West.

Yell, M. L. (1995). Clyde K. and Sheila K. v. Puyallup School District: The courts, inclusion, and students with behavioral disorders. *Behavioral Disorders, 20,* 179–189.

Chapter 20

Remedies Under IDEA

Judicial Relief Under IDEA

IDEA establishes legal rights and legal remedies for students with disabilities served under the statute. Because of this, it has spawned much litigation. The statute allows students or other parties still aggrieved after pursuing IDEA administrative hearing procedures to bring a civil action in state or federal court. In addition, a civil action is allowed when exhausting administrative remedies would be futile or would provide an inadequate remedy.[1] If a remedy is called for, the court is to "grant such relief as the court determines is appropriate."[2]

Under this broad grant of authority, courts have applied many different remedies for IDEA violations, the most typical of which is declaratory and injunctive relief, that is, orders to take a specific action to comply with the law or to stop acting in a way that violates the law. In addition, reimbursement and compensatory education have become increasingly prominent in the last decade as a means to compensate parents for IDEA violations. These kinds of relief fall under the category of *equitable relief*—relief that attempts to "make things right." On the other hand, monetary damages fall under the category of *legal relief*—providing money to help compensate for harm that cannot be undone, such as pain and suffering and economic harm. Monetary damages have remained essentially off-limits in most jurisdictions. Each major type of relief, and court cases awarding each type, are described below, so that educators and parents can understand the impact on a school district of IDEA violations.

Chapter Outline

Declaratory and Injunctive Relief

The most common relief under IDEA is declaratory and injunctive relief, where the rights of the parties are declared and illegal actions prohibited. Injunctions can take two forms: an order to do something and an order to stop doing something. Parents seek declaratory and injunctive relief to keep a school district from continuing an illegal behavior and to force a district to take action, such as changing a placement, providing appropriate services, or otherwise complying with IDEA.

Schools also seek court injunctions, especially to keep disruptive students from remaining in their current school placement. In such cases, the injunction lasts until a due process hearing determines whether to return the student to the placement from which he or she was removed or place the student in a different setting.

Sometimes a court orders an extensive set of actions—"affirmative remedies"—in an attempt to prevent past illegalities from continuing. In contrast to a fairly simple order, such as an order to develop an improved IEP, courts may issue detailed prescriptions of what is required when the situation is especially complex, when systemic issues are involved, or when the agency is viewed as especially stubborn and reluctant to change. *Jose P. v. Ambach*[3] is one of the best examples in special education law.

Jose P. v. Ambach was a class action in which the plaintiffs alleged systemwide violations of IDEA by the New York City schools, which found themselves ill equipped to fully comply with the law. The federal district court agreed with the plaintiffs and ordered an extensive set of actions to enforce compliance by the school district. Among other things, the court ordered the school district to provide timely evaluations, hire additional staff, provide school-based support teams, provide timely placements, prepare a booklet describing parent rights, translate documents into the native language of the parents, develop a plan to make a sufficient number of facilities physically accessible to students with physical disabilities, submit periodic reports, develop more coordinated and uniform data management systems, and enter into contracts with private providers when necessary to meet the evaluation timelines and provide related services. As a result of the decision, New York City agreed to hire 1,200 more special education teachers and clinical staff.[4]

More recently, a federal court in *Reusch v. Fountain*,[5] in response to a school district's inadequate procedural and substantive standards for extended school year (ESY) services, ordered the following set of remedies: extensive notice to parents at least 10 days before review of an IEP, establishment of an ample timeline for decisions and appeals concerning eligibility for ESY services, annual review of ESY decisions, a specific standard for ESY eligibility, individualized programming and placement decisions for each ESY student, staff training, ongoing monitoring, and a yearly progress report filed with the court.

Clearly, if a court determines that it is necessary to give multiple orders to a school district to bring about systemic change, it can do so in great detail. Most school districts, of course, would prefer never to be in the position of having to comply with such an extensive set of judicially imposed requirements. The requirements in the above cited cases remind one of the detailed requirements issued in desegregation cases and illustrate what can happen when systemic violations are occurring.

Reimbursement

We noted in chapter 18 that the Supreme Court ruled in *Burlington School Committee v. Massachusetts Department of Education* that parents can be reimbursed for the reasonable costs of a unilateral private placement for their child when FAPE is not available in the public setting and when the parent's placement is "proper."[6] In *Florence County School District v. Carter*, the Court went one step further in holding that a parentally selected private placement did not have to meet the FAPE requirements because FAPE is required only when the placement is made by a public agency.[7] Reflecting these decisions, reimbursement is now authorized by IDEA '97 as well.[8]

The Supreme Court explained in *Burlington* that reimbursement is not a monetary damage award but rather a way for a school district to pay for what it should have been providing all along.[9] In short, it is an equitable remedy. In both *Burlington* and *Carter*, the Court made clear that equitable considerations are relevant in fashioning the amount of monetary reimbursement and that not all a parent's educational costs are necessarily reimbursable.[10] One illustration of this principle is reflected in *Lascari v. Board of Education*,[11] where the New Jersey Supreme Court determined that the parents were entitled to reimbursement for their child's tuition at an out-of-state residential school but not for room and board expenses.

By extension, the reasonable costs of related services that a school district should have provided are also reimbursable if parents have to obtain them on their own. Such parentally obtained services as transportation,[12] private tutoring,[13] private counseling,[14] occupational therapy,[15] and speech therapy[16] have all been reimbursable. Even lost earnings by a parent as a result of time spent protecting the child's rights have been reimbursable.[17]

Compensatory Education

Compensatory education allows an extension of a student's entitlement to IDEA services beyond the statutory age limit. ESY services and additional tutoring are also options. These types of relief are a means of compensating for a school district's failure to provide FAPE to a given student during a period of time in which the child was eligible.

The recognition of compensatory education as a legitimate judicial remedy for the failure to provide FAPE accelerated after the Supreme Court's decision in *Burlington*. With the recognition that only affluent parents could afford to place their children in private school and sue for reimbursement came the recognition that an alternative remedy had to be available for less affluent parents. Compensatory education is that alternative. Some have called it the "poor-person's *Burlington*."

Numerous circuits of the U.S. Court of Appeals have acknowledged the viability of compensatory education as an equitable remedy for FAPE violations.[18] If you live in a state without a circuit court ruling, you should ascertain whether a state court decision limits the extent of compensatory education available in your jurisdiction.[†]

Due process hearing officers and the SEA have the authority to order compensatory education if necessary

†For instance, in *Natrona County School District No. 1 v. McKnight*, 764 P.2d 1039 (Wyo. 1988), the Wyoming Supreme Court held that no compensatory education was possible past a student's 21st birthday. The ruling was based on Wyoming law.

to remediate the denial of FAPE.[19] Therefore, litigation to achieve this result is not necessary in many instances.

Compensatory education will not be available after a student graduates from high school with a regular education diploma. The OSEP position is that because IDEA does not require states to provide postsecondary education, eligibility for IDEA services can end after receipt of a regular education diploma, assuming proper notice of the termination of special education services.[20] This means that a procedurally proper and bona fide graduation will terminate any obligation for educational services, even if a student has been denied FAPE sometime during the course of his or her public school education. This is because, notwithstanding a temporary denial of FAPE, the student went on to meet the required standards for graduation from public school. On the other hand, a pretextual "graduation" contrived to exit a student prematurely from the public school system or graduation with only a certification of completion could still subject a school district to the possibility of compensatory education after a student graduates.[†] In the past, the court cases have not always made this distinction explicit, but the 1999 IDEA regulations do.

Monetary Damages

As a general rule, monetary damages have not been available for violations of IDEA. Monetary damages are typically of two kinds: compensatory and punitive. *Compensatory damages* would include payments for pain and suffering resulting from illegal school district policies and practices; they could also include economic harm, such as lost future earnings. *Punitive damages* are more difficult to obtain and are imposed to deter a liable party from repeating behavior deemed malicious or especially reckless.

The majority view has been that these two types of damages would take money away from school districts that should be spent on educational programs and that Congress did not intend such a remedy when it enacted IDEA. Instead, injunctive relief has been seen as the appropriate remedy in most circumstances, with reimbursement or compensatory education available when necessary.

†If the statute of limitations (a law fixing the time within which parties must bring their lawsuits) has not expired, even a student over the statutory age may be able to bring a lawsuit in some jurisdictions. See, e.g., *Pihl v. Massachusetts Department of Education,* 9 F.3d 184 (1st Cir. 1993), and *Lester H. v. Gilhool,* 916 F. 2d 865 (3d Cir. 1990).

A 1992 Supreme Court decision in a Title IX sex discrimination case has raised some doubt as to whether the trend against monetary damages will hold. In *Franklin v. Gwinnett County Public Schools*,[21] the Court ruled that monetary damages were available for violation of Title IX's prohibition against sex discrimination in schools. The Court stated that without clear direction to the contrary from Congress, "we presume the availability of all appropriate remedies. . . ."[22] The ruling, however, also indicates that the violation must be intentional. The statutory language of Title IX relief is similar to that of IDEA, leading to speculation that the Court would uphold an award of monetary damages under IDEA in appropriate circumstances if the violation were intentional.

Several lower courts in the years since the *Franklin* decision have held that compensatory damages are available under IDEA,[23] while several others have held that they are not.[24] The issue is still unsettled.

Damages Under 42 U.S.C. Section 1983 for IDEA Violations   42 U.S.C. Section 1983 is a provision of the Ku Klux Klan Act of 1871, a post–Civil War statute initially intended to provide remedies for federal civil rights violations against African Americans. It has been revitalized in recent decades and now has far wider application. It provides that "[e]very person who, under color of [law], custom, or usage, of any State," deprives a U.S. citizen of any rights secured by the Constitution and laws "shall be liable to the party injured in an action at law, suit in equity, or other proper proceeding for redress."[25] In other words, those whose federal civil rights have been violated can sue for monetary damages as well as equitable relief. The allegedly violated rights are not named in Section 1983 itself but are found elsewhere in federal law—either in the Constitution or federal statutes. LEAs, along with other local governmental units, are considered "persons" for Section 1983 purposes.[26]

A provision of IDEA, first passed in 1986 and amended in 1990, seems to indicate that Section 1983 is available as a source of monetary damages in cases of IDEA violations. The provision states that

> Nothing in [IDEA] shall be construed to restrict or limit the rights, procedures, and remedies available under the Constitution, the Americans with Disabilities Act of 1990, title V [section 504] of the Rehabilitation Act of 1973, or other Federal statutes protecting the rights of children and youth with disabilities, except that before the filing of a civil action under such laws seeking relief that is also available under [Part B of IDEA], [administrative hearing procedures] shall be exhausted to the same extent as would be required had the action been brought under [Part B of IDEA].[27]

This language indicates, among other things, that if allegations of ADA and Section 504 violations are not independent of alleged IDEA violations, then a plaintiff must use the IDEA hearing procedures before going to court. What is ambiguous is whether the language referring to "other Federal statutes protecting the rights of children and youth with disabilities" actually includes Section 1983.[28] Some courts continue to view damages for IDEA violations as unavailable under Section 1983 because they find a comprehensive scheme of remedies available under IDEA,[29] while other courts have concluded that Section 1983 remedies are also available.[30] The argument may seem somewhat abstract, but what is really at stake is the availability of monetary damages under Section 1983 in a jurisdiction where they are unavailable under IDEA.

Court recognition of the viability of a Section 1983 claim for IDEA violations is not the same thing as actually obtaining an award for damages. Few cases have resulted in such awards because proving school district liability under Section 1983 for IDEA violations is difficult. Damages only follow actual provable injury, and only compensatory damages, not punitive damages, can be levied under Section 1983 against school districts.[31] Also, simple negligence or individual teacher error will not create liability for the school district. Damages can be awarded against school districts only if school boards or other policy makers violate the law as a matter of "policy or custom."[32] This is unlikely, although blanket separation or blanket inclusion policies that ignore the individualization requirement of IDEA might create damage liability if plaintiffs could prove their resultant injuries. Similarly, reckless failure to train teachers in the face of obvious need—for instance, to effectively manage behaviorally disturbed students—may open a district to liability for injuries flowing from the lack of training.[33]

School personnel can be sued under Section 1983 in their individual as well as their official capacities. If they ignore "clearly established" rights of which a reasonable person would have known, they may find traditional "good faith immunity" unavailable to them and be held personally liable.[34] Because the basic IDEA rights of students with disabilities are well established, ignorance of them is likely to be no excuse.

A Case of Individual Teacher Liability

A notable example of individual liability appears in *Doe v. Withers*, 20 IDELR 422 (W. Va. Cir. Ct. 1993), where a state court awarded $15,000 in damages in a Section 1983 suit against a public school history teacher for refusing to implement an IEP of a student with a learning disability. In direct contradiction to the IEP, the teacher declined to allow the student to take his exams orally and untimed, as a result of which the student failed the course. Of the award, $5,000 was in compensatory damages and $10,000 in punitive damages. This decision alerts teachers to their vulnerability if they refuse to implement a student's IEP.

Judicial Enforcement
Options for Noncompliance

In spite of the split of opinion as to whether Section 1983 provides a source of monetary damages for IDEA violations, courts agree that Section 1983 is available in one specific situation: when school districts or school officials refuse to carry out a court order or hearing decision in an IDEA case. In other words, Section 1983 is a mechanism to enforce a court order or administrative ruling under IDEA. Actual noncompliance with judicial or administrative rulings by either a school district or an individual clearly fits the Section 1983 requirements for damage awards: adoption or implementation of an illegal policy or custom, or an individual's violation of "clearly established" rights.

Other enforcement mechanisms are also available when an education agency refuses to comply with a court order. If damages are not the only fair way to provide a remedy, injunctions to force compliance will be preferred.[†] Other mechanisms include contempt and the appointment of a special master. Contempt usually involves fining or even jailing a party for failure to comply with a court order. A special master is a person with specific expertise who is appointed by the court to oversee and implement court rulings in especially complex cases.[‡] Such an appointment is authorized pursuant to Rule 53 of the Federal Rules of Civil Procedure. Use of contempt and/or a special master is quite rare in special education cases, yet instances do arise.

In *Duane B. v. Chester-Upland School District*,[35] a Pennsylvania school district and the State Board of Education failed to comply in a timely manner with the court's remedial orders. The court observed that fining defendants in special education cases is not an effective means to coerce compliance or remedy past noncompliance, so instead it appointed a special master to oversee the implementation of the court's earlier orders.

Similarly, the plaintiffs in *Jose P. v. Ambach* asked the judge to hold the New York City schools in contempt after several years of noncompliance with aspects of the original *Jose P.* order and judgment. The court agreed to do so but referred the noncompliance issues to a special master rather than imposing a fine or jail sentence.[36]

Another alternative to a fine or jail sentence for contempt of court was applied in *Murphy v. Timberlane Regional School District*.[37] There, because the district failed to comply with the original order, the court ordered additional compensatory education beyond the 2 years previously ordered.

[†]In *Battaglia v. Lexington School Committee*, 762 F. Supp. 416 (D. Mass. 1991) the court granted a preliminary injunction to parents and ordered a student placed immediately in a private school in order to enforce a hearing officer's order for private school placement.

[‡]A special master can also be appointed to manage parts of complex litigation. The federal district court in *Jose P. v. Ambach* appointed a special master to help with fact-finding and to make recommendations to the judge in the course of the litigation. See 669 F.2d 865 (2d Cir. 1982).

Administrative Enforcement
Options for IDEA Violations

The SEA is charged with responsibility for assuring that local school districts comply with IDEA.[38] In connection with this responsibility, the IDEA regulations require each SEA to adopt written procedures to investigate and resolve written complaints alleging substantive and/or procedural IDEA violations.[39] The procedure is an alternative to the due process hearing and can be essentially cost free to the complaining party (see chapter 13). If a public agency is out of compliance, the SEA may provide technical assistance and impose corrective actions. Ultimately, the state has the authority to withhold IDEA funds from a noncomplying school district.

The option of requesting the state to investigate noncompliance has been underutilized. It deserves more widespread use and offers a less adversarial means of resolving a dispute than due process hearings and litigation. As mentioned in chapter 13, anyone may bring a complaint alleging a violation of IDEA, including a teacher or teacher's association. The SEA can be asked to rule on a matter that concerns districtwide policies or on an individual matter that would otherwise have been subject to a due process hearing. No attorney has to be involved.

If the SEA rather than the LEA is out of compliance with IDEA, DOE is authorized to enforce compliance by withholding a state's IDEA funds or a part thereof until a state-level violation is remedied.[40] DOE has asserted its authority in several instances. One was in response to a North Carolina law that denied hearing officers the right to decide parents' reimbursement claims. As a result, North Carolina amended its law in 1990.[41] Another was in response to Virginia's insistence that it could terminate all educational services to misbehaving students with disabilities if the misbehavior did not result from the disability.[†]

†In *Virginia Department of Education v. Riley,* 86 F. 3d 1337 (4th Cir. 1996), the Fourth Circuit upheld the decision of the Secretary of Education to withhold IDEA (Part B) funds until Virginia's policy allowing expulsion of students with disabilities conformed to the DOE interpretation of the law.

Attorney's Fees

With passage of a 1986 amendment to IDEA entitled the Handicapped Children's Protection Act (HCPA), courts were authorized to award attorney's fees to a parent or guardian who was a "prevailing party" in an IDEA lawsuit.[42] The attorney's fee provision in the HCPA is not so much a remedy for a wrong committed as a means of giving parents access to court if they have a viable claim but insufficient financial resources. The attorney's fee provisions appear in the due process safeguards section of the statute. Because school districts tend to see it as a financial "remedy" available to parents, however, it is included in this chapter.[†]

†The HCPA nullified the Supreme Court's holding in *Smith v. Robinson*, 468 U.S. 992 (1984), that IDEA did not create a right to attorney's fees.

The definition of a "prevailing party" is technical. In general, it does not require parents to win on all issues or even the central issue but rather to have gained a significant benefit for their child that would not have resulted but for their action.[43] Of course, if a school district loses at the hearing stage and appeals in court, the parents must continue to prevail in court; if ultimately the school district wins, then the parents are not the prevailing party. One seeks legal fees only at the point that no further appeals are pending.

Rulings in five circuits of the U.S. Court of Appeals, plus dicta in two others, have concluded that when the school district chooses not to appeal an adverse hearing decision, the HCPA permits an independent action in court for attorney's fees by parents who prevailed at the hearing stage.[44] No circuits have rulings to the contrary. IDEA does not authorize a hearing officer to award attorney's fees, so the parent must go to court to collect them unless state law provides otherwise. Reimbursable fees will then extend not only to the parent's legal costs at the hearing stage but also to the legal fees for work in court to gain the fees for the legal work done at the hearing.

Attorney's fees are available for certain kinds of work done prior to the administrative hearing stage. Several cases have awarded fees for work done in obtaining settlement agreements.[45] IDEA '97 has resolved a judicial split over legal work at IEP meetings by specifying that attorney's fees may not be awarded in connection with any IEP meetings unless the meeting is convened as the result of a hearing or court action.[46] The rationale is that an IEP meeting is not a legal proceeding but an opportunity for joint problem solving by the IEP team and that legal representation at the meeting runs counter to the intent of the statute.

The actual amount of attorney's fees is determined by the court based on "rates prevailing in the community."[47] The court will also consider the extent to which the parent prevailed, the efficiency and competence of the legal representation, including the adequacy of documentation of time spent; the complexity of the issues, and similar factors. Ultimately, the amount set is to be "reasonable" under the circumstances of the case.[†] No fees are to be awarded if a parent rejects a timely settlement offer that turns out to be as favorable as what a court or hearing officer orders in the way of relief.[48]

Several courts have ruled that parents who are attorneys cannot receive fees for representing their children in IDEA actions because the purpose of the attorney's fee provision is to provide access to outside counsel, not to pay parents.[49] Other courts have ruled that parents who are not attorneys cannot represent their children in court but must obtain an attorney.[50] Parents will want to ascertain the law in their own jurisdiction in these matters before deciding to litigate.

[†]In *Beard v. Teska*, 31 F.3d 942 (10th Cir. 1994), the court reduced the reimbursable hourly rate from $200 to $125 to reflect what it determined to be the rate prevailing both within the community and the nation as a whole for work done on IDEA matters.

Implications

Both state and local school officials should be aware of the cost implications of equitable remedies available under IDEA. Reimbursement and compensatory education frequently cost more than FAPE would have, and they are widely available for both procedural and substantive violations of IDEA.

If relief short of monetary damages will provide a sufficient remedy, it is likely to be used. Monetary damages, where recognized, are likely to be reserved for situations in which another form of relief is insufficient to redress the grievance.

Monetary damages under Section 1983 can be invoked in some jurisdictions and not in others for IDEA violations when the IDEA remedies prove insufficient. Monetary damages require provable injury and are available against a school district only for intentional violations or perhaps for reckless indifference to a student's

IDEA rights. They are especially likely to be awarded when a court order or hearing decision is flaunted.

If a school district implements an illegal policy or if a teacher fails to honor a student's clearly established IDEA rights, neither ignorance of the law nor good intentions will provide an excuse under Section 1983.

Overall, the law is still unsettled with respect to the availability of monetary damages, and you should keep abreast of current case law in your own federal court jurisdiction.

The best defense against monetary damages, reimbursement, compensatory education, and other costly remedies is to provide FAPE in the first place and to comply with the procedural safeguards of IDEA. When disputes arise, negotiation, mediation, and a complaint to the SEA are tools that can prevent the need for more costly and adversarial hearings and litigation.

Review

1. What are the common forms of remedies that courts order for IDEA violations?

    These are declaratory relief, injunctions, reimbursement of educational costs at private schools, and compensatory education.

2. Under what circumstances are monetary damages most likely to be awarded?

    This occurs when IDEA violations are intentional, such as when a school district declines to implement a court ruling. The money is likelier to be awarded under Section 1983 than under IDEA itself.

3. What remedy can the SEA impose for IDEA violations?

    It can order compensatory education and monetary reimbursement; it is also authorized to take "other corrective action." Ultimately, it can withhold IDEA funds from a noncomplying LEA.

4. When can attorney's fees be awarded to parents?

    This can happen when the parents are ultimately the prevailing party.

Notes

[1] *See, e.g.*, Honig v. Doe, 484 U.S. 305 (1988).

[2] 20 U.S.C.S. § 1415(i)(2)(B)(1998).

[3] 669 F.2d 865 (2d Cir. 1982). The appellate decision contains a description of the lower court's unpublished December 1979 order and judgment.

[4] M. B. Fafard, R. E. Hanlon, & E. A. Bryson. (1986). Jose P. v. Ambach: Progress toward compliance, *Exceptional Children, 52,* 313–319.

[5] 872 F. Supp. 1421 (D. Md. 1994).

[6] 471 U.S. 359 (1985).

[7] 510 U.S. 7 (1993).

[8] 20 U.S.C.S. § 1412(a)(10)(C)(ii); 34 C.F.R. § 300.660 (1999).

[9] 471 U.S. at 370–371.

[10] *Id.* at 374; *Carter,* 510 U.S. at 16.

[11] 560 A.2d 1180 (N.J. 1989).

[12] Hurry v. Jones, 560 F. Supp. 500 (D.R.I. 1983), *aff'd in relevant part,* 734 F.2d 879 (1st Cir. 1984); Egg Harbor Township Bd. of Educ. v. S.O., 19 IDELR 15 (D.N.J. 1992); Northeast Central Sch. Dist. v. Sobol, 572 N.Y.S.2d 752 (1991), *aff'd as modified,* 595 N.E. 2d 339 (N.Y. 1992).

[13] W.G. v. Target Range Sch. Dist. No. 23, 960 F.2d 1479 (9th Cir. 1992); *In re* Conklin, 946 F.2d 306 (4th Cir. 1991).

[14] Straube v. Florida Union Free Sch. Dist., 801 F. Supp. 1164 (S.D.N.Y. 1992).

[15] Rapid City Sch. Dist. v. Vahle, 922 F.2d 476 (8th Cir. 1990).

[16] Johnson v. Lancaster-Lebanon Intermediate Unit 13, 757 F. Supp. 606 (E.D. Pa. 1991).

[17] Board of Educ. of Cabell County v. Dienelt, 843 F.2d 813 (4th Cir. 1988).

[18] *See, e.g.,* Pihl v. Massachusetts Dep't of Educ., 9 F.3d 184 (1st Cir. 1993); Lester H. v. Gilhool, 916 F.2d 865 (3d Cir. 1990); Burr v. Sobol, 888 F.2d 258 (2d Cir. 1989) (awarding compensatory education as a remedy for procedural violations); Jefferson County Bd. of Educ. v. Breen, 853 F.2d 853 (11th Cir. 1988); Miener v. Missouri, 800 F.2d 749 (8th Cir. 1986). *See also* Parents of Student W. v. Puyallup Sch. Dist., 31 F.3d 1489 (9th Cir. 1994) (acknowledging compensatory education in appropriate circumstances); Hall v. Knott County Bd. of Educ., 941 F.2d 402 (6th Cir. 1991) (approving, in dicta, the availability of compensatory education).

[19] See 34 C.F.R. § 300.660.

[20] *Id.* § 300.122(a)(3).

[21] 503 U.S. 60 (1992).

[22] *Id.* at 66.

[23] *See, e.g.,* Padilla v. School Dist. No. 1 of Denver, 35 F. Supp.2d 1260 (D. Colo. 1999); Emma C. v. Eastin, 985 F. Supp. 940 (N.D. Cal. 1997).

[24] *See, e.g.,* Sellers v. School Bd. of Manassas, 141 F.3d 524 (4th Cir. 1998); Fort Zumwalt Sch. Dist. v. Missouri State Bd. of Educ., 865 F. Supp. 604 (E.D. Mo. 1994).

[25] 42 U.S.C. § 1983 (1994).

[26] *See* Monell v. Dep't of Soc. Serv., 436 U.S. 658 (1978).

[27] 20 U.S.C.S § 1415(l)(1998).

[28] *See e.g.* Sellers v. School Bd. of Manassas, 141 F.3d 524 (4th Cir. 1991).

[29] *See id.*

[30] *See, e.g.,* W.B. v. Matula, 67 F.3d 484 (3d Cir. 1995); Mrs. W. v. Tirozzi, 832 F.2d 748 (2d Cir. 1987); Jackson v. Franklin County Sch. Bd., 806 F.2d 623 (5th Cir. 1986); Sean R. v. Board of Educ. of Woodbridge, 794 F. Supp. 467 (D. Conn. 1992).

[31] *See* City of Newport v. Fact Concerts, 453 U.S. 247 (1981). *But see* Woods v. New Jersey Dep't of Educ., 796 F. Supp. 767 (D.N.J. 1992) (stating that punitive damages may be available against the school district for IDEA violations even though unavailable under Section 1983).

[32] *See* Monell v. Dep't of Soc. Serv., 436 U.S. 658 (1978).

[33] *See* City of Canton v. Harris, 489 U.S. 378 (1989).

[34] *See* Harlow v. Fitzgerald, 457 U.S. 800 (1982). *See also* P.C. v. McLaughlin, 913 F.2d 1033 (2d Cir. 1990)

[35] 1994 U.S. Dist. LEXIS 18755 (E.D. Pa. 1994).

[36] 669 F.2d 865 (2d Cir. 1982).

[37] 855 F. Supp. 498 (D.N.H. 1994).

[38] 34 C.F.R. § 300.600.

[39] *Id.* §§ 300.660–.662.

[40] 20 U.S.C.S. § 1416; 34 C.F.R. § 300.587.

[41] *See* S-1 v. North Carolina State Bd. of Educ., 21 F.3d 49 (4th Cir. 1994).

[42] 20 U.S.C.S. § 1415(i)(3)(B–F).

[43] The majority view of what constitutes a prevailing party in IDEA lawsuits is the definition of prevailing party applied to Section 1983 lawsuits. *See* Texas State Teachers Ass'n v. Garland Indep. Sch. Dist., 489 U.S. 782 (1989); Hensley v. Eckerhart, 461 U.S. 424 (1983).

[44] Moore v. District of Columbia, 907 F.2d 165 (D.C. Cir. 1990); McSomebodies v. Burlingame Elementary Sch. Dist., 886 F.2d 1558 (9th Cir. 1989), *as supplemented*, 897 F.2d 974 (1990); Mitten v. Muscogee County Sch. Dist., 877 F.2d 932 (11th Cir. 1989); Duane M. v. Orleans Parish Sch. Bd., 861 F.2d 115 (5th Cir. 1988); Eggers v. Bullitt County Sch. Dist., 854 F.2d 892 (6th Cir. 1988); Counsel v. Dow, 849 F.2d 731, n.9 (dicta) (2d Cir. 1988); Arons v. New Jersey, 842 F.2d 58 (dicta) (3d Cir.1988).

[45] *See* E.M. v. Millville Bd. of Educ., 849 F. Supp. 312 (D.N.J. 1994); Eason v. Cullman County Comm'n. on Educ., 21 IDELR 739 (N.D. Ala. 1994); Masotti v. Tustin Unified Sch. Dist., 19 IDELR 480 (C.D. Cal. 1992).

[46] 20 U.S.C.S. § 1415(i)(3)(D)(ii).

[47] *Id.* § 1415(i)(3)(C).

[48] *Id.* § 1415(i)(3)(D)(i).

[49] *See, e.g.,* Erickson v. Board of Educ. of Baltimore County, 29 IDELR 478 (4th Cir. 1998); Rappaport v. Vance, 812 F. Supp. 609 (D. Md. 1993).

[50] *See, e.g.*, Collinsgru v. Palmyra Bd. of Educ., 161 F.3d 225 (3d Cir. 1998); Wenger v. Canastota Cent. Sch. Dist., 146 F.3d 123 (2d Cir. 1998), Devine v. Indian River County Sch. Bd., 121 F.3d 576 (11th Cir. 1997). A lay advocate, however, was allowed to represent the parent in *Connors v. Mills*, 34 F. Supp.2d 795 (N.D.N.Y. 1998).

Selected Supplementary Resources

Dagley, D. L. (1995). Enforcing compliance with IDEA: Dispute resolution and appropriate relief. *Preventing School Failure, 39,* 27–32.

Fisher, R., & Ury, W. (1991). *Getting to yes* (2nd ed.). Boston: Houghton Mifflin.

Goldberg, S. S., & Huefner, D. S. (1995). Dispute resolution in special education: An introduction to litigation alternatives. *Education Law Reporter, 99,* 703–711.

Zirkel, P. A. (1995). The remedy of compensatory education under the IDEA. *Education Law Reporter, 95,* 483–488.

Afterword

Law is a tool of society, providing order and setting expectations for our behavior. Although it is meant to provide stability, it is not static. It evolves over time to reflect changing needs and aspirations. Sometimes it gets it right; sometimes it gets it wrong. Sometimes we cannot agree on whether it gets it right or wrong. This is no less true for special education law than for any other body of law.

Court decisions will continue to interpret ambiguity in federal statutes and regulations. Statutes will continue to be amended, and regulations will reflect those amendments. Although state special education rules must conform to federal laws, they can go beyond the federal law to serve children with disabilities even better than the federal law requires. All of this means that there is a need for continuous learning, training, reflection, and assessment on our part.

IDEA '97 represents a considerable shift from its predecessors. It is more interested in results for children with disabilities, and it is more prescriptive than earlier versions. Some would say it represents a great deal of micromanagement by the federal government, with the disciplinary and IEP provisions leading the way. Whether the shift is wise or not is not the most important question. In general, a retreat to earlier positions does not provide a good solution for the 5.8 million children with disabilities currently being served, nor for those who come after them.

The level of federal funding has not kept pace with the level of government mandates. More resources are needed to meet the expectation that the individualized needs of the vast majority of children with disabilities can be met in regular classrooms with supplementary aids and services. More resources are needed to reduce teacher-pupil ratios in key areas, to recruit and train teachers who understand functional behavioral assessments and behavior intervention plans, to train and supply related service providers, such as school nurses or health care aides to work with children who are medically fragile, and so on.

More than financial resources are needed, however. As expectations mount and the law continues to evolve, we need to invest more of our personal resources in the education of children with disabilities if we want to achieve good results. There are many ways to invest. We can be constructive critics as well as supporters of the law. We can share our insights with policy makers. We can improve our skills in working collaboratively with one another. We can improve our behavior management skills or our skills in a given curriculum. We can improve our understanding of a particular disability or a particular child. Any one of these investments would be worthwhile.

Like all of us, children with disabilities are a diverse group; like all of us, they can learn and grow. Public schools are a good place for this to happen, but it requires continuing efforts on our part. Laws and regulations cannot make this happen alone; students with disabilities need people like you and me to convert their legal rights into educational realities.

Glossary of Legal Terms

adversary process: the method courts use to resolve disputes in which each side presents its case, subject to rules of evidence; an independent fact-finder (judge or jury) determines which side's evidence is most persuasive.

affirm: to uphold the opinion of a lower court on appeal.

allegation: an unsupported assertion made in a legal proceeding by a party who expects to prove it in court.

alternative dispute resolution: procedures for settling disputes by means other than litigation; e.g., by arbitration or mediation. Such procedures are usually less costly and faster.

appeal: a party's request to a higher court to review a decision by a lower court. In cases where the right exists, the appeal must be made according to certain procedures and limitations.

appellate court: any state or federal court empowered to review and amend the judgments of a lower court over which it has jurisdiction.

arbitrary: without rational basis, underlying reason, or guiding principle; nonrational, capricious, whimsical.

case law: a primary source of law or legal authority formed by the body of reported court cases.

certiorari (abbreviated as cert.)**:** a petition for a superior court to review the decision of a lower court. Review may be granted or denied at the discretion of the superior court.

citation: in legal writing, a notation that directs the reader to a specific source of authority, such as a court case, statute, regulation, or journal article.

civil action: a lawsuit, as opposed to a criminal prosecution, commenced in order to recover a private or civil right, or to obtain a remedy for the violation of such a right.

civil rights or civil liberties: personal, natural rights guaranteed and protected by the constitution; e.g., freedom of speech, and press, freedom from discrimination.

class action: a lawsuit commenced by one or more members of an ascertainable class who sue on behalf of themselves and others having the same complaint and seeking the same remedy.

code: a written collection of laws or regulations arranged according to an elaborate subject-matter classification scheme (e.g., the U.S. Code and Code of Federal Regulations).

color of law: generally, the semblance, without the substance, of legal right; misuse of power made possible because the wrongdoer is clothed with the authority of the State.

common law: law deriving its authority not from legislative enactments, but from ancient and continuing custom or from the judgments and decrees of courts enforcing those customs.

complaint: the original pleading that initiates a lawsuit and that sets forth a claim for relief.

consent decree: a judgment entered by consent of the parties whereby the defendant agrees to stop alleged illegal activity without admitting guilt or wrongdoing.

counsel: a lawyer or team of lawyers; both parties to an administrative hearing or lawsuit in special education disputes are entitled to counsel.

court: a governmental body authorized to decide disputes concerning the law. Judges are often referred to impersonally as "the court."

damages: the monetary compensation awarded by a court to the prevailing party in a lawsuit for injury, loss, or other harm done to their rights, their property, or their person through the illegal or wrongful conduct of another. **Compensatory damages** are meant to pay for the actual and projected harm (loss of wages, hospital expenses, etc.). **Punitive damages** are in addition to compensatory damages and are used to punish a defendant for intentional wrongdoing and to deter the defendant (and other potential wrongdoers) from committing the same wrong again.

declaratory relief: a judgment or opinion of the court that merely sets forth the rights of the parties without ordering anything to be done.

defendant: the defending party in a civil action who must answer the complaint; the plaintiff's opponent.

dictum/dicta: any statement in a judge's opinion that is not essential to the determination of the case; conclusions on which the decision does not turn. Dictum, unlike the holding, is not binding in subsequent cases.

discrimination: unfair treatment or denial of normally available privileges to individuals because of their race, age, color, sex, national origin, religion, disability, or veteran's status.

dissenting opinion: a court opinion, written by a judge or minority of the judges sitting on a court, setting forth news that contradict and often criticize the judgement and reasoning of the majority opinion. Only the majority opinion has the force of law.

due process of law: a phrase from the Fifth and Fourteenth Amendments of the United States Constitution that generally refers to the reasonable, fair, and equitable application and administration of the law. "Procedural due process" refers to constitutionally guaranteed rights to fair notice, fair hearing, and other fair procedures in any legal proceedings that might jeopardize one's life, liberty, or property.

enjoin: to command, especially a court's command or order forbidding certain action; the word also can be used to mean require certain action.

equal protection of the law: the constitutional guarantee that no person or class of persons shall be denied the same protection of the laws that is enjoyed by other persons or other classes in like circumstances.

equitable relief: court relief in the form of an injunction, a declaratory judgment, or some other form of redress other than money damages.

evidence: information in oral testimony or written documents presented to persuade the fact-finder (judge or jury) of the correctness of one side or the other's point of view.

finding: a conclusion or decision upon a question of fact reached as a result of a judicial examination or investigation by a court or jury.

good faith: a term referring to a party's honest intent. A good faith undertaking is one devoid of any fraud or any motive to take unfair advantage. **Bad faith** is the opposite.

hearing: a proceeding with definite issues of fact or law to be resolved, in which witnesses are heard, the parties confront each other, and an impartial officer presides.

holding: a judge's binding decree upon a particular issue of law in a case. (Cf. *dictum.*)

informed consent: consent based on knowledge of what action(s) will result from giving consent; informed consent requires full disclosure by the person seeking to obtain consent.

injunction: a court order requiring a party to refrain from engaging (or to engage) in some particular conduct.

judge: a government official with authority to decide lawsuits brought before courts.

jurisdiction: (1) the legal authority of a court to hear and decide a case (e.g., federal courts have jurisdiction to decide issues that involve federal law but not to decide issues that involve only state law); (2) the geographic area within which the court has authority to decide legal issues.

liability: a party's legal obligation, duty, or responsibility.

liberty interest: an interest protected through the due process clauses of state and federal constitutions. Although defying precise definition, liberty interests have been declared by courts to include the liberties guaranteed by the first eight amendments of the U.S. Constitution as well as such rights as the right to one's good name and the right of individuals to contract, to engage in any of the common occupations of life, to acquire useful knowledge, to marry, establish a home and bring up children, to worship God according to the dictates of their own consciences. More generally, it is the right to enjoy those privileges long recognized as essential to the orderly pursuit of happiness by free people.

litigation: a civil action of an adversary nature.

majority opinion: a court opinion, usually written by one judge, in which the decision is set forth and in which the reasoning behind the decision is agreed to by a majority of the judges.

moot case: a case that no longer rests upon existing facts or rights and in which a judgment would be without practical effect; also an abstract or pretended case.

negligence: conduct that either (1) falls below the degree of care that a reasonably prudent person would exercise in the same situation, (2) falls below a standard of care fixed by law, or (3) falls below a standard of care fixed by a profession or trade and about which the allegedly negligent party knew or should have known. If it causes injury to person or property, negligence will become a tort. Otherwise it remains careless behavior.

parties: the plaintiff(s) and defendant(s) to a lawsuit.

plaintiff: the party bringing suit in a court of law by the filing of the complaint.

precedent: any decided case that may be used as authority in deciding subsequent similar cases.

privacy, right of: the right to live without unwarranted interference by the public in matters with which the public is not necessarily concerned; the right of a person to be free from unwarranted publicity. The term encompasses a number of rights recognized as inherent in the concept of "ordered liberty." The right is not absolute.

private right of action: the legal right of a private person to file a lawsuit and seek a remedy for a violation of a law; some statutes do not create a private right of action but allow some other remedy such as withholding funds for noncompliance.

procedural due process: (See *due process.*)

property interest: an interest protected through the due process clauses of state and federal constitutions. It safeguards the interests that a person has acquired in specific benefits. Property interests are created by statutes that support individual claims of entitlement to specific benefits. A property interest includes far more than ownership and possession of tangible property. For instance, state statutes entitling youth to a public education have been held to establish a property interest.

qualified immunity: immunity from liability conditioned on meeting a certain standard of conduct; an affirmative defense that shields public officials from liability for damages if their conduct does not violate clearly established statutory or constitutional rights of which a reasonable person would have known.

quasi ("nearly, almost, like"): a modifying prefix used to designate a resemblance or similarity to the object or conduct modified. For example, administrative hearings under special education law are "quasi-judicial" in nature; they resemble judicial hearings in many respects but are not conducted by a judge and lack some of the formalities of the courtroom.

question of fact: any question in a lawsuit that relates to the factual context out of which the controversy arose, such as conduct, time, place, duration, physical cause or effect, that gave rise to the adversary proceedings. Questions of fact traditionally have been left for the jury to determine, although in special education suits, the judge is both judge and jury. (Cf. *question of law.*)

question of law: any question in a lawsuit relating to the meaning, relevance, interpretation, or application of any law. Questions of law are for the court to decide. (Cf. *question of fact.*)

reasonable: having a rational basis; fair; not arbitrary.

regulation: a rule or direction written by an administrative agency or department in order to implement a statute, and having the force or authority of law.

remand: an appellate court's return of a case to a lower court for further proceedings there.

remedy: the means by which a right is enforced.

restraining order: a temporary order issued by the court, sometimes without notice and without hearing, commanding the party or parties to maintain the status quo until a more certain judicial remedy can be determined.

settlement: an agreement wherein the parties to a lawsuit resolve their differences without having a trial or hearing.

statute: a law enacted by a federal or state legislature.

stipulation: an agreement made between parties in a lawsuit to accept certain facts as uncontroverted or true or to submit to some proceeding or arrangement; usually the agreement is possible because it is mutually beneficial.

subpoena: a writ issued by a court to a witness commanding the witness to appear and testify in court; failure to obey is punishable by fine or imprisonment for contempt of court.

suit or lawsuit: an action or proceeding brought by one person or persons against another or others in a court of law in order to redress an injury or enforce a right.

summary judgment: a judgment given before the case comes to trial, based on the fact that there is no genuine dispute regarding the material facts and therefore no need for a trial to determine them. On the basis of the preliminary proceedings, the judge abbreviates the full proceedings to avoid waste and inefficiency, and rules as to the law governing the given set of facts.

tort ("a wrong"): any wrongful, noncriminal conduct that causes injury to another's person, property, or reputation; the conduct is wrongful if it is unlawful or amounts to a breach of legal duty existing between the wrongdoer and the injured party.

vacate: to render void; often applied to the action of an appellate court when it sets aside or voids the judgment of a lower court and either substitutes its own judgment or remands the case to the lower court for further proceedings.

Appendix A

U.S. Supreme Court Decisions Concerning Services Under IDEA

1982   *Hendrick Hudson District Board of Education v. Rowley*, 458 U.S. 176 (1982).

The Supreme Court held that a free appropriate public education (FAPE) meant an education that was provided at public expense for children of school age, met state standards, was delivered in conformity with an IEP, was individualized, and was calculated to provide some educational benefit. The Court held that an appropriate education need not maximize the potential of students with disabilities in a way that was commensurate with the educational opportunities provided to nondisabled students.

1984   *Irving Independent School District v. Tatro*, 468 U.S. 883 (1984).

The Supreme Court held that clean intermittent catheterization (CIC) of a young student with spina bifida was a related service, needed to enable the student to benefit from special education, and that CIC could not be excluded as a medical service.

1985   *Burlington School Committee v. Massachusetts Department of Education*, 471 U.S. 359 (1985).

The Supreme Court held that the "stay-put" provision of IDEA did not preclude parents from removing their child from public school and placing him or her in a private school. In such a situation, if the courts ultimately decide that the student did not have FAPE available in the public setting, then the parents may be reimbursed for the costs of a "proper" private placement. If, on the other hand, FAPE was available, then the parents will not be reimbursed.

1987   *Honig v. Doe*, 484 U.S. 305 (1987).

The Supreme Court held that dangerous and disruptive special education students could neither be suspended from school for more than 10 days nor expelled without parental consent or a court order, if their misbehavior related to their disability. To do so would violate the stay-put provision of IDEA and constitute a unilateral change of placement.

1993   *Zobrest v. Catalina Foothills School District*, 509 U.S. 1 (1993)

The Supreme Court held that the establishment clause of the First Amendment does not prohibit a publicly financed sign language interpreter for a deaf student at a religious school when: (a) the services are part of a general government program that distributes IDEA benefits neutrally to any child who qualifies, (b) the child is the primary beneficiary, (c) the school receives only an incidental benefit, and (d) the school was not selected by the state. The Court also reasoned that the interpreter is merely a transmitter of the instructional material and neither adds to it nor subtracts from it.

1993   *Florence County School District Four v. Shannon Carter*, 510 U.S. 7 (1993)

The Supreme Court held that when a special education student is denied FAPE by a school district, the parents can be reimbursed for the costs of an "otherwise proper," unilateral private placement of their child, even in a school that does not meet state standards.

1999   *Cedar Rapids Community School District v. Garret F.,* 119 S. Ct. 992 (1999)

The Supreme Court held that IDEA requires continuous one-on-one nursing care for a medically fragile student because it is a related service and is not an excluded medical service under the regulations. The Court said that accepting a cost-based standard would require it to create a standard that is not present in the statute.

Appendix B

Selected Internet Sites With Information on Special Education and Disabilities

These Internet sites are well-established ones. Occasionally, when you try to access a site, you will receive a message that it cannot be located or is temporarily out of service. In either case, try again later because these sites were correct and active as of the date of publication of this book. You will find that many of these sites will link you to other sites as well.

http://www.ed.gov/offices/OSERS/IDEA/

U.S. Department of Education Web page for IDEA

http://www.ed.gov/offices/OSERS/OSEP/

U.S. Department of Education Web page for the Office of Special Education Programs

http://www.ed.gov/offices/OCR/

U.S. Department of Education Web page for the Office for Civil Rights

http://www.ideapractices.org/

Home page of ASPIRE and ILIAD, federal grant projects that share ideas and practices that work for educating children with disabilities

http://www.members.aol.com/casecec/

Home page of the Council of Administrators of Special Education

http://www.cec.sped.org/

Home page of the Council for Exceptional Children

http://www.dec-sped.org/

Home page of the Division of Early Childhood of the Council for Exceptional Children

http://www.aerbvi.org/

Home page of the Association for the Education and Rehabilitation of the Blind and Visually Impaired

http://www.air-dc.org/

Home page of the American Institutes for Research (special education is among their research interests)

http://www.nichcy.org/

Home page of the National Information Center for Children and Youth With Disabilities

http://www.protectionandadvocacy.com/

Home page of the federally mandated state protection and advocacy systems for individuals with developmental disabilities

http://www.autism.com/

Home page of the Center for the Study of Autism

http://www.autism-society.org/

Home page of the Autism Society of America

http://www.nfb.org/

Home page of the National Federation of the Blind

http://www.afb.org/

Home page of the American Foundation for the Blind

http://www.agbell.org/

Home page of the Alexander Graham Bell Association for the Deaf and Hard of Hearing

http://www.biausa.org/

Home page of the Brain Injury Association USA

http://www.chadd.org/

Home page of CHADD, a national organization representing Children and Adults with Attention Deficit/Hyperactivity Disorder

http://www.gallaudet.edu/~nicd

Home page of the National Information Center of Deafness of Gallaudet University

http://www.ldanatl.org/

Home page of the Learning Disabilities Association of America

http://www.naeyc.org/

Home page of the National Association for the Education of Young Children http://www.thearc.org/

Home page of the Arc of the U.S. (formerly the Association for Retarded Citizens of the U.S.)

http://www.ucpa.org/

Home page of United Cerebral Palsy

http://www.fcsn.org/

Home page of the Federation for Children With Special Needs (the Massachusetts parent center, with links to other parent centers across the country)

http://www.reedmartin.com/

Home page of special education attorney Reed Martin

http://www.edlaw.net/

Home page of Jim Rosenfeld's EdLaw services and EdLaw Center

http://www.ucpa.org/fctd/

Home page of the Family Center on Technology and Disability

http://www.irsc.org/

Home page of Internet Resources for Special Children

http://www.spedex.com/

Home page of Brad Walker's Special Education Exchange

http://www.iser.com/

Home page of Internet Special Education Resources (a directory of professionals serving children with learning disabilities and other disabilities)

http://www.parentpals.com/

Home page for Parentpals, a division of Ameri-corps Speech and Hearing

http://dssc.org/

Home page of the Disability Studies and Services Center of the Academy for Educational Development

http://www.law.cornell.edu/

Home page of Cornell University's legal information institute http://www.lsi.ukans.edu/beach/beachhp.htm

Home page of the Beach Center on Families and Disability, University of Kansas

General Index

Index of Court Cases

About the Author

Dixie Snow Huefner is a professor in the Department of Special Education at the University of Utah. She is one of the few professors of special education who is also an attorney, and her training and perspective give her an unusual advantage in teaching and writing about special education law. She has an undergraduate degree in political science from Wellesley College and graduate degrees in special education and law from the University of Utah. After receiving her law degree and being admitted to the Utah State Bar, she served a prestigious clerkship with the Honorable Stephen H. Anderson, U.S. Court of Appeals for the Tenth Circuit, before joining the Special Education Department as a full-time faculty member.

Professor Huefner teaches and writes in the areas of special education law; home, school and community partnerships; and disability law and policy. Her articles have appeared in leading education and law journals. In addition to *Getting Comfortable With Special Education Law,* she is a co-author of the book *Education Law and the Public Schools: A Compendium,* also published by Christopher-Gordon. She is a frequent presenter at national and regional conferences and training institutes.